HARVARD STUDIES IN BUSINESS HISTORY

Harvard Studies in Business History
XXII

Edited by
RALPH W. HIDY
Isidor Straus Professor of Business History
and
HENRIETTA M. LARSON
Professor of Business History, *Emerita*

Graduate School of Business Administration
George F. Baker Foundation
Harvard University

ISAAC HICKS

*New York Merchant
and Quaker*

1767-1820

ROBERT A. DAVISON

HARVARD
UNIVERSITY
PRESS

CAMBRIDGE
MASSACHUSETTS

1964

TO R.W.D.

CONTENTS

ILLUSTRATIONS

Sarah Hicks's wedding gown (worn by a descendant).

The Westbury Meeting, of which Isaac Hicks was a member. The meetinghouse, shown as it appeared in 1869, was destroyed by fire in 1901.

Letter of Captain Judah Paddock from Mogador, Morocco, informing Isaac Hicks of his capture by "wild Arabs."

Letter of February 8, 1803, from Isaac Hicks to Captain Judah Paddock, then in Savannah awaiting the loading of the *Thames* for a voyage to Russia. *Courtesy of the New-York Historical Society, New York City.*

Isaac Hicks and his brother Valentine were among the stockholders in the Jericho Turnpike Road which still borders Hicks property in Westbury.

FOREWORD

A N Y historian of business learns, soon after beginning his study, that a multiplicity of considerations influence decision-making by businessmen. Among these influences, so the record indicates time and again, is the set of religious beliefs and practices of an individual acquired through early family and church training. Altogether appropriate, therefore, is a study of a Quaker as a businessman and as a citizen. That numerous members of the Society of Friends have attained prominence in business, particularly in the United Kingdom and the United States, lends additional significance to such a study as *Isaac Hicks, New York Merchant and Quaker, 1767–1820,* by Robert A. Davison, Assistant Professor of History at Hofstra University.

In the course of testing the relation between Quaker mores and business practice, Professor Davison analyzes the pragmatic behavior of Hicks as a merchant. Utilizing both partnerships and joint ventures, Hicks shifted the emphasis of his activities from general mercantile activity to commission agency business to international trading on his own account. Having acquired a competence for himself and his family after seventeen years of astute management, he retired from business enterprise to forward the aims of his cousin Elias Hicks within the Society of Friends.

For a number of years the undersigned editors have had an intimate interest in this manuscript. One supervised the writing of a widely different version as a doctoral dissertation at New York University, later making suggestions for revising the first product. The second editor assumed the primary responsibility for final editorial modifications lead-

ing to publication. This pleasant task constituted her swan
song as Editor of the *Harvard Studies in Business History,* a
service she had performed jointly or alone for fifteen years.

July 1963   Ralph W. Hidy
                                     Henrietta M. Larson
                                               Editors

PREFACE

ISAAC HICKS was not a Quaker Saint suffering at the hands of a world not yet ready for perfection. Though he grew up a Quaker in an environment which produced noted leaders in the Society of Friends, in 1789 the twenty-one-year-old Hicks chose a business career. For seventeen intensive years in New York City's rapidly expanding mercantile community, this former resident of rural Westbury sagely moved his funds and talent among a number of different businesses: grocer, dry goods importer, whale oil and candle seller, commission agent for ship owners, cotton merchant, investor in the Russian trade, and bank director. Still, Hicks's Quakerism was important in his business life. Despite his ambition for financial success during times when business ethics were not always clear or enforceable, he always conscientiously applied Quaker standards to his business practice. The very informality of the times may have given Hicks a special advantage because of his conspicuous reliability. Because he was a known member of the Society of Friends, Hicks had the additional advantage of preferential treatment from his fellow-Quakers. By 1805 he had a modest fortune and retired.

The story of Isaac Hicks is business history—in part an account of how Hicks and his contemporaries conducted various trades; in part a description of the services he performed as a concerned Friend. Inevitably the question arises: "Which commitment, the love of gain or dedication to a religious ideal, controlled Hicks?" In this book I offer my speculation about what may be an unanswerable question and present for the reader's judgment the evidence of Hicks's active life both as a businessman and as a Quaker.

Because Marietta Hicks and Grace Hicks of Westbury

generously gave me free use of Isaac Hicks's remarkably ample and nearly virgin records, I had the pleasure of writing this history. The Hicks collection contains 10,000 pieces of incoming correspondence, over half-a-dozen bound volumes, and thousands of other business documents. Most of these manuscripts were untouched, and bound or sealed as their painstaking owner first left them. Mrs. Frederick W. Seaman of Roslyn similarly permitted me to use her several volumes of Hicks material.

I wish also to acknowledge with gratitude a different kind of debt to those who particularly helped me in thinking and writing about Isaac Hicks. Frederick B. Tolles's excellent book about the Quaker merchants of colonial Pennsylvania explores their problem and Hicks's in the fashion suggested in his title, *Meeting House and Counting House.* Heavy borrowing from his extensive research and felicitous prose as indicated by many footnotes gives only a partial indication of my indebtedness. I gained useful insights into Isaac Hicks's period of Quakerism as well as intimate facts about Hicks himself from Bliss Forbush's study of Isaac's cousin Elias Hicks (*Elias Hicks: Quaker Liberal*).

Ralph W. Hidy helped me innumerable times from the inception of the study to its completion with steadfast encouragement, fruitful questions to explore, and criticism which forced me to alter certain conclusions. Henrietta Larson's challenging questions and detailed suggestions helped greatly to make me happier with the results. Besides offering encouragement Frederick Tolles read several chapters and called my attention to errors in an earlier version. To my colleagues who let me think out loud and offered advice, particularly Daniel Fusfeld, and Linton S. Thorn, my gratitude. My special thanks to Professor John T. Marcus who read part of the manuscript, Miss Marie Becker of the New York Historical Society and Hofstra University, and

Professor Gerrit P. Judd, IV, who read all of the manuscript and gave me both new ideas and detailed advice for improving the clarity of the work.

Assistance toward publication was graciously furnished by the Book Association of Friends, the Friends Historical Association, George Morton Levy, and Hofstra University. Edwin W. Hicks of Westbury arranged for assistance from the descendants of Isaac Hicks.

R.A.D.

ISAAC HICKS

*New York Merchant
and Quaker*

CHAPTER I

Isaac Hicks's Advantages in 1789

D A Y S A F T E R George Washington's inauguration as the first President of the United States on April 30, 1789, an obscure young man from Westbury, Long Island, trudged into New York City, the new nation's capital. This new arrival, twenty-two years old—dusty, plainly garbed, and somewhat peculiar in his speech—hoped to become a businessman. And so he did. Within a decade he had made a reputation among businessmen in New York and in a number of American and foreign cities for his wealth and business skill. Within sixteen years of his start, a prominent merchant, he had decided to exchange his successful business for the calm of retirement in rural Westbury. During his fifteen years of retirement Isaac Hicks gave unstintingly of his time and energy to serve the Society of Friends. A fervent Quaker, he accompanied his cousin Elias on arduous religious journeys to all parts of the country until he died suddenly in 1820. This, in germ, is the story of his life.

The reasons for Hicks's fairly rapid business success were, of course, various. Some had nothing to do with him as an individual but lay in the nature of the business environment at that time; other reasons had a great deal to do with Isaac Hicks, the individual: his training, his character, his connections. This chapter has to do with some of the more important factors which influenced his rise to modest fortune.

Hicks and his contemporaries lived during a time in our early national history most propitious for launching business careers. Successful starts were made in this period by a number of American businessmen of note. A few years before Hicks arrived in the city John Jacob Astor went through an initiation of peddling baker's goods on New York streets. In precisely 1789 he made his first investment in New York real estate and laid the basis for his fortune. In Baltimore the merchant Robert Oliver, who started his business in 1783, had to endure six lean years while American business was mired in a depression, but after 1789 his firm prospered rapidly to make him one of America's foremost merchants. Thomas Pym Cope, a Philadelphia Quaker, built his store in 1790 and with it his name, which would be noted for both business success and philanthropy. The family firm which started another Philadelphia Quaker, Nathan Trotter, on his way to a fortune of close to a million dollars also had its start in the propitious year of 1789.[1]

American businessmen found the times improving after 1789, in part because there was a new government. Businessmen in the United States had not appreciated fully the benefits of nationhood until after the adoption of the Federal Constitution and the commencement of Washington's administration. Between the end of the Revolutionary War and 1789 the disadvantages of loose confederacy had been borne in upon many traders. Agrarian and state-minded legislatures all too often made use of their prerogative to tax or obstruct goods shipped from other states. Under pressure from debtors and speculators, state legislatures sometimes issued excessive quantities of paper money. The merchant class also felt that the government under the Articles of Confederation was ineffective in improving American trading rights and in protecting commerce with foreign countries.

After the adoption of the Constitution many of the practices most feared by the merchants were proscribed. "No State shall . . . coin money; emit bills of credit; make anything but gold or silver coin a tender in payment of debts;

pass any ... law impairing the obligation of contracts." This was language to hearten the merchant. Furthermore, the Constitution created the framework of a government capable of enforcing prohibitions against the states and of carrying on its own enterprises.

Men sympathetic to the aims of the Constitution serving in the new government worked with vigor to enhance commercial opportunities in the United States. Certain measures passed were purely domestic. In 1792 the bullion valuation of the American dollar was established. More significant as a measure for regulating the currency was Hamilton's Bank of the United States. Though this bank did not perform all the functions of a modern central bank and did little as a clearinghouse for international or even domestic exchange, it still provided useful services for both the government and the men of commerce. Similarly, the payment of the internal debt at full face value solidly established the credit of the government and created an investable windfall in the hands of the businessmen who held government obligations.

Effective action by the government aided the merchant class in their relations with foreign nations. American diplomacy has not always been praised sufficiently for the Jay Treaty with Britain. If ever a weak neutral could gain from what was considered a conciliatory gesture, certainly it was the United States in 1794. The unprecedented growth of American commerce during Isaac Hicks's career would never have occurred if Britain had used her enormous sea power in a fashion more hostile to American shipping. "Until 1806, the yoke of Britain's sea-power was an easy one." [2]

As a further advantage to American merchants, the new government passed certain revenue measures injurious to foreign shippers in American ports. Britain, particularly, lost shipping to Americans as a result. The tariff of 1789 granted a 10 per cent reduction to importers who brought goods in on ships built and owned in this country. Even more discriminatory, the tonnage duties passed in this same year charged only six cents a ton to American-owned and -built ships in contrast to fifty cents a ton charged to ships owned and built abroad. Americans in the coastal trade received additional assistance from this act because they paid the tonnage duties only once a year; foreign shippers, on the other hand, had to pay on entering each successive American port. These nationalistic measures greatly diminished competition from British ships in American ports and strongly encouraged the expansion of the American merchant marine. Morison, in his *Maritime History of Massachusetts,* notes that government figures for that state suggest that the tonnage of Massachusetts-built ships doubled between 1789 and 1792.[3]

Besides being blessed with an energetic new government, American businessmen who began their careers at the same time as Isaac Hicks could take advantage of the beginnings of a new business era. Up until the early national period individual merchants, acting alone or in groups, had been performing almost all needed business services for themselves. In America, during the seventeenth century and most of the eighteenth, an economic era sometimes referred to as "mercantile capitalism," a merchant who wanted a safe place to deposit his money stored it in his own or another merchant's strongbox. If merchants, or for that matter the general public, wanted money, they borrowed from fellow merchants. If a merchant sought to insure a ship or its cargo, he relied on the willingness of other merchants to underwrite part of the risk. In this era the all-important sedentary merchant operated a web of side-line ventures which serviced the whole business community. The seller and buyer of goods, in short, was also a banker, an insurer, and many other things for his fellow businessmen. There were no agencies specialized to act as banks, as insurance companies, as stock brokers, as commission agents, or as advertising consultants; there were only merchants working together.

When Isaac Hicks began his career in 1789, businessmen were in the process of developing more specialized agencies. A greater degree of merchant experience, an ever larger volume of trade, and finally the industrial revolution, speeded this specializing process in the nineteenth century. In Hicks's day the movement was only beginning. By 1789 only three banks had made their appearance. The Bank of North America pioneered in the Philadelphia community in 1781. The Bank of Massachusetts and the Bank of New York opened for business in 1784. By 1800 there were twenty-nine banks chartered and operating in the United States.[4] Hicks himself would use the services of the "Branch Bank" (the New York branch of the Bank of the United States), the Bank of New York, the Bank of the Manhattan Company, and the Merchants Bank.

The banks helped Hicks and his fellow merchants in a variety of ways. As Hicks's bank books demonstrate, these banks welcomed the deposits of the merchants. These deposits were not exclusively cash but contained many merchants' notes made to the order of the depositor. Because the banks rather than individual merchants collected the payment on the notes, financial transactions were more dependably scheduled. When banks discounted notes for the merchant, this short-term commercial credit represented an increase in the total amount of credit available to the business community.[5] The thousands of notes and checks that passed between Hicks and his banks show how active a merchant's relations with a bank could be in these years.

Not long after Hicks started in business the Baltimore merchant, Alexander Brown, began to concentrate on a kind of banking very useful to commercial people. Alexander Brown & Sons found the volume of its international trade large enough to support a special business of buying and selling bills of exchange.[6] Heretofore, merchants had had to depend upon other merchants' chance demands for exchange, demands made known by advertising of casual buyers and sellers or by word of mouth. As merchants did more of this banking, or even became bankers, the handling of bills of exchange became more convenient and the price less erratic for importers and exporters.[7]

During the beginning years of his business Hicks had to rely on his fellow merchants to underwrite his insurance risks. In the latter part of his life as a businessman, however, Hicks found it convenient to make extensive use of the specialized companies which had come into existence during his own business lifetime. In 1796 Archibald Gracie organized the New York Insurance Company. Responding to the tremendous demand for fire insurance and highly speculative marine insurance, Gracie's company soon found competition in New York from the United Insurance Company, the Columbian, and the Mutual Assurance Company of New York.[8]

Symptomatic of this growing specialization and regularization of business which characterized Hicks's active years as a merchant was the reconstituting of the New York Chamber of Commerce in 1784. This institution made business run more smoothly through its efforts to define and enforce its own conception cf proper business practice. Out of self-interest the established merchants attempted to sharpen the conscience of all merchants with a specific code of business ethics which was of their own creation.[9]

All of these changes taken together helped to regularize and to stabilize trade. The Constitution made contracts more dependable and the emission of currency less capricious. Specialized institutions stood ready at all times to offer more efficient and economical service than the older, unspecialized merchant community could muster. Hicks, then, had the advantage of starting when many, but not all, aspects of business were becoming safer, and when a merchant needed less personal initiative simply to organize the details of trade. Ready-made systems were available; the old order was fading.

Isaac Hicks's business, along with the businesses of all other American merchants connected with American shipping at this time, profited from the still plentiful supply of timber near the coast of the North Atlantic states. Hicks was a merchant during the first phase of a period in which the owners of American-built ships enjoyed a very significant advantage over rivals who owned foreign-built ships. American ships cost less to build than ships made in Britain or other prominent maritime nations. British ships were more expensive because centuries before Hicks's time England had virtually exhausted her own growth of timber and had, in consequence, to import. During the time that the Thirteen Colonies belonged to the mother country, Britain came to make considerable use of colonial-built ships and ship timbers. Independence meant that Britain had to rely more heavily upon imported Baltic timber and ships and timber from her remaining colonies. The new United States, on the other hand, for several decades longer possessed an ample supply of forests on the Atlantic seaboard which supplied ship timbers. As a result, merchants who bought their vessels from American shipbuilders paid less than for similar vessels constructed in other countries. Even the higher wages of American seamen did not prevent American ship owners from having lower total operating costs than their rivals with foreign-built ships.[10]

The mercantilist policies pursued by Britain, France, and

America's other maritime competitors which forced their merchants to purchase only domestically built vessels made the difference in shipbuilding costs an exclusive advantage for American ship owners. In 1786 Britain extended her navigation acts to exclude American-built ships from the British ship-buying market. To add to the woes of her shipping industry the British government in 1793 added a heavy duty on Baltic timber in order to encourage the purchase of her colonial products.[11] This same year French national pride also closed the door to French merchants who wanted to buy cheap American ships. Thus foreign nations excluded their own merchants from the source of cheaper ships and weakened their competitive position with American ship owners, who now had an uncontested call on American shipbuilders. This advantage lasted all through Hicks's time and did not disappear until the forests of the Eastern seaboard had been depleted—long after Hicks's retirement.

But access to cheaper ships and a blind mercantilist policy in Britain were only minor advantages to Hicks and his contemporaries compared to the benefits derived from a huge increase in the volume of American commercial activity which coincided exactly with the years of Hicks's career. Some of this increase can be attributed to the expansion of America's population and to the development of her internal economy; most of it came as a result of the Anglo-French wars, which increased Europe's demand for certain goods that America could supply. Unquestionably they interfered with the normal production of goods in Europe, particularly foodstuffs, and with the normal delivery of goods by water. Fortunately, American agriculture and American commerce were in an ideal position to take advantage of this disruption: the American frontier was expanding rapidly westward; American merchants, fortified by the recent changes in their own government and business institutions, were avid to exploit each new trade opening.

It might be wondered why Britain, with her large navy to protect her, did not expand her merchant marine in proportion to these new opportunities. One part of the answer is that eventually she did. The British merchant fleet was much larger at the end of the Napoleonic Wars than it was in 1793. This increase was not immediate, however, nor was it large enough to absorb the enormous over-all growth of trade in Europe and America. England's buildup in shipping did not get fairly started until several years after the turn of the century.

In the early stages of the long conflict there seems to have been a decline in British shipping. Between 1793 and 1800 the enemy captured 4,344 British merchant vessels. Furthermore, many merchant vessels entered the war service as carriers and as privateers. A measure of the British failure to provide for her own shipping is the fact that in 1792 only 18 per cent of the ships in British ports were of foreign registry, but by 1797 the percentage of foreign ships, most of them American, had risen to 41 per cent. By 1806 the average tonnage of British ships in foreign trade did not equal the 1792 tonnage.[12]

Until the Embargo and other preliminaries of the War of 1812 dampened American commercial exploits, this country's tonnage increased spectacularly. As a side effect of the Anglo-French wars the percentage of foreign ships in American ports dropped noticeably during this period as Table I shows.

A corresponding increase in the value of imports and exports paralleled this increase in shipping activity. In 1790, the United States, with a population of slightly less than four million, imported $23 million worth of goods. In 1807, the last year of relatively unobstructed shipping, when the

Table 1. American and Foreign Tonnage in American Ports[a]

Year	American	Foreign	Percentage American
1789	124,000	110,000	53
1790	355,000	251,000	59
1791	364,000	241,000	60
1792	415,000	244,000	63
1793	448,000	164,000	73
1794	526,000	83,000	86
1795	580,000	57,000	91
1796	675,000	47,000	94
1797	608,000	77,000	88
1798	522,000	86,000	85
1799	626,000	110,000	85
1800	644,000	124,000	82
1801	799,000	158,000	83
1802	799,000	147,000	84
1803	787,000	164,000	83
1804	1,133,000	122,000	90
1805	922,000	88,000	91
1806	958,000	91,000	91
1807	1,020,000	87,000	92

[a] Hutchins, *American Maritime Industries*, p. 250.

nation's population was about six million, imports amounted to $138 million. Exports followed imports. In 1790 exports stood at a modest $20 million, but by 1807, exports, including re-exports from the West Indies, soared to $108 million worth of goods.[13]

The times were right for Americans in commerce when Hicks began his career. The sheer increase in the volume of America's business guaranteed enlarged opportunities; improved business institutions made success that much easier. But it would be a mistake to assume that all Americans in business succeeded between 1789 and 1807. Many owners lost ships in storms at sea. Pirates, privateers, and capricious belligerents levied their heavy tolls on men in commerce. At home, country buyers were highly unreliable and almost always dilatory about paying city merchants. City merchants, themselves often victims of the chaotic war situation, not uncommonly reneged on their obligations. Bankruptcies and pathetic letters from debtors' prisons were as much an accompaniment of the times as the success stories. The very condition which helped to make profits so high on completed transactions made the risks commensurately high.

In any honest appraisal of a businessman's performance in these days luck must be conceded its role. Much was unforeseeable. What rational calculation could inform an owner of two ships leaving port on the same day for the same destination, possessed of equal speed, maneuverability and armament, and captained by skippers of equal experience and character, that one would be captured and the other arrive safely? Certain phases of the merchant's operation were inherently risky. On the other hand, "luck" cannot explain why some individuals persistently sought and found the most profitable avenues of trade, nor why some merchants were able to mitigate the effects of bad luck with protective measures.

The times Hicks lived in were a constant challenge to a businessman's mettle: the more perspicacious expoited favorable opportunities; the prudent found ways of making risks bearable. The character of each individual businessman, his alertness, his intelligence, his prudence, determined how he met the challenge of both the opportunities and dangers of the 1789–1805 period. Isaac Hicks's business practices accurately reflected his character.

On first consideration Isaac Hicks's beginning years seem improbable training for a merchant's life. Born in 1767, Hicks grew to manhood in a Long Island farming community, miles from countinghouses, busy wharves, or banks. Instead of ambitious commercial bustle, he breathed the calm air of Westbury, an area which had changed few of its ways since its founding by English settlers one hundred years earlier and which seemed in spirit a world apart from the marketplace. Relatively isolated and unprepossessing, it was scarcely an obvious place to nurture an international mercantile career.[14]

But when Isaac Hicks walked to New York in the spring of 1789 he was no illiterate country bumpkin, eager and untutored. Isaac's birthplace had been a farm community where, indeed, his father, Samuel, owned a modest farm. Samuel Hicks's principal occupation of tailoring, however, changed the atmosphere in the Hicks home. It seems reasonable to believe that Samuel, who was considered "prosperous," [15] had developed a more flexible and accommodating manner in dealing with people than had his farmer neighbors with their fewer occasions for bargaining. Isaac absorbed certain lessons from his father's example and learned more from the direct experience of being a tailor himself. For three shillings a day he stayed with local farm families, mending old clothing and making the year's new supply of garments. These experiences meant that Isaac left Westbury with a personality presumably more amenable to the ways of trade than if he had been raised in a farmer's family and had spent much of his time in solitary hours working in the fields and barns. At any rate a dozen years later Isaac Hicks had the reputation of being a genial host and a better talker "than any Alderman." [16]

Though the exact amount of Hicks's formal education cannot be determined, his learning was evident. Hicks, the businessman, kept accurate books from his first year in business, wrote in a clear, forceful, and occasionally engaging style, and read some literature of quality. Indeed, family accounts insist that Isaac had taught school for a year in Westbury before his departure for the city at twenty-two.[17]

This school-teaching experience, so the story runs, was just what Hicks needed to make him a businessman. After serving his year with a recompense of twelve dollars a month, he allegedly asked for sixteen. Following immemorial custom, the school board turned down the "unreasonable" request, and pushed its capable employee into earning his sixteen dollars a month in New York City.[18]

In 1789 Isaac Hicks's manner of speaking marked him as different from most New Yorkers and placed him as a member of a significant minority group: the Quakers. Isaac's father, Samuel, had been born in Rockaway, Long Island, into a Quaker family from which descended Isaac's two famous contemporaries, Elias Hicks, the preacher, and Edward Hicks, the primitive painter. Mindful of the Quaker injunction against mixed marriages, Samuel Hicks had married Phoebe Seaman of Westbury, from as venerable a Friends family as his own.[19] Here in Westbury the couple settled among their many Quaker neighbors and raised their family: Isaac, the first born, his sister Elizabeth, two brothers, Samuel and Valentine, who would follow Isaac with distinguished business careers of their own, and Valentine's twin, Phoebe.

As birthright Quakers all of the children automatically became members of the Westbury Friends Meeting and subject to its care. Isaac's parents reinforced the effects of Meeting membership by being upstanding, conscientious Friends. Though Samuel was no Quaker Saint, he won the approval of the Meeting. In 1763 he had been censured for the improper behavior of some of his wedding guests who had played ball after the ceremony,[20] and the year after Isaac was born Samuel found himself in more serious trouble for selling a slave to William Titus, another member of the

Meeting.[21] Nevertheless, the Meeting noted with satisfaction that in 1780 Samuel Hicks and several other Friends had "suffered for conscience sake" when their goods were confiscated by the authorities for their refusal to pay war taxes.[22] Periodically the Westbury Minutes tell of Samuel serving the Meeting in positions of honor and trust. The Meeting, the community, and the parents exerted a strong influence on the Hicks children in predisposing them toward Quaker habits of life and mind.

Hicks's speech peculiarity, the consistent use of the then archaic form of the second person pronoun, "thee" and "thou," and other Quaker idiosyncrasies, may strike one as incompatible with the shaping of a worldly businessman. In Hicks's day part of the Quaker reputation was as a quaint people, curious in dress, likely to abstain from the pleasures of patriotic celebrations, or the ritual of oath-taking. But Hicks's contemporaries also recognized another Quaker: the rich, respectable Quaker merchant. The names Gurney, Lloyd, Cadbury, and Pease remind historians of the eighteenth-century concentration of Quakers in English banking, manufacturing, and shipping. The Quaker historian Frederick B. Tolles notes that in the prosperous Philadelphia of 1769 when no more than one seventh of its population was Quaker, eight of the seventeen richest men were Quakers, and four others had been brought up as Friends,[23] which suggests the historical commonplace that for all their quaintness many Quakers made good businessmen. Hicks's Quaker upbringing, however unlikely it might seem at first mention, may well have given him a set of values and habits unexpectedly appropriate for business.

Many historians have been impressed by the obvious economic implications of the Quaker belief in pursuing diligently one's earthly "calling." From the inception of Quakerism in an England strongly colored by Calvinist precept, Friends had stressed this obligation. "Train up . . . children in the fear of God," exhorted the founder, George Fox, "and as they are capable, they may be instructed and kept employed in some lawful calling." In eighteenth-century America a traveling minister, Thomas Chalkley, who had preached in Isaac Hicks's home Meeting shortly before his birth, gave the same earnest testimony. "I followed my Calling; and kept to Meetings diligently; for I was not easy to be idle; either in my spiritual or temporal Callings." [24] One's work was no longer God's curse on sinful man, the lot of the unfortunate, or a scourge for pride; work in the Quaker view had become a source of earthly satisfaction which enjoyed strong religious sanctions.

The advice Benjamin Franklin made famous through Poor Richard is similar to many of the virtues preached by the early Quakers. William Penn's *Advice to His Children* offered a close model for Franklin. "Diligence is [a] Virtue useful and laudable among Men," Penn admonished. "It gives great Advantages to Men: It loses no Time, it conquers Difficulties, recovers Disappointments, gives Dispatch, supplies Want of Parts." Sounding a different note he continues: "Shun Diversions: think only of the present Business . . . *Solomon* praises Diligence very highly . . . it is the Way to Wealth." [25]

Frugality and a moderate asceticism were the logical extensions of a belief in diligence. The Quakers urged their members to avoid indulging too heartily in the pleasures of this world lest they wreck the orderly simplicity of their lives. "Frugality is a virtue too," Penn explained, "for it has less Toil and Temptation." "It is proverbial," Penn wrote his children, "*A Penny sav'd is a Penny got.* For many get that cannot keep, and for Want of Frugality spend what they get, and so come to want what they have spent." A worried Philadelphia father advised his son who was sailing for

London: "Come back plain," wrote Isaac Norris. "I always suspect the furniture of the Inside Where too much application is Shewn for a Gay or Fantasticall outside." [26] If the Quaker felt that "plain dress and address" served his Lord, it also saved his cash.

It also followed for both Calvinist and Quaker that the conduct of life should be rationalized and orderly. Denied the consolation of a theology tolerant of occasional backslidings, or the humane convenience of indulgences, the Calvinist was commanded to glorify God with a lifetime of obedient service.[27] Such a demand required systematic discipline, and this compulsion for systematization spread to all things, the New Model Army, one's time, and account books. Following a God less dread the Quaker still felt with equal strength the inexorable demand to live up to the leadings of the "Inner Light." All aspects of life were ordered "that none may dishonor Truth." Tolles mentions that a French visitor to Philadelphia, Jean Pierre Brissot de Warville, was particularly struck by "the order which the Quakers are accustomed from childhood to apply to the distribution of their tasks, their thoughts, and every moment of their lives." In consequence their behavior "economizes time, activity, and money." [28] Penn's *Advice to His Children* anticipated the modern secretary's fractioning of her boss's time. "And that you may order all Things profitably, divide your Day, such a Share of Time for your Retirement and Worship of God," Penn advised, "such a Proportion for your Business . . . so much Time for Study, Walking, Visits, etc. And to be more exact (for much lies in this) keep a short Journal of your Time." [29]

Order paved the way for prudence. A man whose records were ample and accurate could be expected to tell better the difference between a cautious and an incautious business position. Friends were admonished by their meetings in

Queries and Advices not to push their credit too far or to be guilty of "over-trading." Quakers, along with the Calvinist sects, gave prudence a religious sanction, and if a lack of prudence forced a Quaker merchant into bankruptcy his meeting was likely to disown him.[30]

"Honesty is the best policy" was no stale maxim for the early Quakers. Enjoined to make their "yea, yea" and their "nay, nay," Friends went to great length to demonstrate their obedience to this order. Plain speech and the refusal to take oaths to increase the apparent veracity of their statements testified to their belief in a single standard of truth. But, as George Fox noticed in his own day, Quakers did not want for customers. "In a world that was unstable . . . and business morals . . . generally lax, the stability, honesty, and independence of the Quaker attracted business to him. It was this unshakable honesty of the Quaker," one authority contends, "that made people willing to place their money in his hands when most other people were suspect." [31] Quaker training, then, would seem to have a relevance to preparing young men for business careers.

It must be recognized that much of the public reputation of the Quakers in Hicks's time had been created by their behavior in the seventeenth and early eighteenth centuries. Quakerism, however, like any other movement, had not stood still, but had altered both its practice and its policy in response to internal pressures and to changes in the wider non-Quaker world. In Pennsylvania, after a period of soul searching in the 1750's, Quakers sought a new direction. Writing of Isaac Hicks's period a century later, the Quaker historian William Hodgson lamented that American Quakerism had lost much of its early character. "In many places— perhaps to some extent in all quarters—the spirit of the world, and the fascination of affluence and ease, had made successful inroads; and the love of many for [their religion's] self-denying life had grown cold."[32] A similar change often occurred with English Quakers as wealth led to Anglican ties and tastes.[33] City life and wealth, it would appear, often menaced the purity of traditional Quakerism.

One cannot simply assume, then, that Isaac Hicks's Quaker upbringing encouraged the traditional values which had such evident application to business success. His exposure to Quakerism might have been in an atmosphere of the sort provided by some of the New York City "Friends," such as the Benjamin Bagnalls who celebrated the marriage of a daughter with a kind of elaborate pomp which included the use of the governor's special chariot.[34]

Nevertheless, Hicks's community, as well as his parents, *did* retain conscientiously the significant features of a Quaker way of life. Although some city Friends lost themselves in the currents of the times, country Friends, if only because of their relative isolation, tended to be more conservative. In fact the quietism which spread among Quakers after 1756 had its distinctive home in the country, especially in places like Westbury. This movement of quietism was counter to the sometimes more learned currents of American Protestantism which were absorbed by city Friends, and antithetical also to the sybaritic materialism of certain rich Friends whose Quakerism had become purely nominal.

Quietism is the term which describes the condition of the Society of Friends after much of its crusading zeal had burned out. Reacting to certain of their own failures, Pennsylvania Quakers after 1756 declined full active responsibility for the world by favoring a more passive political role. Though they became more sensitive to humanitarian concerns, they would be a peculiar people "living in the world but not of the world."[35] Very often quietism meant that Friends made a fetish of observing the outward signs that marked them off from the world's people. Evidence abounds for the predominance of quietism in the Westbury Meeting before and during Isaac Hicks's boyhood. In 1783 the Westbury Meeting recopied its oldest minutes and noted with a degree of smugness that rules had been obeyed. "In . . . Meetings there appear to have been a concern for the support of good order and discipline . . . where any slackness was manifest . . . Care appears to have been taken to labor with such, and to extend a watchful eye over the lives and conversations of . . . Members." [36] Other pages tell of censures for lack of plainness in dress and address, and of expulsion for disturbing the purity of the tradition by marrying out of Meeting.

Besides a somewhat disappointing insistence on certain externals, quietism also described the preference for an untutored mystical approach to worship. This was the more positive side of quietism. In any event the proof is positive of Isaac Hicks's connection with this stream of Quakerism. His letters on religious subjects are filled with the special idiom that marked these believers. Later, the unhappy schism which separated the Society of Friends in 1828 tended to mark the difference between the more mystically inclined country Friends and their more evangelical brethren in the city. That Isaac Hicks's cousin, neighbor, and companion inspired the so-called "Hicksite" part of this division, is, of course, of profound significance in analyzing Isaac Hicks's religious persuasion.

The Isaac Hicks of 1789 must be considered a young man nurtured in a Quaker community which strove to inculcate most of the traditional values and outward habits of Quakerism. When Hicks received a certificate to transfer his membership from his local Meeting to the city, the testimony of the certificate stood for more than routine acknowledgement that he had been imbued with the fundamental tenets of Quakerism.

To: the Monthly Meeting of the Friends in New York

Isaac Hicks a member of our Society having with our approbation removed to New York, we Certify that Enquiry hath been made, whereby we don't doubt but that his Life and conversation is in a good degree orderly, that he is steady in attending our Religious Meetings, clear of Marriage Engagements and his Outward affairs settled, we therefore recommend him to your Christian care with desires for his Increase in the Truth and remain your loving Friends.

Signed by order and on behalf of said Meeting by
Gideon Seamon, Clerk[37]

Quite apart from any direct benefits which Quaker nurture reputedly bestowed upon a man's character for orderliness and hard work, membership in the Society of Friends was useful for Quaker businessmen in Hicks's day. Public knowledge of a person's membership could in itself be valuable to him. The public reputation of the Quakers for honesty, for example, sometimes prompted distant non-Quaker customers to single out Quaker businessmen as correspondents without knowing anything about their individual honesty. Hicks would have this experience. In addition, Quakers themselves preferred to do business with their coreligionists. Perhaps they were susceptible to their own reputation. Hicks, in any event, carried on an overwhelming proportion of his transactions with other Quakers.

But it was a deeper reason than their reputation for honesty that prompted Quakers to associate with each other in business. As members of a corporate religious body, Friends had from the beginning a strong sense of being in a family. Their beliefs made them aware of a "living union with one another because of common convictions and a common search. Fellowship . . . of a most intensive kind resulted from . . . the centripetal forces inherent in the doctrine of

the Inward Light." [38] Early persecution drove them together
into a special community of "sufferers for Truth's sake."
Certain practices worked to perpetuate this communal bond.
The Meetings shared with parents a concern for the proper
education of the young. More than meddlesomeness moti-
vated a Meeting's oversight of adult behavior; love, pride,
and a sense of unity encouraged Meetings to strive for internal harmony and to labor with the wayward. The injunction not to marry out of Meeting did not reflect simply
intolerance.

Ritual and organization further strengthened the familial
sense which existed among Quakers. "Light" was shared by
the corporate body as it sat in silence with a certain number
of its members sitting, looking at the rest of the Meeting
from the "Facing Benches"—a significant label. The way
in which the Meeting functioned without a formally constituted clergy again emphasized for the Quakers that religion was a responsibility of the "family." Even the geo-
graphically separate bodies of Friends could have some of
the feelings of being members of a primary group, or a
large family. With no hierarchy to hold them together,
Quakers met the problem of physical separation in a variety
of ways. Individual Quakers felt it incumbent on them to
write their friends in distant places in order to maintain
spiritual bonds and to inquire after a friend's spiritual welfare. More inspired members of the Meeting received a
"Minute" to travel as lay preachers to other Meetings, sometimes oceans apart.[39] A sense of geography guided the
collecting of Meetings for Worship into Monthly, Quarterly and Yearly Meetings. At these Meetings, which covered
successively larger territories, Friends met together, face to
face, to worship and to decide important matters of policy.
Yearly Meetings, such as those in London or Philadelphia,
published "Advice," and issued "Queries" which were to be

read in local Meetings for the guidance of all Friends. A Quaker was likely to feel a very special bond with other members of the Society of Friends.

This bond had prime economic significance because it encouraged Quakers to associate with each other for business purposes. Other businessmen whose religious affiliations happened to create a less cohesive association possessed less in-group feeling and lacked this special advantage. Because Hicks's business world had not yet developed familiarity with large, impersonal corporate institutions, men in business still had to conduct most of their affairs on an individual basis. Merchants still habitually used partnerships rather than stock companies as devices to pool talent and capital, even though the partnership was fraught with risks. To minimize the danger from unlimited legal liability for a partner's acts, businessmen hesitated before entering these unions or tended to stay within their immediate families in search for suitable partners.[40] Obviously, a Quaker with a host of already established connections in which mutual trust could be expected possessed a telling advantage.

In his study of the eighteenth-century brewing industry in England, an enterprise which attracted considerable Quaker management, Peter Mathias has demonstrated the importance of what he called the "social" or "kinship-environment." Access to wealth and talent was made easier for many of these entrepreneurs if only because the familial quality of the Society of Friends so often produced blood ties as well as spiritual bonds. Quaker brewers, Mathias shows, received substantial aid from Quaker bankers. But this banker-brewer association was based on more than dispassionate approval of investments as such; family ties paved the way. For example, the merchant David Barclay "stood at the head of a vast clan. Through his second wife, Priscilla Freame (the daughter of John Freame, banker of

Lombard Street), and through the marriages of his fourteen children, Mathias points out, "he was related to the Quaker merchant and banking families of Kett, Barclay, Freame, Gurney, Lloyd, Bevan, Willett." As a result, "this whole extended kinship group was rapidly consolidating its wealth in banking circles in London, Norwich and the Midlands, and a comparison of their genealogical tables with the ledgers of the brewery which lists invested capital," Mathias concludes, "shows at once the reliance of the enterprise upon the resources of this extraordinary group of relatives." [41]

When Hicks started his business in 1789 he benefited immediately from the presence of this "community amongst the faithful." He benefited, too, from the existence of a vigorous commercial-minded government, from newly organized banks and their services, and from his own Quakerly predisposition to hard work and honesty. In addition, a long series of wars in Europe soon gave increased employment to Hicks and all of his fellow Americans in commerce.

CHAPTER II

From Grocer to Dry Goods "Specialist" — 1789-1794

U P O N moving to New York, Isaac Hicks promptly put all his advantages to use in launching his career as a businessman. He arrived in May, 1789; by June he had presented the New York Meeting of Friends with his certificate from the Westbury Meeting. This formality maintained the currency of his greatest single intangible asset.

Hicks soon found a very tangible asset, however, in this "familial" Quaker relationship. He met Sarah Doughty, a member of the Meeting. By April of 1790 the pair made their first commitment when they "appeared and declared" before the New York Monthly Meeting "their intentions of marriage with each other." Opposed to haste in these matters, the Meeting followed its usual procedure and appointed Andrew Underhill and Benjamin Haviland "to make the necessary enquiry respecting Isaac's clearness on account of Marriage," and requested written permissions from the parents of both parties. Convening again in early May, the Meeting received the written approval from the parents and satisfactory reports from their investigators. In consequence, Sarah and Isaac were "left at Liberty to accomplish their said intentions agreeable to the good order established among us." [1] A week later Isaac and Sarah stood before their friends and broke the silence of the Meetinghouse to exchange their solemn vows. Isaac's "dearest Sally" was his lifelong partner.

The New York Meeting of Friends thus became a guide

to Isaac, and formally recognized his marriage to one of its members within a year of his move to New York. But Isaac was able to marry and to take a house on Everitt Street in Brooklyn, near Fulton Ferry and his wife's parents, because he had prospered during this year. Upon his arrival in 1789, Isaac had had sufficient funds to go into business at once. This twenty-two-year-old youth did not need to start his career as a laborer at fifty cents a day, or as a sailor, or even as a merchant's clerk.[2] Quaker industry and thrift had their advantages. What he had saved from his jobs as a three-shilling-a-day tailor and as a ten-dollar-a-month schoolteacher and what he may have been able to borrow from his father[3] made it possible for him to rent a small store at 78 Water Street, a part of the mercantile center of Manhattan just one block from the East River. Here, according to the New York Directory for 1789, he was a "grocer."[4]

To be called a grocer in the late eighteenth century could mean a lot of things. Typically, Hicks imported the luxury items which had been considered a grocer's staple before the Revolution: teas, spices, sugar, and chocolate, for example.[5] Perishables were not "groceries" but goods purchased in the city's markets. But Hicks was no narrow grocery specialist. Tobacco, wines, assorted dry goods such as calicoes, muslins, corduroy, diaper, and wool and cotton cards also appeared on his counter. Hicks's ledger suggests the actual profusion of stock found in the latest combination markets: shoes, hats, garters, shoe buckles, pins, needles, buttons, combs, chalk, indigo, ink powder, writing and wrapping paper, and finally such hardware items as bar iron, gunpowder, nails, shovels, and scythes.[6] These were the goods this city grocer sold in 1789 and 1790, many of them to Long Island farmers who bartered their produce for a supply of Hicks's merchandise.

If the variety seems modern the tempo was quite unlike a modern supermarket. More wholesale than retail in character, the eighteenth-century grocer saw few customers each day. The quantities purchased by farm families on their infrequent trips to the city differed little from the purchases of the shopkeepers who bought goods from Hicks's grocery store. The following order from a country shopkeeper for over £60 worth of merchandise indicates the typical commodities and quantities sold by Hicks in this trade.

14 pounds indigo	42 pounds lump sugar
25 pounds pepper	2 dozen wool cards
20 pounds allspice	4 bladders snuff
3 reams of wrapping paper	20 pounds chocolate
125 pounds of Bohea tea	6 dozen shaving soap
1 tierce of tea	1 barrel wine[7]

To handle the demands of his wholesale trade Hicks had to make fairly large purchases of certain items. One such was 384 pounds of pepper which cost £50. Perhaps purchases of this order pushed the firm into commodity speculation. In any event, in 1790 Hicks's firm bought £419 of flour on its own account and another £271 worth as agents for someone else's account. In addition to these 300-odd barrels of flour the firm also speculated in 2571 bushels of wheat and 1400 gallons of molasses.[8]

Hicks had still another distraction from the business of being a grocer. Hicks brought his trade of tailoring with him to New York. Family accounts have him "seated cross-legged on his rear counter," his shutters drawn and his goods dusted as he sewed some sea captain's britches.[9] His early rising, industry, and reputation for honesty brought customers in such profusion that Hicks had to abandon this side line after a few months.

Hicks's apparent lack of concentration on the announced business of being a grocer, however, was typical of his times. If Hicks did tailoring in his grocery store, Astor hired out as a fur beater at the same time he was managing his shop, which sold musical instruments. Later in his career Astor advertised his business in furs, musical instruments, "ten thousand wt. of best English gun powder," "a few casks of water colors," "some elegant looking glass plates," and "24 cannons." [10] The proper label for Astor's business is hard to find. Apparently the lack of real specialization among merchants in pre-Revolutionary America, as described by Virginia Harrington, still prevailed among Hicks's contemporaries after the Revolution.[11] Certainly Hicks's grocery trade in 1789 and 1790 serves as a case in point.

Before his business was a year old Hicks reaped one of the business advantages of his membership in the Society of Friends. In 1790 he was able to use the time-honored mercantile device of increasing working capital by adding a partner. The key feature of this partnership, however, was the fact that it was with another Quaker, in fact a former member of Hicks's Westbury Meeting, Richard Loines. Thanks to his established web of Quaker connections, Hicks had been able at short notice to find someone he could trust and who would trust him.[12] Early in 1790 the two young men published the name of their firm, "Hicks & Loines, Grocers, Number 15 Fly Market." [13] If Hicks had continued to use only his own limited capital in the grocery trade his prosperity might have been long delayed.

From this partnership Hicks derived three benefits. When Richard Loines entered to form the firm of Hicks & Loines he contributed £70 toward the stock and a month later £100 more.[14] The evidence suggests that this $425 of 1790 dollars increased the capital in Hicks's firm by somewhere between 50 and 100 per cent. Loines brought talent as well as cash to the partnership. Later, with his brother James as his partner, Richard became one of the successful owners and operators of America's famous "Second," or "Red Star" line of packets.[15] Richard Loines's third contribution to Hicks was to provide entrance to a still more interesting partnership, one which was to add considerable breadth to the business experience of both men.

Hicks & Loines dissolved before the end of 1790 when the two young men joined with two older men to create a new firm, Loines, Alsop & Company. William Loines, just arrived from Westbury, was the principal partner in this new firm and the father of Isaac's original partner, Richard Loines.[16] The web of Quaker ties and kinship did not stop there because John Alsop, Jr., the other principal, was the elder Loines's brother-in-law and had also been a member of the Westbury Meeting. Only Hicks lacked the tie of kinship with these men, but evidently the Quaker tie sufficed.

The repute of Hicks & Loines and of Loines, Alsop & Company as Quaker firms gave them the advantage of a receptive Quaker market. An analysis of the meager records left by these firms indicates that only about 40 per cent of their business was with non-Quakers.[17] This figure reflects disproportionately the religious identities of American businessmen in those years because the Quakers in the general population were estimated at only 2 per cent.[18] In short, Hicks and his associates did not operate in a market in which the only preference or prejudice was a rational calculation of profit; the Quaker merchants had an additional motivation to seek each other out for business purposes.

The merchant firm of Loines, Alsop & Company opened its store at 39 Queen Street (the old name for Pearl Street) a short way from Astor's first shop, a music store at 81

Queen, but only five doors from a fellow Quaker merchant, John W. Haydock.[19] Loines, Alsop & Company invested the major portion of its capital in British dry goods. For Isaac Hicks this was a new experience, even though as a grocer he had carried a small assortment of dry goods. Instead of picking up a few items locally as a garnish to another trade, the new firm imported wholesale quantities from half-a-dozen large English suppliers.[20] When Loines, Alsop & Company dissolved, Hicks made immediate use of both the experience in selling this merchandise and the established connections with these British firms.

But Loines, Alsop & Company was no more specialized as a dry goods firm than Hicks had been as a grocer. As a result Hicks learned something from the side ventures of this firm. It rented business properties, it owned part of a mill, it operated a wharf. Thanks to Alsop's presence in the firm it was responsible for the sloop which he had owned at the commencement of the partnership.[21] Finally, on an international scale, Loines, Alsop & Company speculated in the American commodities with which Hicks and young Richard Loines had just begun to experiment.

Loines, Alsop & Company, however, soon proved an unsatisfactory alliance for so many men of talent. Richard Loines and Isaac Hicks, relegated in the firm's title to the ignominious designation "& Company," were young and ambitious; the two senior partners were close to retirement from business. Furthermore, the records indicate that some of the firm's ventures resulted in sizable losses. Undoubtedly if the combination had earned high profits its members would have borne more patiently with their own ambitions to run businesses. But a tone of discontent marked the dissolution of Loines, Alsop & Company.[22]

When the partners settled the affairs of the late firm in August 1791, Isaac Hicks's share was calculated as £359

7s. 5d., the third largest amount. Richard Loines received £149 5s. 3d., a smaller amount than he had invested (£170) in his earlier partnership with Isaac Hicks. William Loines and John Alsop, Jr. held balances respectively of £1137 and £600.[23] These were modest sums indeed when compared with John Hancock's reported legacy of £100,000 Massachusetts currency,[24] but they were large enough to classify the two Friends as businessmen and not mere shopkeepers. The elder Loines was not listed in the New York Directory after 1791 and presumably retired. At Number 38 Water Street Richard Loines joined with his older brother, James, to start a distinguished mercantile partnership.[25] Isaac Hicks and John Alsop, Jr. decided to continue as partners in the dry goods line, the principal business of the late firm of Loines, Alsop & Company. Opening under the fortunate omen of a gilt sign painted by Cornelius Roosevelt for 15 shillings, the new firm bore the name of Alsop & Hicks, Isaac's most enduring partnership. During the first three years of its existence the firm conducted its business on the first floor of John Alsop, Jr.'s house at 58 Water Street, a location right next door to another Quaker merchant, Willet Seaman.[26]

During the next three years Isaac Hicks's business career remained relatively stable. He did not change partners. Not until 1794 did the partners change the public designation of the firm as being "in the dry goods line."[27] With more extensive records of the firm available for this period, a fuller view of the dry goods operation is possible.

When Alsop & Hicks conducted business, only a couple of dozen firms listed themselves in the New York Directory as dry goods establishments. Alsop & Hicks, along with many other New York merchants, preferred the simple listing: "merchant."[28] Because specialization could be only relative during those days the term chosen by Alsop & Hicks fit well.

Hicks as a dry goods merchant appears little more specialized than Hicks the grocer. In the dry goods trade itself, although there were stirrings of change during the last decade of the eighteenth century, most of its operations resembled closely the business methods of pre-Revolutionary America.

In typical mercantile fashion, Alsop & Hicks continued to do a little bit of almost everything. In three years' time the firm, acting as an international importer, brought in some forty-one dry goods shipments from Britain. Disposing of these goods in a number of basically different fashions, it sold to customers scattered from Maine to Georgia. To absorb its domestic collections and to make its foreign remittances, Alsop & Hicks was forced into enterprises not at all akin to dry goods merchandising. Furthermore, during lulls in the selling year, the firm deliberately ventured into fields totally unrelated to its specialty. True specialization would have to wait for still greater development of the British textile industry, a transportation and communication revolution in America, an adequate American currency, and an enlarged market made possible by an increased American population.[29]

In the specialized trades of later decades the various operations of business moved in well-worn tracks. The dry goods trade of Alsop & Hicks, however, was still marked by considerable moment-to-moment improvising which comes through clearly in the firm's arrangements for obtaining goods. In the beginning Alsop & Hicks augmented its initial stock, which had been inherited from Loines, Alsop & Company, by making sizable spot purchases in New York. Though granted six to eight months' credit by these New York firms, Alsop & Hicks made only temporary use of this source because it meant dealing with rival wholesale jobbers whose function was similar to its own.[30]

An example of this improvising was in the firm's relations

with its regular British suppliers. There was no established routine. The British textile manufacturers had not yet begun the practice of a decade or so later of dumping dry goods on the New York auction market at the manufacturer's risk. During the days of Alsop & Hicks the British houses experimented with agents in America to assist the American merchants in importing on thir own account and risk, but with the help of long credits from the British houses.[31]

Four agents of British houses, John Warder, Ralph Mather, John Travis, and Philip Nicklin & Company, played various roles in handling the dry goods orders of Alsop & Hicks.[32] When the firm first opened its doors it wrote to three of these agents to introduce itself, to offer its credit references, and to request orders from the British houses these agents represented. In a letter to John Warder, however, the firm admitted that it had already by-passed him by sending a letter directly to his London house, "as the Brig *Peter* . . . sails this day." [33] Save for distributing pattern cards and samples the agents do not appear to have been very vital to the ordering process after the initial order was passed. Alsop & Hicks sent all subsequent orders directly to the overseas houses.

The firm also sent some orders to British suppliers without any prior assistance from or credit rating by resident agents. When Alsop & Hicks wanted an order of notions in 1791 they simply wrote to Waldo, Francis & Waldo in Bristol and stated their needs. In this case Alsop & Hicks relied on the implied recommendation of a local house which was one of the Bristol firm's customers. "Our mutual friends C. and J. Sands," explained Alsop & Hicks, "proposed yours to us and offered to mention us to you." [34] To the extent that Comfort and Joseph Sands were placing their relations with the English house at the mercy of future acts by the newly recommended customers, it is interesting to note that this responsibility was assumed by a wealthy Quaker establishment for another much less wealthy. In any event, Alsop & Hicks received the buckles, buttons, and jackknives without further letter-writing.

In addition to shipments from British houses of textiles and related items, the firm bought some of its dry goods from American manufacturers. Benjamin Chase of Hudson, New York, wrote that he was sending "forty eight napt hats, eighteen of the same stomp of excelent qualety . . . the others marchentable." Sylvannus Hussey of Lynn, like other shoe-makers in the firm's circle, delivered to the New Yorkers shoes by the barrel, in exchange for the shoe binding and Florentines which he bought from them. Jonathan Mix, an early American inventor, whose account with Alsop & Hicks amounted in 1794 to £294 15*s*. 4*d*., sent the firm large quantities of buttons from his New Haven plant. Other pioneer New England manufacturers, such as John Reynolds of East Greenwich and the Quaker firm of Pliny Earle & Company of Lewiston, used Alsop & Hicks as an outlet for their jennet and cotton cards.[35]

The lack of real specialization in the dry goods trade is also shown in the way Alsop & Hicks picked up odd items during the peak sales periods. Inventories declined rapidly during the spring and fall as orders were filled. As a result certain specific items demanded in late orders might not be in stock. To fill these late orders Alsop & Hicks and other dry goods wholesalers eked out their collective supplies by maintaining barter accounts with each other, reckoned at wholesale cost. Again it is interesting to note that religious ties affected the prevailing mercantile tendency toward self-help, for Alsop & Hicks's most active barter accounts were all with firms of fellow Quakers.[36]

The nature of the inventories carried by these dry goods "specialists" during America's early national period was both the cause of this frantic bartering and evidence of the undeveloped state of the industry. For Alsop & Hicks, a firm with limited capital, to order ten different grades of black silk or quantities of "olive pillow" in thirteen grades ranging in price from 16s. 6d. to 29s, would have been reasonable if cloths of these types had been its specialty.[37] But the firm's inventory continued in characteristically uninhibited fashion through many varieties and grades of cottons, woolens, silks, linens, hats, shoes, and novelty items. By this extensive ordering the merchants were bound to run out of some of their items before many sales had been made. At the same time such practices had the added disadvantage of tying up a merchant's capital in some slow-moving, unprofitable items. Alsop & Hicks had to follow this custom of carrying everything in the catalog so as not to inconvenience the retailers who otherwise would shop at a number of different importers in order to acquire their own overelaborate assortment.[38]

From a look at these characteristic practices it becomes obvious that Alsop & Hicks and the dozens of other similar firms were not true specialists.[39] More rational inventories were unlikely as long as the volume of dry goods was limited by America's sparse population. And this limited volume, in turn, discouraged dry goods merchants from trying to make profits by concentrating efficiently on a manageable number of items. Eventually the manufacturers themselves were driven by economic pressures to simplify their lines. But in the days of Alsop & Hicks the prevailing custom was for the merchants, however "specialist" they might claim to be, to carry a litle bit of everything that the manufacturers offered.

To a modern merchant, Alsop & Hicks's methods of assembling its stock might well seem improvised rather than rational. In its sales methods, too, the firm was necessarily ignorant of modern merchandising precepts. But the uneconomic practices which were forced on a dry goods wholesaler in those days sprang from the nature of the times.

The dry goods trade, unlike the modern fashion industry, did not have to provide goods suitable for each changing season, but sold bolts of cloth which usually served a variety of purposes. Nevertheless it was the seasons that determined the timing of deliveries. Because a voyage on the North Atlantic was a fearsome undertaking in winter for eighteenth-century ships, British goods did not arrive until the spring. By the time the vessels had turned around with their cargoes of American goods for disposal in England they had time for just one more round trip delivery, which was made in early fall.[40] Spring and fall, then, became the times when new stock filled the shelves.

Selling, too, followed the rhythm of deliveries. After the ice had melted, reopening the rivers to navigation, and the snows no longer blocked the roads, country merchants made their way to the city to contract for their spring selection. In the fall they made a second trip to replenish their stocks from the newly arrived merchandise in the hands of the wholesalers. If a merchant were lucky, his stock would move in and out of his store a maximum of twice a year. Until a transportation revolution occurred it was impossible for a dry goods merchant to achieve the economies made possible by frequent deliveries in and out, by a low inventory, and a consequent reduction of unit costs. Furthermore, frequent deliveries to retailers would have no justification until an increase in the population created an enlarged demand at the retail level.

Within the limits imposed by this semiyearly sales pattern, Alsop & Hicks appears to have been successful in moving its goods out on time. When Robert Bolton of Savannah requested goods in November, the firm, replying on the 29th, had to tell him that his order had come "so late that it is out of our power to execute it in full, as the greater part of our goods were disposed of before it came to hand." A week later, in a reply to a similar request, the firm declared that its "goods were almost all sold off." Blotter entries recorded dry goods sales in the fall of 1791 amounting to £3810 1s. 5d. but by January 1792 the entry came to only £350 of "sundries."[41] The low January inventory speaks well for the firm's sales effort.

The limited size of the local market was another handicap to tight, rational control of Alsop & Hicks's operation. The bulk of the firm's customers came, as might be expected, from the city and Long Island, and from the towns in the Hudson River Valley. But in order to unload more of its goods within the established sales period, Alsop & Hicks sold goods in such distant places as Lewiston, Maine, and Savannah, Georgia. The New Yorkers could not wait for orders from these places to find their way to 58 Water Street; the firm had to take the initiative by proposing consignment shipments to the merchants in these distant places. Consignments, however, were risky and decreased the firm's control over such a vital item as the selling price of the goods. Once the partners had incurred the transportation costs, they were virtually forced to be content with whatever price the distant merchant obtained. As a result, Alsop & Hicks seems to have used this measure only as a last effort to unload stock.[42]

Partly because of poor transportation and communication and partly because of the business methods of the times, Alsop & Hicks had trouble controlling transactions with merchants, even those closer to New York. Discounts were no particular problem since only a few of the firm's largest customers enjoyed them; credit, on the other hand, was almost impossible to control. The partners frequently extended from three to six months' credit, but country customers had the habit of writing their orders and casually stating their own credit terms. When Eli Whitney of Cortlands Town requested some "ground calico," he cheerfully added, "I will pay for it when I come down which I expect some time next month." Shadrach Sill's order dated in Loonenburgh, November 1791, extracted longer terms. "If you have any diaper coverlets . . . I will pay the money when I come down in the spring." To accept this kind of business—and the wholesaler had little choice—merchants in the dry goods line had to improvise their cash position until the crossroads storekeeper deigned to pay his bill. No wonder Alsop & Hicks had to write to Peel Yates in England in 1794 that the firm had "failed in . . . [its] calculation of remittances from our country customers." [43]

The informality and near-illiteracy of country customers plagued Alsop & Hicks with more than just credit control. Laconic notes frequently forced the firm to guess the intentions of the back-country storekeepers. William Mitchell's scrawled request, for example, hints at the commodity wanted, but gives no limits on the price. "In rememberance of former acquaintance I take the freedom to propose some small business to thee. I stand in nead of a peace of white sheating sutable for countery use." At another time the firm let Thomas Howland of Newport know that he had put Alsop & Hicks at a disadvantage. "Thou was so short in the description of many of the articles, that we were much at a loss in the choice of them. Should any of the articles in which we have deviated from thy order prove not agreeable, thou art at liberty to return them." Such concessions could incur expensive transportation charges if the goods did "prove not agreeable" to the customers. "The black broadcloth is by no means agreeable," complained William Lamb of Savannah, "as also the piece of elastic cloth which I did not order." [44]

If constant improvisation marked Alsop & Hicks's ordering and selling, "uncertainty" characterized the firm's collections from its customers. Even in times of general prosperity business failures were numerous. When not actually bankrupt, country merchants suffering from America's chronic currency shortage seemed never to have enough money at hand to make prompt cash payments. If Alsop & Hicks accepted barter payments in lieu of cash, which was usual, the firm could never be certain what price the barter goods would fetch on the market.[45] Consequently, whenever the firm sold dry goods the management always wondered: will the customer pay on time; will he pay at all; will he offer goods which are difficult to dispose of or do not even cover the cost of his purchase?

Insolvent customers meant not only an economic loss to the firm but usually in addition a long, enervating struggle. To force a collection from the wily debtor, Alexander Leslie, Isaac Hicks consumed two months' time traveling to Savannah, ferreting out Leslie, applying legal measures, and then returning with nothing more than the debtor's promise to pay. The prelude to struggles of this sort often started with an outburst of righteous indignation from the customer upon receiving a dunning letter. "As unaccountable as it may appear to you," blustered Jonas Morgan of Lansingburg, New York, "I believe there has been other instances of other persons procrastinating payment as much as I have." If things went badly—as they did in the Morgan case—the firm's collecting agent soon sent a note which confirmed the partners' worst suspicions: "Said Morgan is in gaol and is good for nothing."[46] Now that the firm's funds were lost, the merchant still had to endure the inevitable and piteous plaints from the debtor's prison:

The unhappy situation of my family, my child at this time lying at the point of death, and my distress'd wife without my assistance to administer the necessary consolation at this painful moment impels me forcibly [to] address you.

Parental sensations, under circumstances like these, are too painful to be suppressed. Permit me to hope that you are not less sensible than myself in an exigency like this, [and] will not fail to use that humanity which the Father of mercy hath inculcated we should show to one another.

Let me hope that upon the receipt of this note you will take the trouble to call and see me. I shall then make such proposals respecting the payment of my proportion of our debt to you as may be found . . . acceptable. I would say more, but the painful sensations of domestic distress prevents.[47]

Businessmen could not have enjoyed the prospect of separating a hapless debtor from his earthly possessions. Because John Hutchinson failed to pay his debts to Alsop & Hicks, Minturn & Champlin, and the creditors represented by Alexander Hamilton, he lost everything. Such "merchantable" commodities as Hutchinson's goods in store, iron, cider, cut timber, book debts worth £408 5s., together with such unmerchantable items as "one cow, house furniture, buildings, and two span of horses" were seized.[48] And disastrous as these situations were from the debtor's point of view, the merchant, also the loser, had traded salable goods for deteriorated "house furnishings."

Even when customers made payments which were punctual and voluntary but in the all too frequent form of barter, dry goods merchants still had the problem of disposing of these commodities. This was a situation little changed from the days of Thomas Hancock and his pre-Revolutionary contemporaries who also wrestled with this problem.[49] Customers sent Alsop & Hicks almost all the common American staples: from the northern states grains, barrels of beef and pork, potash, lumber, butter, porter, and beeswax; from the South, tobacco, rice, indigo, and cotton. Even West Indian sugar found its way into a good number of barter accounts. Perhaps the storage space used for dry goods could also house barrels of potash, tobacco, or porter, but it is hard to imagine how a dry goods merchant's store could accommodate Robert Perrigo's shipment to Alsop & Hicks of

"20,000 feet of square lumber in a raft." [50] Wherever they stored barter goods and however they sold them, these dry goods merchants had to act as merchants of a very general description. As soon as a dry goods "specialist" sold his goods he exposed himself to the necessity of accepting goods in payment which drove him from his chosen specialty. The following advertisement of William Bowne's fairly represents the nonspecialized character of the goods in the store of this dry goods merchant:

Cheap India Goods. Ten bales Coffas, etc. European Dry Goods as usual. He has also remaining on hand, 50 tons Pig-iron, 200 Kettles for Maple Sugar, 200 barrels Beef and Pork. [51]

Alsop & Hicks shared with all American merchants of the eighteenth and early nineteenth centuries the difficulties in repaying European suppliers. In those days the American merchants had no banks where they could make a deposit to establish a line of credit in a correspondent British or Continental bank. Individual merchants, in the usual mercantile fashion, cooperated by using the time-honored medium, the foreign bill of exchange, to make their payments. This instrument passed from exporter to importer to make the flow of trade possible. The transaction began when an American importer received a shipment of British goods and made himself indebted to a British house. At the same time, other American merchants shipping American goods to Britain or the Continent had been acquiring credits on the other side of the ocean. Bills of exchange became available in America when some of the American exporters wanted cash or purchasing power in America in preference to their overseas credits. By writing a bill of exchange against the foreign house which had bought his shipment the American exporter could now sell the bill to some American who had to pay an overseas debt. Finally, after the British exporter had received this bill purchased by the American importer, the British house presented the bill to the firm against whom it had been drawn and demanded payment.[52]

Although the bulk of young America's growing trade with Europe was facilitated by this financial instrument, the foreign bill of exchange had its deficiencies. If imports and exports exactly matched during any short-run period, the bills theoretically sold at par. Because exports and imports seldom did balance within any given year the bills of exchange sold either at a premium or at a discount. No American merchant wanted to decrease the profits on his entire importing operation by having to buy bills at a premium. No exporter wanted to sell bills at a discount. A further deficiency in this method of paying for trade was the fact that the American had an imperfect market for bills. In some ports, such as the southern tobacco outlets, there was almost no market for bills because so little importing went on. Only in the principal commercial cities—Boston, New York, Philadelphia, and Baltimore—could merchants expect to offer or to purchase bills with any regularity. A. H. Cole notes that not until 1795 did American periodicals publish the local price of London Bills.[53] American merchants in Isaac Hicks's day were seldom satisfied with the operation of the foreign bill-of-exchange market.

Because Nicholas Biddle had not yet put the Second Bank of the United States in the foreign exchange business and because private merchant-bankers, such as Alexander Brown of Baltimore, Stephen Girard of Philadelphia, and Prime, Ward and King of New York were barely starting, Alsop & Hicks had to improvise its own methods of making remittances abroad.[54] When the firm began to face this problem the bill market was working against their interests. An excess of American imports over exports made good bills on British houses sell at a premium. In August 1793, for example, Alsop

& Hicks, instead of sending a valid bill of exchange to Peel Yates in Manchester, gave the British firm an analysis of the American bill market's "unreasonable" soaring prices. Later that year the New Yorkers put off John & Thomas Watson in a similar fashion: "We intended to have handed you by this conveyance the amount of your last invoice, but" the firm lamented, "exchange being so much above par, and a prospect of a fall within a month, that we expect by a little delay to reap the advantage of it." [55] Alsop & Hicks shared with other American importers an aversion to seeing what might have been an otherwise profitable importation and sale jeopardized by premiums on bills at the point of making the final remittance.

Alsop & Hicks experienced another difficulty with foreign bills of exchange. Since the firm began its business in 1791, conditions both at home and abroad had endangered the reliability of many of the merchant houses. In the United States optimistic speculation in 1790 and 1791 was followed by a fall in prices in the American market which prevailed until 1794. Further trouble came to American merchants when the European markets yielded a poor return on American produce in 1791. Bills of exchange drawn by American houses became suspect. In Europe the outbreak of war between France and England in 1793 caused financial strains and a wave of bankruptcies among British houses, bringing into question the ability of British merchants to honor the bills presented to them for payment.[56] In 1792 the New Yorkers had had the bad luck to have a bill made to the order of Peel Yates protested for nonpayment by another British house. When Alsop & Hicks talked about the "difficulty of procuring bills drawn by such as can be relied [upon]," or about the "many failures which have taken place [which thereby] renders a double caution necessary in purchasing bills," the firm had a point.[57]

Alsop & Hicks discovered that it could use the American agents of British houses to take the responsibility for the actual overseas remittance. Late in 1792 John Warder, in Philadelphia, took the first steps which were to lead to this new method. He sent the New York firm a low-pressure dunning letter: "Not being certain that you have received your account current from my London House . . . I now enclose the same balance." Sometime during the next year Warder must have proposed to Alsop & Hicks that it had the option of making a payment directly to the agent. In any event, Warder wrote the still delinquent partners in January 1794: "The reasons given need not have had the weight you apprehended to prevent you either making the remittance to London or paying the same to me." Nevertheless, Warder met them halfway: "As it is not convenient to you to pay the balance until next Spring . . . I am willing to accommodate you, but at the same time it is necessary to have the time of payment fixed." To do this Warder declared his plan: "I have drawn on you for £70 0s. 11d. sterling at *four* months sight for account of our friend Edmund Prior . . . and . . . I doubt not but you will duly honor said draft." This was a neat stroke because Hicks and Alsop were not likely to endanger their reputation for financial probity by refusing to pay an obligation on time which was drawn in favor of a member of the New York Friends Meeting. The real point is that Alsop & Hicks now could make the payment a purely domestic matter by placing in Prior's hands something equivalent in value to £70 sterling.[58]

That Alsop & Hicks was improvising and not simply making use of an established practice comes through clearly in the firm's relations with other agents of British houses. First the New Yorkers wrote Philip Nicklin: "The difficulties attendant in remitting bills of exchange induces us to query whether thee will receive money for and on account of some of the houses thou represents." When Nicklin made no immediate reply Alsop & Hicks pursued the inquiry by asking Peel Yates in Manchester "whether his [Nicklin's] arrangements with you may not be such that he will receive cash of us."[59] Both Philip Nicklin and John Travis, also of Philadelphia, did agree to accept funds and thereby relieved the New Yorkers of the risks attached to purchasing foreign bills of exchange.

Domestic drafts were the principal means used by Alsop & Hicks to put funds into the hands of these agents. The drafts, in essence domestic bills of exchange, were three-party affairs in which one party drew against another in order to pay a third. For example, in the transaction arranged by the New Yorkers in the spring of 1794, Alsop & Hicks began the transfer by drawing against a Philadelphia firm which acted as their banker. "We have this day taken the liberty to draw on you two drafts, one in favor of John Travis and the other in favor of Philip Nicklin & Company, the first for $234.44 and the other $1,040.48." By the same post the firm sent two agents the drafts in their favor and told them at what advance over sterling the exchange was calculated. Travis was told: "We now . . . inclose a draft on Joseph Anthony of your place for $234.44 which at 5½ per cent above par is £50 sterling . . . please to pass to our credit with them [John & Jeremiah Naylor of Wakefield] ninety days after payment." Apparently horse-trading determined the exchange rate at any given time because the hard-bargaining Nicklin was offered a 6 per cent advance with the comment "we hope [this] will meet your approbation, or we will adjust it hereafter."[60]

A. H. Cole and others have noticed that in order to escape paying any premiums on bills of exchange many importing merchants themselves became exporters.[61] Early in 1794 Alsop & Hicks took the plunge with a shipment of American produce by the ship *June* to Caspar Voght, a Hamburg commission merchant. Voght was told that the articles were worth "£1,257 3*s*. 0*d*. currency of New York" which they wished him to dispose of "as we shall be under the necessity of drawing for it in short time in favor of some of our friends in England." Clearly this shipment was not intended primarily as an independent speculation.[62] Nonetheless, Alsop & Hicks by improvising this method of paying for its dry goods had put itself in the export business and further destroyed the meaning of the label "dry goods specialists." [63]

If the shipment to Hamburg was made for the purpose of paying off British dry goods suppliers, the truth is that Alsop & Hicks did a noticeable amount of buying and selling that had no connection with the dry goods line. Hicks had shown his fondness for investing in commodities during his early partnership as a grocer with Richard Loines, and apparently continued to have this interest as a partner in a dry goods concern. Before the fall selling season was over in 1791, Alsop & Hicks made a modest purchase of molasses and then within a week sold all 30 hogsheads at a profit. In December, with even more time on its hands, the firm formed a temporary partnership with the Quaker merchant, Robert Mott, to take advantage of the still rising market for molasses. This time its purchase of 105 hogsheads netted an even higher profit.[64]

Irregularities in commodity prices between New York and other coastal cities occasionally lured the firm into this more complex kind of investment. In November 1792 Alsop & Hicks tried to interest a Philadelphia merchant in sharing the risk of sending 6,000 bushels of wheat to New York if this could be obtained at 7*s*. 3*d*. On its own account the firm shipped, in the spring of 1793, a consignment of 40 barrels of flour to Theophilus Breed of Boston. When Samuel Coates in Philadelphia wrote that "barley is suddenly rose to . . .

9/ . . . you may interest me one half," the New Yorkers promptly bought 311 bushels in New York at 8s. 3d. and shipped them out on the sloop *Tryal*.[65] The dates indicate that once Alsop & Hicks became involved in these investments it no longer limited such activity to the slack periods of the dry goods trade.

Occasionally Alsop & Hicks tied up its capital and energy in "speculations," as the firm called them, to foreign markets. In the spring of 1792, on its own account and aboard its own vessel, the *Hudson Packet,* the firm entrusted its captain, William Bunker, with the job of disposing of 150 kegs of crackers, 15½ barrels of flour, 86 barrels of bread, 1,550 bunches of onions, and 165 pounds of tobacco. This assorted cargo for Curaçao was a far cry from the commodities one would expect a dry goods merchant to be handling. The next year the firm seems to have restricted itself to a single exportation of 60 barrels of flour to Granada. This adventure, which had been made in concert with another New Yorker, Tiddeman Hull, netted the firm £30 1s. 8¼d. In 1794 the firm was much more energetic, for besides the shipment to Hamburg on the ship *June,* Alsop & Hicks chartered the ship *Peggy* for Cork and loaded her with a cargo of approximately 98,000 staves, 18 barrels of potashes, and a quantity of strained lamp oil consigned to the Cork commission merchant, Edward Forbes. In view of the fact that the firm could not wind up the affairs of the *Peggy* until 1796 it is clear that these transactions represented a serious distraction from handling dry goods.[66]

John Alsop, Jr.'s *Hudson Packet,* a sloop which he had owned at the commencement of the Loines, Alsop & Company partnership and then put into Alsop & Hicks, presented the firm with another distraction from its announced specialization. Existing records would indicate that the sloop never carried a single bolt of dry goods. When the partnership was two weeks old, Alsop & Hicks chartered the vessel to its neighbor at 71 Water Street, Peter Schermerhorn, for a period of two months and a fee of $111. After some minor repairs the firm let Thomas Jenkins of Hudson, New York, charter it for four months under the command of Daniel Paddock. Next, after a feeler from Uriel Coffin of Hudson to use the sloop for fishing had come to nothing, the partners decided on the Curaçao venture. Actually, this move was an unsuccessful attempt to get rid of the vessel. Writing to the head of a Curaçao commission house, B. H. Phillips, the firm asked him to sell her and gave the reason with damaging frankness: "she is not large enough to profit either in the Curaçao trade or any other part of the West Indies." Not unexpectedly, the vessel returned to New York and spent the rest of the year under Captain Bunker's command going up and down the Hudson between New York City and the thriving river port which gave the sloop its name. After selling her in the spring of 1793, in the course of a trading expedition to Charleston, the firm could count a small profit from the rather bothersome task of managing the sloop.[67] To its credit as a dry goods specialist the house of Alsop & Hicks did not put its money in another vessel for the remainder of the partnership.

"Scratch an early private banker and you find a merchant," was the dictum of a famous student of business history.[68] As dry goods merchants, Alsop & Hicks shared the common fate of virtually all merchants of those days of being pushed into acting as a part-time bank. Simply by extending credit in the process of selling the firm's advertised line of merchandise, it in effect "sold" money as well as goods. A more recognizable form of banking, however, became a part of the activities of these dry goods wholesalers. The firm accepted the obligation of paying small, check-sized pieces of paper called drafts, or bills, or orders.

The firm of Alsop & Hicks was in the banking business because merchants since the days of the Medici, or even earlier, had been acting as private bankers. Throughout the colonial period in America there had been no true banks, nor had there been an adequate supply of currency. Colonial merchants solved their domestic difficulties produced by these deficiencies by using the credit and debit side of their ledgers to record three-way transfers of funds. Thus, one merchant with a credit on the books of the banker-merchant could order the banker to pass this credit to the account of still another party who held a claim against the first merchant.[69] Little slips of paper to request the transfers and the books of the intermediary—the banker—were the only tools needed to carry on these banking services in a bankless and almost moneyless economy.

Even though the supply of currency had improved and banks had made their appearance in New York by the time Isaac Hicks became a merchant, the essential pattern of this private banking remained the same. Alsop & Hicks's creditors or out-of-town business acquaintances wrote their drafts and requested the firm to make payment to a third party. A sample order read:

To Alsop & Hicks

Please to pay John & Reary King the sum of twenty pounds when you receive the proceeds of our flour.

New York, 12th mo. 1793   Henry and John Hull[70]

The Hulls' claim against the firm is expressed in the bill itself. Another stated:

Messers. Alsop & Hicks

£122,10,0

Ten days after sight be pleased to pay Messers. Selden and Jones or bearer one hundred and twenty-two pounds ten shillings New York currency and place the amount to

Hudson,   Gentlemen,
November 22, 1792   Your real friends
                                Thomas Jenkins & Sons[71]

In this case Thomas Jenkins, who was much involved in the affairs of the New York firm, would be expected to provide some form of reimbursement to Alsop & Hicks if he did not already have a credit on the books of the firm. Both of these orders have in one form or another stated the amount of time Alsop & Hicks had to pay these demands. In the slower-paced colonial world there was less attention to details of this kind because a month or two did not make very much difference to these more casual debtors and creditors.[72] Later, as banks and better means of communication began to exert a regularizing effect on all financial transactions, it is interesting to notice this transaction even in the limited experience of Alsop & Hicks. Of the seventy-eight drafts Alsop & Hicks accepted while in the dry goods trade, forty-three were undated. This gave the banker some leeway in making payment and, indeed, on one draft the firm signed its willingness to pay but added "accepted to pay in forty days." [73] By 1794, however, almost all of the drafts received carried a specified time for payment.

Banks served as useful adjuncts to this private means of transferring funds by offering immediate cash to the holders of reliable drafts. Once Alsop & Hicks had written a dated acceptance on the face of a bill, the holder could take it to a New York bank and receive the face value of the draft, less the bank's discount. This discount was calculated on the basis of the length of time the bank had to hold the bill until maturity and the anticipated ease of collecting. The reverse side of a bill so handled bore the following legend:

579 [the bank's number for the transaction]

Thomas Tom [signature of the endorsing bearer of the bill]

Bank of New York
Received
Charles Wilkes
Assistant Cashier[74]

Alsop & Hicks did not turn the quest for fees for accepting drafts into a major portion of the firm's business. Some merchants, following the lead of the Medici, subordinated their mercantile or manufacturing interests to some phase of banking. The Philadelphian Nathan Trotter, for example, retired from the family metal company in order to concentrate his funds in the discounting of merchant's bills. Stephen Girard made a similar exit from commerce to manage his banking operations.[75] Alsop & Hicks never changed an enforced sideline into a specialty, although in the three-year period, 1792 to 1794, the firm accepted for payment over $12,000 in bills.[76]

By 1794 Isaac Hicks and his partner John Alsop, Jr. had had enough of being unspecialized dry goods specialists. The evidence suggests, although no record states their specific reason for changing, that dry goods merchandising had not been a very profitable enterprise. Though over-all figures are not available, the firm fortunately took inventory and sales figures during its operation in 1791, the first year of its existence. The results show an unexciting anticipated gross revenue:[77]

	£	s.	d.	
Sale of dry goods	3,810	1	5	
Opening inventory	500			
British invoices	2,335	17	4	
Domestic purchases	673	0	6	
Total purchases	3,508	17	10	
Closing inventory	350			
	3,158	17	10	
Cost of goods sold	3,158	17	10	(83%)
Gross margin (revenue)	651	3	7	(17%)

The 17 per cent margin seems modest in the extreme compared to other reports of the period, especially those of retailers. Yet this figure is probably close to what Alsop &

Hicks aimed for. Telling Robert Bolton in Savannah that the firm sold "as reasonably as any person in the city," the firm declared its terms: "Sterling cost and 25 per cent advance." This mark-up, equivalent to a 20 per cent margin, the New Yorkers explained, "leaves us but little if any more than 5 per cent profit after paying all charges." [78] An examination of the mark-up on a number of random samples from the British invoices further confirms the intention of Alsop & Hicks to come close to a 20 per cent margin. [79]

Two additional transactions had to take place, however, after the above calculation of 1791 operations, before the results were final, and the £651 margin realized. In the first place, the sales figure of £3,810 was only tentative. The firm arrived at this figure on the basis of sales agreements with its customers, not on the basis of money collected. In those days there was many a slip twixt customer and cash and Alsop & Hicks had the misfortune to have more than one bankrupt on its list. Partial payments or long-delayed, expensive collections, such as Hicks's trip to put pressure on a Savannah debtor, necessarily affected subsequent calculations of the sales figure.

The other loose end at the time of the 1791 calculation was the figure for the cost of the British invoices (£2,335). This figure would hold only if bills of exchange sold at par when Alsop & Hicks was ready some year or more later to make its overseas payments. If bills sold at a discount, the previous estimate of cost would be lowered and the margin enhanced. If bills sold at a premium, however—and Alsop & Hicks's complaints about this phenomenon were constant—this amounted to a delayed increase in the cost of the goods sold and a consequent reduction in the gross margin. Fortunately for Alsop & Hicks, no income tax law forced American merchants to unscramble their accounts for an annual calculation of profits.

Dry goods importing, of course, did constitute a major segment of American importing and did make money for many American merchants before, during, and after the experience of Alsop & Hicks. Nevertheless, some American merchants such as Jonathan Jackson, a member of the famous mercantile family of that name, failed in this trade in the post-Revolutionary period.[80] Alsop & Hicks met a better fate. The partners did not become rich, but they paid off all their British creditors by 1796, although they did not have an altogether pleasant time in the dry goods trade between 1791 and 1794. The correspondence of the firm indicates the pressure the partners must have worked under as the demands of the British suppliers became more and more insistent while at the same time the firm's country customers procrastinated and procrastinated and procrastinated.

In spite of this trying experience, however, the very diversity imposed by the nature of this trade gave the management a view of many lines of business. Isaac Hicks's first three years in partnership with John Alsop, Jr. had, perhaps, had its advantages. At any rate, after one year as a "grocer" and three as a partner in a dry goods house, Hicks, in September 1794, announced with his partner a new mercantile venture for the firm of Alsop & Hicks.

CHAPTER III

"We Are in the Shipping and Commission Line"

WITH THIS statement[1] the firm announced its shift from the dry goods trade to commission work. It was an important change. As dry goods merchants the partners had been able within the limits of the credits extended by the generous British suppliers to cram their store with as much merchandise as they chose. From samples and pattern cards the partners had ordered exactly what they wanted. Now, as commission merchants, Alsop & Hicks had goods in the store not by virtue of the firm's initiative in ordering but as a result of the firm's reputation with distant merchants who were willing to choose Alsop & Hicks as trusted agents. Instead of handling its own goods, Alsop & Hicks handled the goods chosen and sent to them by out-of-town merchants. Of course, certain commission merchants established reputations in specific areas—cotton, oil, crockery, linens, or paper, for example—and were sought out on this basis.

Yet most of the differences between commission-merchant operations and dry goods' importing might have escaped the notice of a casual stroller in 1794 who glanced at Alsop & Hicks's store on 192 Water Street. Draymen still unloaded heavy crates of merchandise, some of it dry goods. The merchant or his clerk stood at a high desk writing or copying letters and business records. Periodically a representative of the firm took outgoing mail to the Tontine Coffee House and dropped it in the bags of the vessels scheduled for departure, or carried the firm's bank books and bills for deposit either to the "Branch" Bank or the Bank of New York. Externally, little difference was discernible—after all, the dry goods firm had sold items unrelated to dry goods—what was so odd now about Irish linens or Nantucket candles being in the new assortment?

The key differences were internal and of a financial nature. Fewer risks endangered the capital of the partners. In the dry goods business, even though British credit had been generous, Alsop & Hicks had to accept full financial responsibility for the goods it bought and sold. In the commission business it was not Alsop & Hicks but the merchants giving orders to the firm who were responsible financially for the acts undertaken by Alsop & Hicks in their behalf. If Alsop & Hicks purchased goods on a rising market in response to an order from a distant merchant, it was he who had the worry of finding a profitable market for his goods. Whether he succeeded or not, Alsop & Hicks collected its commission for making the purchase. If Alsop & Hicks sold goods below cost on a falling market, the firm received its commission and the principal bore the loss. Even when a customer defaulted, the principal suffered the consequences, not the agent, if he had sold the goods in good faith.[2]

Though no evidence exists which categorically tells why the management of the firm decided to leave dry goods merchandising for commission work, abundant hints appear in the correspondence. In the dry goods business, Alsop & Hicks found itself in the middle of an unpleasant situation. Country customers frustrated the firm's efforts at prompt collection; British suppliers sounded less and less understanding as remittances fell behind. Fluctuations in the market for bills of exchange more often favored the seller than the buyer while Alsop & Hicks was a dry goods firm. Commission work was a less vulnerable business than

importing on one's own risk and account. At least such costs
as a two month trip to squeeze a debtor in Savannah would
not come out of the firm's own pocket, but could be called
an expense chargeable to the customer. Though profits were
to be found in the dry goods trade, neither John Alsop, Jr.
nor Isaac Hicks wanted to commit his limited funds any
longer to the mercies of unreliable retail merchants or to
wait for favorable market movements.

To be sure, a commission merchant could not be a penni-
less beginner. Without a reputation for competence in some
trade and for financial responsibility, new commission merchants could not expect many assignments. Merchants preferred to give their commissions to houses with ample funds
of their own. If a commission house had a sizable capital
and a successful mercantile career behind it, others felt more
secure in using its services. Moreover, a commission merchant could not carry out certain assignments unless he was
able to raise immediate funds for the purchase of such commodities as ironmongery or pot ashes which could not be
bought on long credit.

Fortunately for the partners, their names already had
some currency in the business world. The firm—no slower
than most dry goods importers—was in the process of honor-
ing all of its obligations. It was able to do this because from
all indications the eventual settlement of its dry goods
operation produced a net gain in capital for both partners.
In short, Alsop & Hicks had the funds and some of the
reputation necessary for starting in the commission business.

The firm had a previously unexploited asset in the form
of personal acquaintances in Hudson, New York, in Nantucket, New Bedford, and Philadelphia. Small country retailers rather than the merchants in commercial centers had
been the typical customers of the dry goods firm. The basis
of the connection with these men in Hudson, Nantucket,

and other places was usually the bond of Quakerism, though one Hudson merchant—to note an exception—had made a career out of battling with a Quaker faction on Nantucket.[3]

Isaac Hicks could claim acquaintance with a number of persons in New Bedford, Nantucket, and Philadelphia through his cousin, the famous Quaker minister Elias Hicks. As a "Traveling Friend" Elias delivered his messages in the various Meetings on the eastern seaboard. In many cases a warm bond grew between the visiting Friend and members of the local Meetings who shared his concerns. Letters and exchanged visits attest to the friendship between Elias and such men as Henry Drinker, Joshua and Miers Fisher of Philadelphia, Samuel Rodman, William and Thomas Rotch of New Bedford and Nantucket.[4] "Uncle" Elias of nearby Jericho had been a revered friend of the Westbury Hickses and a frequent visitor to his younger cousin when Isaac lived in New York. It is very likely that men like the Fishers and Rotches found it agreeable to favor the cousin of their much respected friend with business orders. Because both the Rotches and Fishers themselves did some traveling as concerned Friends it is very likely that the conscientious Quaker, Isaac Hicks, had met them in New York in the company of his cousin before he became a commission merchant and had a call to solicit their business.

Although Isaac Hicks's connections would prove more valuable in the long run (in 1799 Hicks had business relations with sixty-three Nantucketers) John Alsop, Jr.'s friends brought more business during the firm's earliest years of commission work. The businessmen and leading citizens of Hudson knew Alsop well because he was in fact one of them. When this remarkable town was founded in 1783 by the Jenkins family and some thirty original proprietors, Alsop was one of these proprietors. In 1785 he was made town Chamberlain.[5] After Alsop left Hudson in 1790 to form a partnership in New York with William Loines, and then with Isaac Hicks, his fellow-townsmen sent his dry goods firm occasional assignments. Once the firm transformed itself into a commission house it was able to welcome a variety of commissions from Hudson merchants.

In early May of 1794, a date which coincided with the firm's entrance into the commission business, a change took place which strengthened the Hudson connections and profoundly altered Hicks's business career. John Alsop, Jr. returned to Hudson. Always a wanderer, Alsop had been born in Westbury in 1753 but had left as a youth for parts unknown. For a while he had lived in Providence, Rhode Island, then in Westchester County, New York, then in 1771 in Flushing, New York. During these travels he met the men who had decided to desert Nantucket in favor of Hudson. Even after his departure from Hudson, Alsop maintained a part interest in his farm. A journal entry for 1792 records the fact that Alsop bought a cow for £9. Later that year he paid the firm for the use of the *Hudson Packet* in bringing his hay down to market. By 1794 he had a mill as well a farm to attend to in Hudson, a testimony of the weakening hold of New York on his interests.[6]

After May 1794 Alsop, as a partner in the firm, encouraged his neighbors to give their business to Alsop & Hicks in New York. After the dissolution of the firm in 1796 he still served the partnership until after the turn of the century by getting what he could from the scattered country merchants in New York and New England who owed the firm for unpaid dry goods.[7]

In New York Isaac Hicks held almost full responsibility for dispatching the firm's business. Alsop wrote letters and made occasional visits to the city but this limited participation could not meet the need of day-to-day decisions. These were Hicks's. For all purposes Hicks had become the active partner in the firm. Alsop might urge Hudson businessmen to give their jobs to the firm, but it was Hicks who executed them. The success or failure of the commission business of Alsop & Hicks rested with Isaac Hicks.

Fortunately for the firm, 1794, 1795, and 1796 were years in which the commerce of New York soared in volume, reflecting and indeed leading the general advance in commercial prosperity of the nation. When American exports increased in volume from $26 million in 1794 to $59 million in 1796, more specialized services of all types were demanded.[8] Though middlemen functions had been performed in America from the earliest colonial days, historians usually date the rise of independent middlemen, such as commission agents, from the turn of the century.[9] Hicks and his partner had chosen a propitious time to enter the commission business.

The firm's business with Hudson arose from the fact that this community, no matter how ambitious and aggressive, just could not provide everything Hudson businessmen needed.[10] Hudson and its hinterland offered a much smaller market for the sale of merchandise than larger and more cosmopolitan New York. Consequently, Hudson merchants usually broke up the cargoes of their incoming ships in New York and brought only a fraction of the cargo up the river. Neither the variety nor the quantity of export commodities nor the ship supplies available in New York could be found in Hudson. Ship owners generally completed the outfitting of their ships, bought insurance, and obtained freights in New York. New York City was where Hudson's debts had to be paid and where money could be found to pay them. The firm of Alsop & Hicks "in the shipping and commission line" stood ready to perform all of these services for the ship owners, merchants and captains who demanded them.

The tasks Thomas Jenkins & Sons gave Alsop & Hicks were almost in themselves a business. As the Hudson firm's vessels, the *Juno,* the *Nancy,* the *Thomas,* the *Friendship,* the *Maria,* the *Apollo,* and the *Betsy,* went in and out of the harbor their passage kept the New York firm busy. In announcements like the following Alsop & Hicks advertised the movements of Jenkins' vessels:

For Liverpool
The Brig *Thomas,* Reuben Macy, Master
Will sail in 15 days, and intended out from there
an early fall vessel.
For freight or passage apply to
Alsop & Hicks, 58 Water Street[11]

Some of the jobs were simple, such as paying the custom bonds, giving the crews their wages, or buying a new boat for a vessel. Others required considerable judgment, as, for example, this discretionary order for the brig *Nancy:* "You will please . . . attend to the dividing of the cargo, as we cannot determine what she may bring," wrote Jenkins. "Can give no other directions than to sell such as you think for our interest leaving some of every article that she brings to come here." [12]

Jenkins called on the New York firm to help the Hudsoners prepare for voyages. Sometimes it was for mundane supplies: pieces of Ravens duck, barrels of rosin, "pulverized verdigrease," or hardware; other times for more colorful items—bunting enough to make an ensign 16 feet by 24 feet, and a pendant burgee and Jack suitable for a ship of 300 tons." From the woodcarver Rush in Philadelphia, Alsop & Hicks obtained several figureheads for Jenkins' ships. Although a whaling voyage might produce nothing more interesting than a request for iron pots, the preparation of the brig *Maria* was reminiscent of *Moby Dick*. Jenkins wanted some Long Island Indians and told the firm to write to Benjamin Hunting of Southampton for "six good hands to come as soon as possible."[13]

Besides using Alsop & Hicks to locate freights in New York for his outgoing vessels, Jenkins relied on the firm to aid him in freighting his ships in Britain. Requested to fill Jenkins's brig *Thomas* in Liverpool, Alsop & Hicks wrote eight of its dry goods suppliers for "at least an equal chance of your freight with the rest of your friends' vessels." It is interesting that in soliciting this freight, Alsop & Hicks stressed the feature which was to characterize the sailings of packets of some twenty-five years later. "As the *Thomas* is intended a constant trader the strictest punctuality with respect to sailing . . . will of course be attended to."[14] This would not be Hicks's only attempt to anticipate the scheduled crossings of the Black Ball Line, the company which initiated packet-boat regularity in Atlantic crossings.

Although Alsop & Hicks received money for the sale of Jenkins' cargoes in New York or from the sale of an occasional vessel, the firm usually spent more than it took in from Jenkins' shipping business. The Hudson merchant paid part of this debt by sending drafts to Alsop & Hicks drawn against other New York businessmen. The rest of the debt Jenkins discharged by shipping to the firm oil processed in his own plant and rum made in his own distillery. The firm of Thomas Jenkins was nothing if not a diversified enterprise.[15]

Although Thomas Jenkins & Sons' activities covered the widest range of any of the Hudson merchants, this was not the only firm to give Alsop & Hicks commissions in the shipping line. Seth Jenkins, Hudson's first mayor, and businessman, requested the kind of services for his brigs *Mohawk* and *Revolution* that had been demanded by his brother. The

Paddock family—Stephen, Daniel, Ichabod, Laban, and Judah—built, owned, and commanded ships. Paddock captains frequently called on Alsop & Hicks to insure, to sell, or to lend them money to buy a portion of the cargo of the ship they commanded. Other Hudson captains, Enoch Barnard, Timothy Bunker, William Bunker, John Church, Reuben Macy, and Solomon Bunker gave the firm similar assignments.

Any connection Hicks had with the Nantucket and New Bedford Quakers had been strengthened by the correspondence of the Hudson Barnards, Coffins, Macys, and Bunkers which mentioned the New York firm to their Quaker namesakes on Nantucket or in New Bedford. Soon after Alsop & Hicks declared itself in the shipping and commission business, assignments began to trickle in from these places for the firm's shipping services.

William Rotch, Jr., son of the Nantucket patriarch and friend of Elias Hicks, requested some business information from the firm in October, 1794. "Captain Benjamin Glover of Nantucket having purchased the ship *Hudson* in Dunkirk . . . is desirous of knowing from you . . . the prospect of his obtaining a freight to Europe?" Rotch continued, "It will oblige him if you will give me the earliest information . . . which will enable him to determine either to go [to New York] or to send the Ship on a Whale voyage." Promptly Hicks wrote assurances that with his aid "a good freight might be had for her either to a French or English port." [16]

Not content to wait for business to come, Hicks visited Nantucket and New Bedford that winter to drum up trade for the firm. From this visit and a series of follow-up letters Alsop & Hicks soon had a steady flow of new commissions from these places. So gratifying was this new business to Hicks that he felt he must thank his friend at court, William

Rotch, Jr. "We feel much obliged to thee for thy kindness in mentioning our house to thy fellow citizens. Fully sensible of its effects," Hicks wrote appreciatively in February 1796, "we have had the address of three square-rigged vessels, and two schooners and have advice of others not yet arrived from your place." [17]

Because Hudson and these New England communities were made up of ship owners with a taste for both whaling and merchant voyages, the firm's commissions from all three places tended to be the same. These commissions varied from David Starbuck's assignment to apprehend three runaway sailors, to the repair of a disabled brig, to the sale of Shubael Coffin's ship *Swan*. [18]

The principal job in the shipping line, of course, was to find employment for the vessels owned by these New Englanders. A view of this work can be had from an examination of the relatively uncomplicated voyage Hicks directed for the ship *Ann*, a vessel owned by Francis Macy and Thaddeus Coffin of Nantucket.

A correspondence of some nine months' duration began with general solicitation of Macy and his neighbors in the early spring of 1796. In glowing terms the firm described the possibilities of freighting a vessel in New York "before the Spring vessels arrive." Hicks urged Macy on with: "We can but flatter thee as we never knew so grate a demand for vessels." [19]

After a spell of cogitation Macy and Coffin did write acceptance to Alsop & Hicks. In mid-March the New England firm requested Hicks to buy provisions for the ship, but by the middle of April the ship had still to make its appearance in New York. News of the vessel arrived but the procrastination forced Hicks to send Macy & Coffin a less glowing report. "By the arrival of Timothy Folger we learn thy ship *Ann* left the Vinyard in company with him. We are sorry freights are grown slack for some days past owing to the arrival of the Spring ships, or rather of the French market's being overstocked." [20]

Though the prospects for a good outward freight for the *Ann* had dimmed, Hicks tried to intrigue his principals, Macy and Coffin, with a project for the future—the suggestion that he had earlier broached to Thomas Jenkins of putting a vessel up for Liverpool "and keeping her a regular trader between the two ports." He was "very confident she will succeed well as Franklin R. [Robinson] & Co. have taken their ship, the *Hunter,* out of that trade to send her to India." In consequence, Hicks pointed out, his English friends, Rathbone, Benson & Company, "will now be without any regular trader from this port." Enthusiastic though he was, the careful New York Quaker did not promise too much too soon. "Although she might not the first trip make so very good freight . . . after she got a little established she would undoubtedly succeed, whereas transient vessels seldom get other freights from there except salt and crockery." [21] How correctly Hicks sensed the shape of the future! If Rathbone, Benson & Company had been willing to break with its custom of distributing its freight among many vessels and to experiment with concentrating its deliveries in Hicks's ship, a packet line might have started in the 1790's instead of 1819.

Ten days after Hicks wrote Macy & Coffin of the diminished chances for a good freight, he chartered the ship *Ann* to Isaac Clason & Company of New York at a satisfactory figure. "We now have the pleasure to advise you," Hicks told Macy, "of having taken a full freight of flour for the ship." The arrangements were to load the ship in New York "as fast as the captain can take in and proceed to Falmouth, there to lay 6 days, if required to wait for orders [from Clason]. If ordered to a port in England, 8/6 per barrel [freight charge], if France, 9/ sterling." [22]

After charter party—the legal document which granted a merchant the right to use another's ship—had been drawn up between Clason and Isaac Hicks, as agent for Macy & Coffin, and the ship loaded, instructions for the captain came next. After a set of these had been sent to the owners, Macy & Coffin responded with gratifying warmth to the enterprise of its New York shipping agent. "Your favors concerning the ship *Ann* came safe to hand all which we were very well pleased with and perfectly satisfied." [23]

The instructions Hicks prepared for the *Ann*'s captain illustrate perfectly the problem of American shippers in the pre-wireless age. As many contingencies as possible had to be foreseen on this side of the Atlantic, and appropriate responses outlined. "Captains' Orders" almost always contained such a maze of alternative possibilities that even the best captains sometimes wondered just what it was they were supposed to be doing.

First, Hicks warned Captain Cartwright that the instructions which would be sent to him in Falmouth by the British agents must specify a "port . . . agreeable to charter party." Second, Cartwright was advised to pay strict attention to the owner's interest in regard to the rate of freight prescribed, lay days, primage, and demurrage. "Make a regular demand of demurrage every day after demurrage begins." Hicks's next advice would have repercussions: "See that freight money is secured . . . to thy satisfaction before thee discharges the whole of cargo."

Once this routine advice had been given, the real struggle with alternatives began. Hicks wrote in the captain's orders: "Should thee be ordered up to London . . . call immediately upon Philip Sansom . . . as to the prospect of a freight. If no freight offers equal to £200 Sterling . . . purchase a load of salt at St. Ubes or Lisbon." Though given this definite advice, Hicks expected Cartwright "to make a proper calculation thereon . . . supposing salt to be worth 3*s*, New York Currency, per bushel as freight."

Then an alternative was covered: "If thee is ordered to Liverpool, we advise thee to address the Ship to Rathbone, Benson & Co." In this case Hicks offered lengthy alternative directions. Finally, "Should thee be ordered to any other port in England," or "in case thee is ordered from Falmouth to . . . France," Hicks offered still another series of instructions.[24] The guidance given to the captain had to be included in these orders because, once the ship cleared Sandy Hook, later advice could not be given without subjecting the vessel to expensive delays in a foreign port.

Even before the ship had been loaded in New York, Hicks wrote instructions to all the English houses likely to be involved in the *Ann*'s voyage. Once again Hicks had to formulate detailed directions. Should earthenware prove to be the best freight, for example, Hicks advised his Liverpool correspondent, Rathbone, Benson & Company: "We should choose the low priced blue and white and cream-colored, such as tea cups and saucers, plates, bowls, chamberpots, tea pots, little or none of the fancy ware, but generally common staple articles as they are much the most salable with us." Quite unexpectedly, at the end of a series of instructions like the above, Hicks might suggest, as in this case, the possibility "of fitting the ship for a whaling voyage."[25]

Having anticipated as many contingencies as possible, Hicks could only sit back and wait for the reports of the plan's execution. The first news came from the captain in Cowes. Cartwright had made a brisk twenty-five-day crossing and found orders from Clason's agent to proceed to London. Things looked unpromising for the owners of the freight. "Provisions of every kind is very plenty here," the captain wrote. "Nothing will fetch first cost."[26] Hicks's principals, Macy and Coffin, however, would get the money for the freight no matter how poorly the exporter fared.

Once in London, Cartwright followed instructions closely and kept a sharp eye out during the unloading of the flour and staves. When Bird, Savage & Bird, Clason's London agent, neglected to pay the freight money with sufficient promptness, Cartwright refused to permit further discharging. Indignantly, Bird, Savage & Bird, a well-known house, which handled all the financial transactions of the United States Government in Britain, protested to Alsop & Hicks about "the improper conduct of Captain Cartwright." The English house fumed, "We flatter ourselves you knew the character of our house too well to have given this caution to your captain."[27] Everyone would have agreed with Bird, Savage & Bird in 1796, of course, but in 1803 this proud firm failed and proved the wisdom of Hicks's universal caution.[28]

With a partial load of coal in her hold and the remainder of the freight money—£909 7s. 10d.—deposited with Philip Sansom, the *Ann* sailed from London on July 14, 1796. Stopping at St. Ubes, Cartwright drew on Sansom to pay for a load of salt which completed the homebound cargo. In due course the *Ann* returned to New York to complete a successful voyage singularly lacking in the drama or unforeseen complications characteristic of those uncertain times. On her very next voyage, however, the *Ann* was captured in the West Indies by the French.[29]

Hicks, having informed the owners of all news about the ship's progress, awaited their next instructions. As a reward for his cautious management, he earned a continuation of the commission. "It is our wish," Macy wrote him, "[for you] to sell the cargo . . . and charter or freight the ship as your prudence shall direct. We have full confidence in your acting for our interest."[30]

This was the pleasant conclusion of one of the many merchant voyages Hicks assisted. In this case Hicks appears to have made most of the managerial decisions himself; in his arrangements with other owners, such as Thomas Jenkins, Hicks made fewer policy decisions. All of these activities, however, fell into the "shipping" phase of the firm's commission business.

When the firm described itself as being in the "shipping and commission line" it is interesting that the partners used a conjunction in the title. This wording indicates that they thought there was a practical division in the kind of work they did. Actually, all of this was "commission" work; in those days a fee of 2½ per cent was charged for collecting a freight for a ship owner, or for a domestic sale or purchase for an American speculator. Many New York merchants, among them Franklin Robinson & Company, Theophylacet Bache, Archibald Gracie, and Robert Murray & Company, followed the same course of handling both shipping commissions and commodities.[31] Nonetheless, a difference in classification is useful for descriptive purposes even though the economic distinction may not be fundamental. Alsop & Hicks earned shipping commissions by taking care of vessels and by serving the ship owner's interests. The agents earned commissions in commodity investments by aiding some distant merchant in buying or selling goods in the New York market.

Before 1794 Alsop & Hicks had done some selling for out-of-town merchants at the going rate of 2½ per cent. Late in 1791 a Quaker from North Castle, New York, sent the firm 90 barrels of Indian meal, which when sold netted the first commission, a slim £1 12s. 3d. Other assignments before 1794 varied from selling blackhead peas from Fairhaven, Massachusetts, to prime pork from the Middle Atlantic states, to tobacco from Augusta, Georgia. In one instance the firm even acted as a commission agent in the dry goods trade. After Hicks's trip to Savannah in 1792 the firm wrote to Robert Bolton of that city a statement of a verbal agreement: "Thee to send thy orders to us to forward to our friends in England," the statement began. After the goods had arrived, "Thee to remit to them [the British suppliers] thyself so that the remittance arrives at twelve months from the date of the invoice." For this modest ordering service Alsop & Hicks requested, "thee to pay us 5 per cent for our trouble." [32] Orders for commission services, however, did not come in great volume before 1794.

Once the firm dropped its dry goods wholesaling, Hicks made strong efforts to increase all kinds of commission assignments. In 1794, to get European customers, he used the time-honored technique of priming the pump. Alsop & Hicks sent small consignments to foreign merchants who might be expected to reciprocate. Following this plan Hicks sent Edward Forbes of Dublin a quantity of strained lamp oil.[33] Forbes returned this favor a few months later by requesting Alsop & Hicks to purchase some potash.

Hicks's response to Forbes's order must have made the Irish firm feel confident that the New York house scrupulously considered the interests of its customers. Instead of executing the potash order right away and collecting the commission immediately, the firm advised delay in buying at least a part of the order. "The French markets has been . . . so flattering as to induce our merchants to purchase nearly all that was on hand. Since . . . what little has arrived is immediately purchased . . . at 61 to 62 pounds per ton," the firm considered the price exorbitant. Later on "in the course of six or eight weeks we presume . . . it will be in large quantities when it is possible that the price will fall." [34]

By showing this restraint Hicks gained a steady customer. In quick succession Forbes consigned two shipments of linens to the New York firm. The second lot gave Hicks another opportunity to show his principal how well the agent guarded his welfare. A few boxes of linen scheduled for re-shipment to one of Forbes's customers in America had been mishandled on shipboard. "We perceived that they were wet on the outside and feared they were damaged," wrote Hicks. "Upon further examination and opening one of the worst we happily found the linen was dry." [35] In a time when a suspiciously large number of shipments were blandly de-scribed to the hapless—and distant—owner as "severely damaged in transit . . . too poor to sell," Forbes must have found Hicks's report a refreshing form of honesty. Hicks then added that the first consignment had been sold "at 25 per cent advance, the purchaser . . . to have no benefit of the bounty." [36] Forbes steadily expanded his favors to Alsop & Hicks by sending consignments of Irish linen and orders to purchase such items as flax seed, cotton, and mahogany.

Occasionally Hicks threw extra business Forbes's way. "We have . . . prevailed on Stansbury and Wood, owners of the brig *Catherine,* to put her up for Dublin . . . and to thy address." [37] This assignment gave Forbes as a shipper's agent a commission on all the work he did to service the vessel and to sell its cargo in Dublin.

For these special favors and for the solid dependability shown by Hicks, Forbes volunteered a testimonial in 1796. "Your prudent caution and attention to your friends' business must insure you their continuance and confidence. When people act for their friends as if the transaction was to be their own," Forbes averred, "such conduct must give satisfac-tion in the end." [38]

Hicks could be satisfied with this Irish customer because he also brought the firm some American business. Joseph Coolidge of Boston paid Alsop & Hicks 2½ per cent for buying the bond to clear his shipments of Forbes's linens through the New York customs before Hicks reshipped them to Boston. Isaac Howland & Sons of New Bedford bought as much as £1,062 18s. 10d. worth of linen at a time from Forbes, then commissioned Alsop & Hicks to sell these goods on the New York market.[39]

By writing directly to George McConnell in Derry, Hicks went after the business of another Irish merchant whom he had heard of through Thomas Jenkins. Before Hicks asked the Derry firm to send Alsop & Hicks commissions, he suggested that he had some plans of his own to make "an annual shipment of a few hundred casks of flaxseed." Hicks also asked a touchy question for the Irish firm when he inquired, "what proportion of the cost" of a shipment purchased by Hicks in New York "thee would suffer us to draw on thee for, payable in London in thirty or sixty days after the shipment here?"[40] Perhaps because the Irish merchants connected with the linen trade lacked financial resources comparable to those of the British merchants, McConnell showed no immediate interest in Hicks's feeler.

The New York firm received a reply only after Alsop & Hicks, acting as a shipping agent for a ship's captain, addressed a cargo of flaxseed on the schooner *Sally* to McConnell in Derry. No funds in advance of the receipt and sale of the flaxseed had been requested. Having served McConnell this plum, Hicks repeated the firm's earlier proposition and further offered to "charge no commission of drawing and selling bills of exchange."[41] When McConnell reported his progress with the cargo of the *Sally* he was frank about his reluctance to grant the New York firm the right to draw against him in advance of the sale of goods in Derry. "I shall accept drafts at ninety days for the half of your consignment . . . I am not fond of coming under acceptance for procuration of consignments, but in order to induce you to try this market, I shall do it for the approaching season."[42]

Though ninety days was not so advantageous as thirty or sixty for Alsop & Hicks, McConnell had demonstrated his eagerness to handle American flaxseed bought by Hicks.

McConnell returned Hicks's favor via the *Sally* by a shipment of linen. "In order to commence a correspondence with you . . . I have enclose invoice and bill of lading for . . . linen cloth which I have shipped . . . to your address." McConnell informed the New York firm that "this place affords great variety of such linens as answer your market. I only want encouragement to induce me to send you a much larger quantity annually." He also urged Alsop & Hicks to send a vessel large enough to take advantage of "the profitable freights that offer here every year of passengers for your country." [43]

By a similar maneuver of assigning the brig *Pearl,* which belonged to his neighbor, Charles Doughty, to Harvey & Lecky of Cork, Hicks added still another house to the firm's list. This firm of Quakers reciprocated by sending Alsop & Hicks sailcloth and linens. To repay the consignments the Cork merchants suggested: "Should good bills be obtainable at or under par we do not know . . . any better or more agreeable mode of remittance, unless," Harvey & Lecky continued, "some . . . vessel was about to come to us, in which case you may ship us pot ashes, all of first quality . . . the second not being liked here, or a few parcels of first quality pearl ashes." [44] For a number of years Hicks and the Cork firm exchanged consignments of potash and Irish linen.

Alsop & Hicks acquired a correspondent in Belfast, James Holmes & Company, on the initiative of the Irish house. A Quaker merchant, Holmes wrote: "Your respectable firm having been recommended to us by our mutual friends, Messers Rathbone & Benson of Liverpool [a Quaker firm which also had relations with Alsop & Hicks] we take this opportunity . . . to offer you the services of our house." [45] This recommendation was followed by several years of business, concluded only when Holmes himself migrated to America.

Not all of Alsop & Hicks's new commission work was with overseas merchants. As New York drew ahead of Philadelphia in the 1790's in the amount of trade carried on, Philadelphia merchants had reason to do business in this larger market. Besides, New York's harbor did not suffer from heavy freezes as did Philadelphia's. It was during the winter of 1795–96 that a Philadelphia Quaker sought the assistance of Alsop & Hicks with an international shipment. George Pennock wanted to send a "parcel" of coffee to Amsterdam. Unable to do this at home, he had Hicks buy some coffee in New York, arrange for freighting it, and secure the drawback on the custom duty. For this service the firm charged Pennock 2½ per cent of the cost of the coffee and netted a tidy commission of £53 9s. 10d.[46] During the remainder of Pennock's life he entered into many business deals with Hicks, particularly during the winter months.

A final comment on the character of this firm's experience as "Shipping and Commission Merchants" should point to the number of Quaker connections running through the affairs of Alsop & Hicks. Most of the Hudson accounts were with Quakers, nearly all the Nantucket and New Bedford accounts were Quaker, and this was true also of a fair proportion of the firm's international correspondents. Certainly the predilection of Quakers to do business with each other explains in part the ability of Alsop & Hicks to find customers. Furthermore, doing business with Quakers had the special advantage for the partners of forestalling certain losses. In 1794, for example, an innocent mix-up concerning a bill of lading threatened the security of the firm's shipment of goods which were on a vessel owned by a fellow New York Quaker, Thomas Clarke. Fortunately, the firm handling the shipment in Ireland was also a Quaker house and

interceded in favor of its coreligionists: "Had Thomas
Clarke not been of our Society, we should have . . . suffered
James Henderson to attach the ship, which he had a right
to do." [47]

Early in the spring of 1796 Isaac Hicks took stock of his
business situation. After two years of conducting the affairs
of Alsop & Hicks in the shipping and commission business
by himself he had reason to be confident. He had had the
experience of managing the firm's expanding business. To
the Hudson accounts, which the firm had handled from its
beginnings when Alsop had been active, Hicks added by his
own efforts new customers in Nantucket, New Bedford,
Philadelphia, and Ireland. He had tangible evidence of the
growth of America's commerce. He also had the significant
reassurance of his membership in an international body, the
Religious Society of Friends. Why then, should he not assume
the risks and take the profits for his own firm? On May 1,
1796, Isaac Hicks, no longer a tyro, dissolved the old partnership despite the protests of his well-satisfied partner, and
opened the books of his new firm.[48]

When Hicks started his firm in May 1796 he took Benjamin D. Doughty, who had been the clerk for Alsop &
Hicks since 1792, a Quaker, and from a Westbury family, as
a partner in the firm of Hicks & Doughty. Unfortunately
Doughty died only a few months later, a victim of the
Yellow Fever epidemic. After this brief alliance Hicks did
business only as the firm of Isaac Hicks until his retirement.

CHAPTER IV

Oil, Candles, and Ships — 1796-1880

THE FIRST advertisement of Isaac Hicks's new firm informed the readers of the New York *Daily Advertiser* that the following assortment was available:

100 bolts of Sail duck
1 bale check linen
100 boxes window glass
10 packages of buttons and cutlery
2 bales woolens
10 pipes Fayal wine
20 boxes soap
200 barrels whale oil
1 box hosiery[1]

Hicks, the master of his own commission house, continued to handle most of the old items that had been traded by Alsop & Hicks. During the next four years, however, Hicks spent most of his efforts increasing his sales of the whale products of the Nantucket and New Bedford merchants. Commissions from these sales exceeded all other sources of revenue until 1800. If Hicks in this period could be called a specialist, it was in oil. As an "oil factor" he obtained his next few years' experience.

Well over 90 per cent of American whale products in the 1790's came from the two towns of Nantucket and New Bedford. Merchants in these communities owned solely or by shares the compact whaling vessels of one or two hundred tons which plied the North and South Atlantic. Later, in larger ships, these merchants sent their captains to hunt whales in the Pacific. Ship crews did some of the processing on board. They cut blubber from the carcass, saved the whalebone and ambergris. In a large iron try pot they rendered the blubber, heating the pot with the smoky flame of the burning blubber which had been processed. Back on shore in Nantucket and New Bedford the cloudy liquid from the rendering was filtered and strained in presses, and the head matter made into candles. After completing the manufacturing, the whale merchants arranged to export some of their products and sold the rest in American coastal cities.

Oil commissions were not new to Hicks. He had his introduction to this trade in 1794 after Alsop & Hicks had declared the firm in the "shipping and commission line." Early that year the Quaker firm of Francis Joy of Nantucket started the flow with a twenty-four cask consignment of the "best strained Sperm Oil," which the Nantucketer hoped would "meet with a ready sale and a high price, which perhaps may be an inducement for some future shipment." [2] The firm's performance in 1794 did give inducement for future shipments by Joy and other oil men who subsequently chose Hicks after he had dropped his partnership with Alsop.

The turning point in Alsop & Hicks's oil commission business occurred in July 1795 when New England's most famous whaling family, the Quaker Rotches of Nantucket and New Bedford, sent an introductory shipment. Previously Hicks had assisted William Rotch, Jr. by arranging a commercial voyage for one of his ships. After this transaction Hicks had maintained this valuable connection through diligent correspondence. On July 17, 1795, William Rotch & Sons wrote to thank the New York firm for one of its letters and added: "We are obliged particularly for the Price Current. Our old correspondents in New York do not uniformly keep us informed of the price at your market." Rotch, however, had not written simply to praise the firm's information service. "The person who has the care of our Manufactory at Bedford informs us he has shipped [you] 50 boxes of candles." [3] Furthermore, Rotch promised an oil shipment as soon as transportation from Nantucket was available. Following Rotch's oil and candle shipments, a small but significant number of Rotch's neighbors, all of them Quakers, also became clients of the New York firm: Abraham Barker, Micajah Coffin, Thomas Hazard, and Jonathan Jenkins. Having impressed these weighty Friends, the firm profited from the word-of-mouth advertising that traveled quickly in these close-knit whaling ports. The Aldens, Barnards, Bunkers, Coffins, Husseys, Macys, Rodmans, Shearmans, Starbucks, Tallmans, and Swains—nearly all of them Quakers— soon added their business to the growing list of accounts the firm enjoyed in Nantucket and New Bedford.

By the end of 1796, Hicks, now on his own, was well on the way to becoming New York's most important oil factor. Aside from whatever effect a shared religion may have had on these merchants, the basic ingredients of Hicks's success seem to have been his own simple honesty and his demonstrable willingness and ability to serve his clients.

As the New York oil market fluctuated, Hicks had to be alert to protect the property entrusted to him. During 1796 he wrote Abraham Barker, for example, that whale oil was going at 3/6 per gallon. "We have, however, had a prospect of asking $15 per barrel [a price several dollars higher]. Unfortunately, ths price was not obtainable at the present because "a quantity arrived from Bedford . . . also from Sagg Harbour which induces us to . . . obtain 3/6 pretty soon for the present parcel." Sometimes when an oversupply threatened the market Hicks was willing to defer his commission by advising against additional shipments. "We yesterday received 400 barrels whale and 110 sperm oil from New Bedford," Hicks wrote Micajah Coffin, "so of course cannot recommend you to make any shipments this way for a month." [4]

Although the size of the New York oil market was limited, no single merchant could effectively control the price. Oil came from too many sources; selling practices were too varied. Nevertheless, Hicks made efforts to bring about the conditions which would diminish wild fluctuations in the price of whale products. His problems are revealed in his communications to William Rotch, Jr. in the early part of 1796. "Although it may be against out Interests to advise thee that a Suspension of Shipping oil this way would be best," Hicks wrote Rotch, "A quantity of that Article is now landing from Barbadoes, it being the cargo of a ship belonging to Cape Ann that put in . . . in distress." This unexpected supply was bad enough, but the trouble was compounded, as Hicks lamented, because "they are shipping her cargo . . . to a house . . . unacquainted with its value and we expect they will fall the price." A few weeks later Hicks wrote gloomily that "the house . . . is now paying it away to their creditors who held papers of theirs protested. Of course it is getting into many hands as the persons who held such notes are glad to get any goods." Hicks's exasperation increased as his prophecies came true: "This is not a little mortifying to us. We used our best endeavours to keep the price up, and had it not been for the ridiculous conduct of the house who ordered that quantity . . . we would have done so." [5]

The selling practices of captains of the large whaling vessels which occasionally came directly to New York posed another threat to a stable price. These men often held a sizable share of a ship's oil in their own names and were always impatient to turn their oil into money. In April 1796, for example, Captain Darling of the *Bristol,* much to Hicks's chagrin, let his oil go for $15 less than the prevailing $110 a ton. [6]

A more frequent source of exasperation was the New England coasting captains. These free-wheeling enterprisers —sometimes part owners of the small vessels they commanded, sometimes simply the masters of vessels owned by the whale merchants—delivered oil and candles to New York from the whale ports. Possessing considerable latitude in their actions, they sold a sizable amount of oil right off the vessel while it was tied up to the dock, but, once they became anxious to get back to sea, they dropped the prices to speed their sales and departure.

Hicks inveighed periodically against these practices which depressed the market for whale products, but the Nantucketers—strangely enough, for they were the principal losers—seemed resigned to them. After one of the aggressive New Yorker's exhortations to change things, Gardner & Mitchell, a large Nantucket firm, observed ruefully in 1799: "Thy remarks on the coasters . . . selling oil we know . . . to be just and have labored in vain to prevent it. We see no way but it must regulate itself until the freighters are willing to see their errors." Hicks's Nantucket friend, Jonathan Jenkins, saw both sides of the case: "As the oil is in so many hands [in Nantucket] it is impossible for the merchants to prevent such things. We are sensible of the difference it would make was the oil shipped regular and consigned." Needless to say, if it were "shipped regular and consigned" to the firm of Isaac Hicks, he, too, would profit. In 1794 Hicks had already made such a plea for centralizing oil distribution in New York for all Nantucket and New Bedford oil. He explained that if all the oil would be consigned "to some merchant here . . . that person might always keep it up. But when it is in the hands of three or four . . . people will beat about and try one another in such a manner as to reduce the price."[7]

If Hicks never managed to convince the oil suppliers to

Sarah Hicks's wedding gown (worn by
a descendant).

The Westbury Meeting, of which Isaac Hicks was a member. The meetinghouse, shown as it appeared in 1869, was
destroyed by fire in 1901.

Mogadore 3rd July 1800

Dear Friend

Isaac Hicks   this will inform you of my disagreeable situation
at loss the Oswego on 3d April about 500 miles to the
Southwestward of this place there we fell in the hands
of what is called the wild Arabs and with much fre-
quency the have that appalation ten of us were marched
of 150 miles there sold as Slaves, four kept at the ship
which I've not heard of since the savage treatment
we received was horried after being with them near
seven weeks and they found we would not work,
was sold again 8 of us and marched on here the two
they kept was blacks which the said was their own people
when we came here found no Consul or Agent acting
for our Country I called on the English Consul who could
do nothing for us I was then very much alarmed
fearing we should fall in the hands of Government
who would be ready enough to ransom us and make
it a Governmental affair of it in that case we should
fare hard and perhaps kept here 2 or 3 years as
Others in the same situation are now - the House of
William Court & Co (who I shall always revere) came volen-
tarily forward and redeemed us, we now only wait
for his Majesty the Emperors permission to leave the
Country I sent immediately to Js Simpson our Consul
General at Tangier who made the application to the

Letter of Captain Judah Paddock from Mogador, Morocco, informing Isaac
Hicks of his capture by "wild Arabs."

ship all oil to one commission agent, he did his best within the existing system to maintain oil prices. He not only suggested limitations on the shipment of oil to New York, at the loss of his own commissions; he also encouraged owners to be patient about their oil already in New York. When the redoubtable Rotch firm urged Hicks to cut the cash price for oil to $110, he gently vetoed this concession. "We make response that owing to the scarcity of money we doubt of being able to effect it, and indeed, should be afraid to offer it at that price . . . as it would undoubtedly have an unpleasant effect upon our market, the which we feel solicitous to keep up to the present or to raise . . . rather than otherwise." [8] Hicks's determination won him the bulk of the New York trade of the Nantucket and New Bedford whaling merchants, the ports which dominated the whaling industry during the last decade of the eighteenth century. [9]

In the eighteenth century, Nantucket, New Bedford, and Providence led the nation in the production of spermaceti candles, the clear-burning candles made from the head matter of sperm whales. Americans preferred sperm candles to the less satisfactory tallow candle, but during the Revolutionary War with whaling at a standstill tallow candles had made inroads on the market for both illuminating oil and sperm candles. In consequence, after the war many of the marketing practices which had been established before the Revolution by the short-lived trust, the United Company of Spermaceti Chandlers, had dropped out of use. [10] From 1794 to 1800 Hicks tried to increase the candle-makers' profit by restoring some of the former marketing practices.

In the past the manufacturers had received 2 shillings for the wooden crate which held the customary 25 to 30 pounds of candles. When Hicks entered this business he strove to reverse the new trend initiated by the coasters of giving away the boxes. "We have latterly sold nearly 100 boxes," Hicks informed the leading manufacturer, William Rotch, and have charged "2/ for each of the boxes, although the latter is hard work, as the coasters make it a rule to give the boxes ... which has almost become a rule not [to] be got over." In a similar letter to Abraham Barker in New Bedford, Hicks celebrated his victory: "Although some made their protestation against paying for them ... we have prevailed and mean to keep it." Part of Hicks's success came because he had been able to enlist the support of other commission merchants. "They say they will endeavor to back us in the attempt." [11] These measures were aimed at the coasters.

When necessary to preserve prices, Hicks battled his fellow commission merchants. To prevent John Adams, the factor of Hudson candle manufacturer Cotton Gelston, from selling below 4*s*., Hicks sent a note to Gelston and innocently remarked that the price current for candles in New York was now 4*s*. A suspicious Gelston infuriated Adams by questioning whether the agent were cheating him by selling Gelston's candles for less. Adams complained vociferously to Hicks, so Hicks, in his next letter to the Hudson merchant blandly assured Gelston that "our only wish was that an uniformity might be kept in the price," and disingenuously added that he did "not wish to throw any blame ... but believe [Adams] to be of fair character." [12] From then on Adams probably thought twice before he sold candles under Hicks's price.

When fighting for the interests of his clients, as the Adams-Gelston incident shows, Hicks, the Quaker, was no namby-pamby. In another instance, a clash with New York's minor officialdom, Hicks set off more fireworks. Since colonial times New York had had official gaugers who measured the contents of barrels intended for export or for local sale. When oil already bearing a New England gauger's official count was offered for sale in New York, a New York customer could demand regauging. Indeed, it was almost traditional for oil coming from New England to New York to be gauged twice. This was one tradition that Friend Hicks did not like. Ruefully he reported to William Rotch & Sons: "You'll perceive that the gauges have not held out," Hicks apologized, "but it generally so happens that the Eastern gaugers fall short. We find our gaugers make an allowance from the apparent gauge, for the 'deception' (as they say) of the casks . . . which deduction appears to us unjustifiable." Hicks let these petty bureaucrats know his opinion. "On our insisting that it was so, it affronted one of them so much that he would gauge no more." [13]

Hicks's business behavior pleased his customers for other reasons. He confined himself to the role of agent and avoided any occasion for competing with the business of his principal. "T. Folger offer'd us his Oil at $110 cash," Hicks informed the merchant Jonathan Jenkins, "but we did not choose to buy when we had any of our friends' oil on hand lest they might think we gave our oil the best sales." In this case propriety was the best policy because "T.F. left his oil with us to sell on commission." [14]

Finally, Hicks's success as an oil factor for the Nantucket and New Bedford whale merchants must be attributed to his simple honesty. In the following instance Hicks demonstrated that there was substance to the Quaker reputation for honesty. "We now hand the annexed account of sales of thy 66 casks of oil received by the *Susa*," Hicks wrote William Rotch, Jr. in 1796, "which thee will find to overrun the invoice 100 gallons." [15] This much oil represented a substantial sum. The error, an untraceable one, had been in the invoices sent by Rotch. Hicks's honesty, in this case, was worth a lot more to Rotch than the commission he paid Hicks on the sale. Such conduct undoubtedly invited further shipments.

From all accounts it appears that Hicks enjoyed the

preference among the nation's leading whale merchants during the years 1797, 1798, 1799, and during part of 1800. Hicks probably handled more oil in those years than any other New York factor.

Table 2. Isaac Hicks's Oil and Candle Receipts, 1796–1804[a]

Year	Oil: Sperm and Whale	Candles
	(gallons)	(pounds)
1796	21,217	9,669
1797	57,927	27,334
1798	49,034	58,725
1799	23,961	15,193
1800	11,033	10,653
1801	4,340	7,130
1802	5,131	8,776
1803	—	6,909
1804	—	—

[a] Invoice Book, H.P.

The statistics of Table 2 are taken from Hicks's invoice books and indicate domestic sales of some importance. In 1797, when Hicks sold 36,530 gallons of whale oil, this amount was only 1,691 gallons less than the total whale oil exports of the United States for that year. Hicks's biggest year for candles, during which he sold 58,724 pounds, compared favorably with total American exports, which in the year 1798 amounted to 144,149 pounds.[16] Hicks's function as an oil factor did not include exporting oil because the whale merchants had both the ships and the experience to handle their own overseas shipments.

The year 1800 was the turning point in Isaac Hicks's relations with the whale merchants. After that time his commissions from this source declined steadily. Part of the reason for this decline lay in the vicissitudes of the whaling industry, part with Hicks's own actions.

Whale products came into being only because a dozen or so men willingly left the safety of a New England or Hudson River port in a small vessel of one or two hundred tons to seek whales in open boats in the Atlantic or Pacific Oceans. These industrious vessels were fair game in any war. Much as many Nantucketers desired neutrality during the Revolutionary War, their wishes were not observed by the British fleet, which captured or destroyed most of colonial America's whaling fleet. With the Treaty of Paris in 1783, Nantucket and other whalers were unmolested until the Anglo-French wars brought new hardships to shipping interests on this side of the Atlantic. By 1798 French war vessels made the sea around the West Indies so dangerous for all American ships that insurance rates rose to prohibitive levels. "Whaling suffered . . . the price of provisions ran high . . . at one time rates as high as 20 per cent were charged for marine insurance when underwriters would assume risks at all." [17] When oil prices failed to rise proportionately, thanks to the competition from alternative products, the results were disastrous for men in the whaling industry. Needless to say, New Englanders sent fewer ships into the service of the whale fishery in 1798 and 1799.

Hicks's correspondents reflected this situation in their letters. Samuel Rodman, complaining about insurance rates in 1799, said "the premiums with the present prospects in the fishery . . . will wholly discourage it. Sperm oil is now worth $100 a ton." Two weeks after writing this letter he ordered Hicks to suspend further insurance on the *Maria,* "which is the only whaling ship I have out. When I hear of her in the Pacific Ocean . . . may . . . endeavor to make myself more secure . . . in that sinking property." At best Rodman was pessimistic. The last completed venture on the *Diana,* he wrote, "brought me a voyage that twelve months ago would have cleared the ship . . . now leaves a balance of

$2,ooo against the venture." [18] All American whalers felt discouraged by the loss of the French market, the rising cost of outfitting a voyage, the soft domestic market for whale products, and, most of all, the exorbitant price of insurance.

By the year 1800 Nantucket whale men were becoming increasingly aware of a situation which was their own special problem. A sandbar crossed the mouth of their harbor which only relatively shallow draft vessels could pass over. As long as the center of whaling was the North and South Atlantic, Nantucket ships small enough to clear the bar were adequate to the service. With the gradual exhaustion of these areas, however, especially after 1800, more ships went to the Pacific to find whales. These longer voyages required bigger, deeper ships. Although Nantucket whale men managed to scrape more ships over their bar during the first decade of the nineteenth century than rival New Bedford was able to clear, Nantucket's days of supremacy were numbered.[19] Though Hicks dealt with both ports—indeed, many Nantucket families had branches in New Bedford—Nantucket was the more important account. The disruption of Nantucket whaling, had Hicks continued in this business, might have had adverse effects on his commissions.

Even before 1800 Hicks had been receiving pleas from his Nantucket friends, eloquent testimony of the plight of the unemployed of this island. In April 1799, Friend Jonathan Jenkins sought Hicks's aid for Resolved Gardner, a kinsman of Jenkins who had been a cooper. "The stagnation of business with us in the whaling line," Jenkins explained, "has put a final stop to the occupation he followed." Another cooper, Thomas Freeborn, received in true Quaker fashion, a cautious recommendation from Obed, Aaron, Richard, and Jethro Mitchell, "as we think he is adequate to the task. He is a Member of our Society, one whom we think will pay proper attention to his business and endeavour to perform his promises." [20]

After 1800 the firm of Isaac Hicks received less oil from New England, but difficulties in the whaling industry constituted only a part of the cause for this falling-off of shipments. By his own acts Hicks was responsible for diverting business from his firm. In 1797 Isaac started his brother Samuel as an apprentice in his firm, and soon made him chief clerk. When Samuel left Isaac late in 1799 to establish the partnership of Hicks & Post with his Westbury friend Henry Post, this new firm inherited with Isaac's blessing much of the older firm's business. With similar generosity Hicks assisted one of his New England apprentices, Jacob Barker, after he had served his term.[21] Barker's subsequent notoriety even brought a kind of fame to his former master, at least in the mind of one commentator: "If he had done nothing but bringing up Jacob Barker, that would have been sufficient to immortalize his name." [22] In any event, both Barker and his brother Samuel drew off a considerable portion of Isaac's oil commissions after 1800.

But Hicks did not give up all of his oil commissions by gracious voluntary surrender. Friend Hicks and some of his most proper Quaker correspondents in New England exchanged sharp words in the course of a series of misunderstandings. At this point it is difficult to know for certain who was at fault—if anyone.

One of these unfortunate exchanges occurred late in 1799 when Hicks sold some of William Rotch, Jr.'s oil on a falling market. The price was not high, but Hicks felt that it would have been even lower if he had waited. Rotch did not see it this way and vented his pique in plain language. "The net proceeds falls far short of our expectations, as we have been confident of a scarcity as to keep some of it nine months on hand, and have since the shipping of that refused $80 per ton here for what remained, knowing that it was in good demand at Philadelphia at 3*s.* per gallon." Here Rotch made a pointed suggestion: "So near as thou are to that market, we apprehended thou would sooner have taken liberty to have sent it there than to have sold it at a price so far below our ideas." Rotch's next cut was the unkindest: "We had rather have given thee a commission for purchasing at that price than to have sold ours so low." [23]

To make matters worse Hicks had the bad luck to accept underwriting for one of Rotch's ships from two firms that declared bankruptcy when the loss of the ship was announced. Although misfortunes of this kind were all too common in those uncertain times, Rotch, understandably, was disappointed: "We . . . having calculated for the whole of the *Eliza's* insurance." [24]

In this same letter of May 8, 1800, Rotch took Hicks to task for still another business misfortune, which suggests genuine neglect on Hicks's part. "We observe charges of $100.56 . . . being our proportion of loss on candles sold John Blagg, eleventh month, 1798," a displeased Rotch wrote. "Now eighteen months having elapsed and this single charge being the only information, we were surprised supposing ourselves at least entitled to information when the sales of our property were involved with failures of this kind." [25] Hicks's accounts with the Rotch firm declined after 1800.

In the spring of 1800 a misunderstanding with Obed and Aaron Mitchell caused more trouble for Isaac Hicks. The Mitchell firm sent an order for insurance which Hicks had misinterpreted. When the big oil firm criticized his interpretation of the order, Hicks did not conceal his own irritation. The Mitchells in their turn assumed a posture of outraged innocence. "In reply upon the subject of insurance upon the ship *Hercules* and calling in question they sincerity and integrity, we do not find anything in our letter sent thee meddling therewith." Taking the offensive, the Mitchells continued: "Thy ideas must be grounded upon jealousy or the want of patience to investigate a subject. We are sorry

our business with thee should amount to such language as
is in thy letter for upon a retrospective view [we] never met
with the like before." In a calmer part of the letter the firm
made an observation which hit close to the mark. "Far from
judging . . . that thou wished to slight our business [we]
but conjecture that thou was overcharged with business and
therefore did not see that the policy was in conformity with
our advice." [26]

Whatever may be said about Hicks's apparent lack of
cautious tact as a reason for his losing some oil and candle
business, the Mitchells were correct in assuming that he had
been busy with many accounts other than those of the oil
merchants. Alert to the risk he ran in pouring all of his
efforts into "that sinking property," as the oil business appeared at that time, Hicks had been spending more and
more of his time on other parts of his commission business.

Although oil and candles had been the firm's major pre-
occupation from 1796 to 1800, Hicks had also carried on all
the other lines of commission work begun in the days of
Alsop & Hicks. In fact, he had expanded the volume in the
shipping and commission line and had added new ventures
after 1796.

As a "ship's husband" serving the needs of out-of-town
ship owners, Hicks became steadily busier after 1796. Along
with most other commission merchants of this period Hicks
obtained insurance for his clients by letting New York's
dozen or so insurance brokers collect underwriting for the
policies from among the many merchants who invested this
way. In the later days of Hicks's career he used the services
of the new insurance companies, such as the New York
Insurance Company or the United, rather than the older
form of underwriting. Between 1796 and 1800 a growing
stack of marine insurance policies testified to Hicks's activity
in this area. During the last two years of the Alsop & Hicks's

partnership, for instance, the firm procured 38 policies; from 1796 to 1798 Hicks obtained 104 policies; by 1804, the year he dropped his commission agency, he had arranged for 338 additional policies.[27]

This business of taking care of ships was sufficiently important for Hicks to provide a separate account in his ledger for each ship. Though some of these accounts were small, such as the twelve-day expenses of $307.30 for the schooner *Anna,* others were substantial. For the New Bedford ship *Sarah,* Hicks disbursed $3,580 in 1799, and $13,282, $7,907, and $1,531 in the next three years. This single account earned Hicks a handsome commission of $1,100.[28]

Hicks's New York location, which had been valued by the firm's pre-1796 Hudson accounts, was also exploited by New England and Philadelphia merchants once Isaac managed his own firm. The firm of prominent Philadelphia Quakers, Samuel & Miers Fisher, in 1797 joined Hicks's old correspondent in that city, George Pennock, in buying and selling through Hicks in the superior New York market. Some of the Fishers' ventures were purely domestic, but often they asked Hicks to sell foreign importations such as Teneriffe wine or Altoona linen and glass sent directly from Germany. In these instances, since the goods had been ventured by the foreign correspondents of the Philadelphia firm, Hicks had to split the usual 5 per cent commission for foreign sales with the Fishers.[29] Although he was more than once invited by these Philadelphia merchants to join in commodity speculations, Hicks refused, apparently preferring to specialize in commission work as an agent.

Because William Rotch, Jr., Jonathan Jenkins, Walter Folger, Gardner & Mitchell, Samuel Rodman, and other New Englanders employed less and less of their capital in whaling, they invested more often in merchant ventures. These firms often called on Hicks to assist their voyages and to sell their

imports. Java sugar and coffee, Chinese tea, India sugar and
silks, Russian iron and shipstores, German linens, and French
plaster of Paris were some of the commodities Hicks sold in
New York for these sometime whaler-capitalists.[30]

In 1797 Hicks added to his overseas accounts the Liverpool
firm run by the Quaker Cropper and Benson families. Like
an earlier Hicks customer, Edward Forbes of Dublin, this
firm bought and sold goods on the New York market. After
selling cargoes of earthenware, salt, and porter, Hicks then
purchased for the account of the English firm such commodities as potash, cotton, and a great deal of wheat. Shipments on this firm's regular ship, the *Albion,* and on other
vessels, kept Hicks busy. In 1800 the Cropper & Benson
account stood at $11,709 and by the next year had risen to
$37,031.[31]

Thanks to this Quaker firm, Hicks was introduced to John
Robinson & Sons, a pottery-maker in Burselm, England,
who induced Hicks to perform another type of commission
service. This relationship is of interest because it was one of
several with a manufacturer rather than with merchants.
Hicks earned a 5 per cent commission for selling Robinson's
pottery and made remittances to this firm by purchasing
London bills. The English firm gave him a number of additional commissions of 2½ per cent simply for conveying
orders from other American merchants for Robinson's ware.
From 1799 until Hicks dropped out of commission work in
1804, the firm sold over £6,000 sterling worth of pottery for
this manufacturer.[32]

Hicks was also earning commissions from two American
manufacturers. The Fishers of Philadelphia arranged to give
Hicks the New York sales for their nephew's Brandywine
paper factory. The nephew, Joshua Gilpin, an early American experimenter in paper manufacturing, used Hicks's services from 1797 until 1798, during which time Hicks sold

about $600 worth of paper.[33] A more enduring and lucrative relationship for Hicks was with the Philadelphia sugar refiner, Morgan & Douglas. Despite competition from a number of sugar refiners with plants in New York, Hicks managed from 1797 on to sell an average of 20,000 pounds of sugar a year for this Philadelphia manufacturer. This business ended for Isaac Hicks only after he persuaded Morgan & Douglas to transfer the account to his brother's firm.[34]

From 1796 to 1800 Hicks's firm prospered. During this period the oil and candle specialty led other lines as income-producers but almost all lines showed gains. In 1797 the firm's revenue from commissions amounted to $7,559. This figure rose successively each year to $8,006, $12,570, and $15,743 by 1800.[35] Other indicators of general business activity, such as bank deposits, drafts accepted, and letters received, all show marked increases. Furthermore, when circumstances at the turn of the century dimmed the immediate prospects in the oil industry, Hicks, if not "overcharged with business," was already well on his way to prominence in the handling of what was to be America's most valuable export during the next half-century.

CHAPTER V

Isaac Hicks Serves the South

THE CLUSTER of devices contrived by John Kay, Lewis Paul, Richard Arkwright, James Hargreaves, and Samuel Crompton revolutionized English textile manufacturing, and created a pressure for still another invention—a "cotton gin." Eli Whitney obliged historical necessity and made the engine which transformed the American South. Before the gin, America had been able to raise along the coast of Georgia only a trivial amount of long-staple Sea Island cotton. After the gin had made the growing of upland short-staple cotton feasible, the cotton culture spread quickly from Carolina to Texas to make the United States the leading producer of baled cotton. Because there seemed to be no limit to the demand for cotton garments and the raw material to make them, cotton was crowned king by American businessmen from the New England mill site to the Delta plantation.

Isaac Hicks was in the commission business handling New England oil and candle shipments when this ground swell in the cotton industry began. As late as 1794 Robert Bolton of Savannah had apologized to the New Yorker for sending him a bag of cotton in payment for dry goods: "I know it is a dull article in New York." As America's cotton exports rose from 189,316 pounds in 1791 to 6,107,000 in 1796, and to 27,501,000 in 1812, Bolton never again felt the need to apologize for shipping this "dull article." Hicks's invoice books record the increase of cotton shipments to him from the negligible ones of 1794 to 9,341 pounds in 1798, and to 76,770 pounds in 1800.[1] As the wave of the cotton future gathered strength, Hicks, settled by 1800 in his new business quarters at 239 Water Street, was in the process of transferring his major attentions from New England to the South. Hicks needed no special decision to make this change because his already established southern connections simply added to his business each year until, for him, too, cotton became "king."

Hicks's role as a commission agent in the southern trade reflects something of the international organization of this trade in its early years. Albion and others have noted certain unusual features in the nineteenth-century financing and transporting of southern cotton to British markets. They speak of a "cotton triangle" in which northerners "dragged the cotton shipments 200 miles out of their normal course" in order to "transship" the cotton in regular New York trans-Atlantic vessels.[2] A part of Hicks's operations followed the course described by this triangle.

Hicks's invoice books and other records demonstrate that he received sizable shipments of cotton in New York. These he handled in the same manner as any other goods on consignment. Hicks sold the cotton, usually to merchants interested in reshipping the goods to Europe, then credited the southern owner with the proceeds of the sale, less his own $2\frac{1}{2}$ per cent commission for conducting the sale. If the southerner wanted his proceeds invested in New York goods for shipment south, rather than converted into currency or left on the books to cover drafts, the commission agent earned an additional $2\frac{1}{2}$ per cent for the service of making these purchases. From Hicks's end the mechanics of this commission transaction might have applied equally well to consignments of oil, linen, or potash, as to rice or cotton.

In addition to this pattern of southern trade, Hicks's correspondence, insurance records, and other papers attest to a different routing of southern goods which did not pull cotton 200 miles off course. Hicks's southern correspondents, particularly Robert & John Bolton of Savannah, sent some of their ships loaded with cotton, rice, and tobacco *directly* to European ports. Many of these vessels, such as the Bolton's ship *Elizabeth,* were fully as large as the regular New York-to-Europe traders.[3]

On return voyages from Corunna, Rotterdam, Liverpool, or elsewhere, the Boltons might order these vessels—even the larger ones—to by-pass New York and to sail directly with their inbound cargoes for Savannah.[4] In Hicks's experience this return routing was, admittedly, less common than the lap charted by Albion for southern shipping. When European goods purchased by the Savannah firms appeared better suited for a New York market, the Boltons and others sent their ships to New York. From 1799 until Hicks left business, however, New York did not act invariably as an entrepôt for the goods traded by his southern correspondents.

To serve these southerners Hicks did much more than simply sell the portion of southern cotton that was routed to New York. The size and development of the New York mercantile community gave Hicks many ways of serving these correspondents. As a resident of the nation's most active port Hicks had access to much more commercial news than was available to his friends in Savannah or Charleston. One of Hicks's simplest but most important services was to send regular advices about his own and foreign markets. In addition he frequently passed on information about the southerners' ships which had come to Hicks from various captains in the port of New York or from his correspondents abroad.

For a while Hicks had a considerable business making insurance for Savannah ships and cargoes, whether or not they were destined for New York. Savannah's mercantile community was far too small to offer the amount of reliable insurance underwriting needed in its own cotton trade. Unfortunately, a series of bad experiences with New York underwriters made the Boltons, Hicks's principal customers, switch to British underwriters.[5]

Undoubtedly Hicks's most important service to the southern businessmen was financial. The leadership in trade probably explains why New York had more banks—the Bank of New York, the "Branch Bank" of the Bank of the United States, and the Manhattan Company—and a greater volume of financial transactions than in any other American city, certainly more than in Savannah or even Charleston. This meant, among other things, that by the turn of the century New York was a leading market for buying and selling international bills of exchange. Hicks used these facilities of the nation's financial capital to perform transactions the southerners were incapable of conducting in their own limited markets.

As early as 1797 Robert & John Bolton had requested Hicks to sell international bills for friends, relatives, and for the firm itself. These bills were the devices used by the southern exporters to obtain money when they did not choose to turn the proceeds of their cotton shipments into cargoes purchased in Europe for sale in the United States. These bills, however, could not be sold in Savannah because the excess of exports over imports in that city meant that almost every merchant wanted to sell bills and almost nobody wanted to buy them. Consequently, Hicks received many requests like the following during his early years of serving the South: "Inclosed [are] the first sixteen setts of Exchange drawn by George Alsop [of Savannah] on Robert Spear [of Manchester] amounting to £2,000 Sterling which have negotiated and forward the money arising from the sales." [6]

Toward the end of 1798 Hicks and his principal customer, Robert & John Bolton, established a more effective arrangement for disposing of bills. Instead of trying to sell in New York the bills of some Georgia exporter who was unknown there, Hicks sold bills drawn in his own name against an English house. "You will receive by Captain Webb a letter," the Boltons explained to Hicks, "authorizing you to draw on Robert Spear of Manchester for £5,000 sterling." Larger sums were usually split up. "We want you to draw on John Gore & Co. for £10,000 sterling at 60 days—say £2,000 per week for five weeks for cash to be immediately sent by post and good vessels." [7] Hicks charged the customary 1½ per cent for this service of selling bills.

Since sailings from Savannah to England were infrequent, Hicks often forwarded the letters sent to him by coastal vessels which authorized his English drafts. "The letter for Rathbone, Hughes & Duncan which goes by the *Hunter* and *Ceres* [New York to Savannah packets] must be forwarded by first (separate) opportunity as they are your authority for drawing." By 1800 Hicks had established such close rapport with the Liverpool Quaker house, Rathbone, Hughes & Duncan, that this firm accepted Hicks's draft even before authorization from the Boltons had arrived. "We have accepted your draft on us for £196 12s. 11d. favor Samuel Blain, and for account of R. & J. Bolton," the English firm wrote Hicks, "although we are without any advice . . . on the subject." [8]

After selling these drafts on English houses Hicks's next responsibility was to send the funds he had acquired in some form convenient for his southern correspondents. Although this was not an international but only a domestic transaction, it was not so simple as it sounds, or would in fact be today. The nature of business in bankless Savannah, together with the lack of any central banking facilities for clearing checks from one area to another, or even of exchanging the notes of one branch of the Bank of the United States with those of another, made remittances between New York and Savannah difficult.

Although there were limits to the quantity of domestic bills of exchange that could be passed, as well as some objections to their use, southerners drew a considerable number against Hicks between 1798 and 1805. In 1797 a mere fourteen bills worth $9,974 were presented to Hicks by houses in the South. Hicks thus passed some nine thousand dollars into the hands of New Yorkers who were creditors of these southern merchants. In 1798, bills worth $22,220 came from the South. By 1801 the figure had jumped to $47,668 and reached a peak of $64,536 in 1802.[9] The principal limit upon the use of these domestic bills of exchange originating in the South appears to have been the scarcity of southern debt in New York. As an exporting area the South paid most of its debts with the commodities it shipped, and hence generated scant demand for bills payable in New York.

Hicks's southern merchants did not like to do business with their fellow southerners when it came to domestic bills of exchange drawn against New York houses. "No calculation can be made on selling bills on you," the Boltons explained. "We are always obliged to wait for applications." Alexander Halliday, another southerner, pointed to a special disadvantage of funds in this form: "Cotton is occasionally sold for bills on New York to people who are well known, but the purchaser is always obliged to pay about two cents per pound more than if he was to buy for cash."[10]

The genteel informality of southerners made domestic bills originating in New York no more serviceable than those originating in the South. If Hicks bought the Boltons a bill drawn by a New York creditor against some Savannah merchant, the Boltons still had trouble in Savannah. "In *confidence*," the firm confessed, "we are seldom enabled to get payment to a day from any person in this place, as we have no bank [to discount notes]." According to the Boltons, the merchants are "all on friendly terms and we are often put to inconvenience by being obliged to give indulgence after the time is expired for it would be disagreeable," they admitted, "to send a bill back even after ten or twenty days over the time and this is generally taken advantage of." Though procrastination was bad enough, they further admitted that "bills on this place, generally, are more unsafe than risks at sea." [11]

Because no form of domestic bills of exchange had wide acceptability in the South, Hicks's final recourse in making remittances to these merchants was to send them actual money. This was not easy. Lacking a national currency, merchants who had to pay debts in cash usually used bank notes. Hicks, however, could not always send the southerners the bank notes that were most available to him, the notes of the Philadelphia and New York branches of the Bank of the United States. In 1799 he was told by Robert & John Bolton: "We find it necessary to mention a circumstance which has lately taken place in Charleston. The Banks there have come to a resolution to take no other bank notes but their own. As our dealings is great with the planters of that state we shall be under the necessity of getting you to procure as much of the notes of that Bank as possible—there is a loss of five per cent on Northern notes in Charleston." [12]

Even though Hicks had to transfer large sums, the Boltons made a further restriction on the size of individual bank notes. "Let the bills be not over $100 and one-half in smaller bills of $50, $20, $10 and $5." [13]

Because southern cotton merchants like the Boltons had to deal with financially unsophisticated farmers, a request for cash from these southern merchants might quite literally mean specie. "Our back country men in consequence of the frequent deceptions in paper," complained the Boltons, "have renewed the cry for specie." Because all of the United States was chronically short of specie in those years, Hicks must have been disconcerted by casual requests like the following: "If you can send us $500 in silver, say Spanish Dollars, they will be very acceptable." Very acceptable—indeed. Despite the repeated southern complaint that there was "a great scarcity of change in Savannah," not all forms of metallic currency satisfied southern demands. Coins as small as quarters would do, but the "twenty cent pieces, or pistareens . . . pass here for but eighteen and three-quarter cents." [14] Southern financial requirements were nothing if not exacting.

After Hicks had availed himself of his city's matchless banking facilities to assemble the exact kind of funds requested by his southern customers, he still had the considerable responsibility of finding a suitable method of delivery. After recording the numbers on the bills, Hicks mailed bank notes of $50 and $100 denominations on "four different post days." [15] This method, costing much more than present-day postage, had considerable risks. Obviously, "$500 in silver, say Spanish Dollars, could not be mailed. Delivery of cumbersome and all too negotiable specie was made by entrusting it to a "confidential passenger" on one of the Savannah packets, to the captain of the vessel who charged from ½ to 1 per cent for the service, or to one of the Boltons' own captains when he happened to be in port. So great was the southerner's craving for hard cash that he always seemed willing to bear the added expense and risk involved in sending specie from New York.

An analysis, then, of Hicks's relations with this principal southern customer between the years 1798 and 1804 suggests that the older notion of a cotton triangle may miss the point. Some southern cotton went directly to Hicks on consignment, but his records give the clear impression that during these years more cotton was shipped directly to Europe from Savannah than was dragged to New York for transshipment. But no matter which route the goods took, New York re-

mained an indispensable corner in the triangular organization of the cotton trade. The city's role was both that of
importer and of financial go-between. Southern credits in
the form of international bills of exchange on British houses
had to be redeemed in the northern cities where the import
trade created a demand for these bills. Northerners had to
"buy" American exports from the South to pay their overseas
debts. Literally, Hicks, the commission agent, and his northern counterparts arranged the payments to the South for
northern imports, for which service he earned his profits.
The mechanics of this financial triangle endured after
Hicks's day regardless of the destination of cotton ships in
southern ports.

A corollary to the assumption that unenterprising southerners allowed their cotton to be dragged to New York for
transshipment is the theory that southerners lacked capital,
and so fell into the clutches of Yankee businessmen. This
was not Hicks's experience from 1798 to 1804. His southern
correspondents were not in a position of colonial dependence
upon his money-lending. The whole tenor of Hicks's business
relations with these people contradicts the view that the
South lacked capital. Hicks's experience does not contradict
the assertion that the South was absolutely dependent upon
the financial *facilities* of the North; it does suggest that they
did not need the North's capital.

In the first place, Hicks never loaned money to, nor arranged a loan for, any of his southern correspondents. In
1802, when the Boltons, his most important customers, found
their firm hard-pressed, Hicks offered to advance them funds.
This offer was declined with thanks. Several years later the
Boltons did invite Hicks to share on even terms in the ownership of a gin. The amount of money involved, however,
was small, and the offer would appear to have been a gesture
by the Boltons to include Hicks in the profits anticipated

from the new operation.[16] This single instance hardly provides evidence in Hicks's case of southern dependence upon northern funds.

On the other hand, the Boltons as southern merchants bought cotton, rice, and tobacco from the planters with their own funds. Furthermore, this firm financed the shipment of the crop to market. Very often the Boltons carried the cotton cargoes in vessels which they owned, such as the *Diana,* the *Nixon,* the *Rachel,* the *Thomas & Robert,* the *Columbia,* and one, the ship *Thames,* which they owned in part. This basic self-sufficiency which characterized the Boltons' operation was matched in varying degrees by the other southern businessmen who employed Hicks as their commission agent.

Hicks's records show that the Boltons not only had enough capital to handle the routine local purchasing of southern commodities from the planters but also enough to speculate through Hicks on commodities in the New York market. Sometimes the Savannah firm chose to speculate in cotton, the commodity with which it was most familiar. "I am informed that a considerable quantity of Georgia cotton is laying in your city and that the sale is dull," Robert Bolton wrote Hicks in 1798. "This induces me to request you will purchase from 100 to 400 bales . . . provided the same can be procured . . . by the negotiation of bills on London. Please ship in the first good vessel for Liverpool, advising Messers, John Gore & Co. . . . and forward them duplicate invoice and Bill of Lading." Bolton did not want the Savannah people to know that he was using his funds for purchases in New York: "I think it prudent to observe that whatever you do in this business I would not wish it to appear as being done from my house—except in the invoices." [17]

The Boltons were alert to the opportunity to invest in commodities other than cotton in the New York market. In

1800 Hicks received an order to buy a stock of another southern staple, rice. "If you can purchase good rice at $5.00 . . . we wish you to . . . ship to London or Liverpool 200 bbls." A day later the Boltons inquired about an item normally out of their experience in local purchasing. "Would not flour be a safe speculation to send to England?" the Boltons asked Hicks. This request was not unusual, for the previous year the southern firm had used part of its English credits to speculate in something completely out of its line. "We observe that you were purchasing ashes on account of our mutual friends. R. & J. Bolton, to ship for this market to our address," Hicks's Liverpool agents wrote early in 1800, "and that it would be necessary to value on our house for part of the amount."[18] Hicks's own commodity speculation to Russia in concert with the Bolton firm, an operation described in the next chapter, offers further evidence of the adequacy of southern business capital between 1798 and 1806.

In Hicks's day, when merchants involved in international or interregional trade were more exposed to the dangers of fraud, close personal relations often grew between men who conducted their business at a distance. Trust was essential in long-distance business. Once mutual confidence became established in the course of trade, the merchants often recognized and encouraged this bond of confidence by exchanging acts of friendship. A. H. Stone, in his study of the American cotton trade, emphasized the close, friendly relation of the southern factor and the planters;[19] however, in the Bolton-Hicks case, the relations between the southern merchant and the northern agent seem no less intimate.

Isaac Hicks and Robert and John Bolton had a somewhat unusual relationship in that they had known each other before they began their extensive trading in cotton. After a brief correspondence with Robert Bolton about the dry goods trade, Hicks, then a partner in the house of Alsop & Hicks, met Bolton in Savannah in 1792. Bolton aided him in his legal pursuit of Alexander Leslie, a delinquent dry goods importer, and most agreeably entertained Hicks at the Savannah merchant's out-of-town farm. At another time, before their numerous cotton transactions developed, Robert Bolton and his family returned Hicks's visit with a stay at the New Yorker's home in 1797. Subsequently, Captain John Bolton made several stops in New York to see Hicks, once in the course of a pilgrimage to "Ballstone Springs" to take the cure, but these visits by the brother came after the cotton business had begun.[20]

These prior friendly face-to-face meetings certainly helped to prepare the three men to trust each other with very large sums of money. Intermittently, the course of the cotton transactions put each firm at the other's mercy. If Hicks's risk as a commission agent may have seemed the lesser because his own capital was not invested, he still made himself liable for the extent of the Boltons' drafts by drawing bills in his own name. If these bills of Hicks's had been refused because the Boltons' delivery of cotton failed to come through, Hicks, as the drawer, would have been liable for the full amount of the bill. The southerners were sensitive to Hicks's position and half-jestingly wrote: "Are you not staggered at putting your cautious hand to so much paper for us—let your faith continue." [21]

The Boltons in turn were dependent upon the honesty and business sense of their New York agent. Frequently the greater part of their active funds were in Hicks's hands. Unable to keep up with the market for international bills of exchange, they had to rely on his judgment to sell their bills for maximum yield. They had to depend absolutely upon his liquidity both to cover their many drafts at short time and to furnish promptly the hard money they needed when their buying season began.

Throughout their letters the Boltons reflect their full confidence in Hicks. "We imagine you must sometimes compare us to Citizen *Talleyrand* for *money, money,* is our only cry in most of our letters," Robert Bolton wrote in a letter requesting more of the same. "The fact is . . . as you are our main stay and *particular* friend you know more of it than any others, in truth . . . we feel as easy in it as though we were speaking to each other. We know your willingness to accomodate us too well." Other letters continued this theme: "We are . . . so fully convinced of your close attachment to our interest that we shall feel satisfied with what you do." "We must say that you have always done our business so well," the Boltons wrote in 1802, "that we feel easy about it, preferring rather to leave to your judgment than offer opinion, convinced that while you are free . . . you will always do as for yourself." [22]

It was customary for these mercantile ties to be accompanied by requests by the parties for small favors and various nonbusiness services. Frequently gifts were volunteered. Each year the Boltons sent Sarah Hicks Georgia watermelons, seasonal fruit, and bushels of her favorite sweet potatoes. Ironically, the Boltons found themselves embarrassed one year because no sweet potatoes were to be had. "Could you believe that our cotton planters are so cotton mad that we have no sweet potatoes to sell?" the firm expostulated.[23] Yet it was the pressure of factors like the Boltons upon the planters which progressively diminished the self-sufficiency of the South.

Hicks cheerfully responded to the Boltons' requests for the many wants they could not satisfy in Georgia and South Carolina. Standard in October was an order for "four barrels best buckwheat and four kegs best butter. The last must be placed in the cabin to prevent turning rancid." [24] Foodstuffs and delicacies such as "three or four dozen of the best claret for our own use," were the most frequently requested items. Occasionally, requests reached Hicks for special medicine. "A female friend . . . troubled with a bad cough thinks some of Doctor Church's Drops would be of service to her." "Please procure me two boxes of Collier's Ointment for Piles—to be had at Philips & Clark, Druggists, No. 66 Maiden Lane." "The enclosed letter," Bolton wrote, "ordering thirty-dozen bottles of the water of Ballton Springs I will thank you to forward. I mean to have an experiment for . . . my old complaint." Even the most trivial items had to be ordered in New York. "My snuff box," wrote Robert Bolton, "wants two of the sweet scented vanilla Beans which please send me." [25]

Northern craftsmanship was much admired by the Boltons. Robert, for one, trusted Hicks's Quaker taste in the furnishing of his own new home. "Mrs. Bolton begs you to have a handsome slab made agreeable to pattern. It's intended for an arch in her drawing . . . room and of course she wants it handsome. She chooses you to be the judge recollecting the choice you made of her carpet." During the house-building the senior partner pleaded: "Robert Bolton's fine house must not be stopped, therefore must beg you to have immediately got in readiness: 2 sets marble for two chimney pieces." John, the junior partner, also put in his confidential request: "I will thank you to send me a set of elegant tea china . . . should they be approved, I will send you the thanks of Mrs. B. . . . this between friends." [26]

Conceivably, all this requested "elegance" may have tried Hicks's Quakerly sentiments favoring simplicity and moderation; however, Robert Bolton's taste in silver must have met with approbation. The Savannah merchant asked Hicks to go to William G. Forbes, "nearly opposite the Trinity Church in Broadway, No. 90," and buy some assorted spoons, "all made strong and plain with the letters 'R B' cyphered on them." Bolton must have had a smile on his face when he wrote the following request which deferred to the Quaker testimony against music. "One of our particular friends wants a Pianna for his daughter. As we don't expect you have much knowledge of those instruments of music, we beg you to get a judge to make a choice." [27]

Actually, Hicks and the Boltons had much in common though the southerners did not belong to the Society of Friends. As public-spirited men, the Boltons were active in organizations. Both of them belonged to the Savannah Cotton Exchange, and Robert was a member of the City Corporation. Interested in improvement, Robert requested Hicks to send him "the ordinances of your corporation" for the last two years "as we wish to gain knowledge from their experience." [28]

Robert Bolton's staunch republicanism produced in him an attitude toward titles of distinction not unlike that to which Hicks had been trained as a Quaker. Improbably, it was Hicks who offended on this score and drew a rebuke from Savannah: "I observed that you *Esquired* me by your last letter," an aghast Bolton exclaimed. "I don't know whether this is considered an indictable offense against the rules of the Friends Society, neither can I suppose so, when deviated from by a man of your gravity, but conclude," Robert Bolton admonished, "there will be no necessity of preferring a bill against you for it, as it is to be supposed the like will never happen again." [29] That round went to Bolton.

These two men, Robert Bolton and Isaac Hicks, had learned to sense each other's reactions. When Bolton asked Hicks to find him a captain in New York, his order sounded almost as though Hicks himself had made it. "Be sure to get a Master famed for modesty, sobriety, morality, *no swearer,* plentiful in the art of patience, etc." But Bolton knew the comment this council of perfection deserved, for he immediately added: "I can almost hear you say, 'This is impossible in our depraved times.' " [30]

A neighborly quality marked the relations of merchants who did business with each other in those days. Separated by hundreds of miles from the Boltons, Hicks often acted as a Bolton relative might, boarding visiting kinfolk. "My nephew, Thomas Newell," Robert Bolton explained to Hicks, "is on his way to Woodstock ... to see a poor relation. On his return to New York it is probable he may have in his charge a little girl. As there may not be an immediate opportunity to send her out by a good conveyance," Bolton then requested, "I beg you to permit her to play with your four little boys until you can send her to us." Bolton did not forget about Hicks's own family and added: "I hope your next will be a daughter which may help the mother to darn stockings for the rough Boys." [31]

At another time the southern family asked Hicks to take special care of young Curtis Bolton during his visit to New York. After Curtis returned to Savannah, the Boltons wrote: "We have this day the pleasure to have Mrs. Gibson, her son, and Curtis, who cannot express too much admiration when speaking of your friendship, but as it was nothing strange to us, we only admired their sensibility." [32]

When it was Robert Bolton's turn to invite Hicks to Savannah, he was exceedingly cordial. "As I have invited you to come to Savannah for *your health*—my house (which has given you so much trouble) is at yours and Mrs. Hicks and the children's service. I am not joking," urged Bolton, "why can't you come and spend a couple of months if the fever appears in your City next summer. I can hardly expect the pleasure of your company, nor do I wish this unhappy event may ever drive you off, but you know your company would be adding to our pleasure." [33]

A final bit of evidence of the closeness of this southern factor and his northern commission agent is John Bolton's letter to Hicks following the death of Bolton's cousin and partner in late 1804. "I am charged by . . . the widow of our dead friend to request your acceptance of a great coat bound with fur (which was imported from Russia and worn by him) as a mark of her great respect for you and the friendship which subsisted between you and the former wearer," Bolton explained. "She has heard me with peculiar pleasure read your letters in which you have made such affectionate mention of herself and family, and it is no small consolation to her that the friendly intercourse which subsisted between you and her dead Husband is continuing through you and myself." [34]

For Hicks, friendship had been no bar to profits during these years when his commission agency shifted its concentration from New England products to cotton and other southern staples. From 1799 to 1804 his total revenue from commissions came to $88,321. Indeed, these results were so satisfying that on February 18, 1804, Hicks issued a circular letter to announce that he was declining further commission work "in favor of Messers. Hicks, Jenkins & Company," the firm managed by his brother Samuel and a former apprentice. [35]

In keeping with the leisurely pace of these times this announcement was simply a statement of intention which let the world know that a transition was in progress. Hicks had thought of this move earlier and had even written abortively to his English correspondents in 1802 of his intention to drop commission work. So gradual was the changeover that during the whole of 1804 the firm earned $11,598 in commissions, just $600 less than for the year previous. Even though the commissions continued for the rest of the year, after the announcement Hicks must have considered himself free of whatever restraint he had felt as a commission agent in speculating in commodities on his own account—the phase of business which concluded Hicks's career as a merchant. [36]

CHAPTER VI

Isaac Hicks Invests on His Own Account

I F   O N E of Isaac Hicks's principal motives for entering the commission business in 1794 had been the desire to safeguard his limited capital, this reason carried less weight some eight or nine years later. Although Hicks was not likely to lose much money as a commission agent, he was not likely to find sudden riches either. His earnings as an agent always were limited to the customary 2½ per cent or 5 per cent no matter how profitable a venture might have been for some distant principal. With money accumulating from his commission business, Hicks by 1802 seems to have been anxious to make part of it available for investments on his own account.[1]

Another probability is that the thirty-five-year-old Hicks had been considering at least partial retirement from business in 1802. Dropping the commission work was a logical first step. Through a single fortunate venture on his own account he could earn as much as he made in a year scurrying around handling the numerous ventures of other businessmen.[2] Having earned over $88,000 from 1797 to 1802, Hicks could think of himself as a successful man.[3] In all probability he was now more willing to slacken his efforts and to give more heed to his health, about which he had been receiving occasional unfavorable reports.

In 1802, when Hicks made his first considerable investment in his own name, he was not entering an entirely new field. Since the founding of his firm in 1796 he had speculated moderately in ventures which did not conflict with the commodity lines he handled in his commission work.

In 1796, for example, Hicks and Jonathan Jenkins, one of the Nantucket whale merchants, bought £1,359 9s. 2d. worth of foodstuffs to be sold on Nantucket by Jenkins. Because too many other merchants decided that 1796 was the year to ship flour and pork to Nantucket, the partners added only 5s. to their ledgers at the conclusion of the venture, if more to their fund of experience.[4]

In collaboration with another New Englander in 1798, Hicks shipped £212 9s. 10d. worth of naval stores to Bristol. More fortunate this time, Hicks realized a 40 per cent gross profit margin on the operation, a sum amounting to £136 13s. 11d.[5] Neither of these two ventures risked an excessively large amount of his working capital and in neither case did the commodities conflict with his handling of whale products or southern produce.

The next year Hicks put more money in adventures of his own and earned a total of $1,429. On an importation of German textiles from Hamburg, Hicks made his largest single profit, $932, on sales totalling $8,167. But the most complicated transaction in 1799, an adventure to St. Petersburg, gave Hicks his taste for the ventures which absorbed his interests during the last part of his career. In partnership with the ship's captain, Judah Paddock, Hicks owned $8,723 as his share of the return cargo from Russia of "White Rope, Ravens Duck, Sheetings, Table Spreads, and Feather Beds."[6] Although the profits from this voyage were not large, both men became intrigued with the possibilities of trade with Russia, an avenue of commerce explored by Elias H. Derby in 1784.[7]

For the next two years Hicks involved himself only sporadically in overseas speculations. Very busy with the commission business which in 1800 and 1801 earned him a total of over $40,000, Hicks did not divert much of his time or money to ventures on his own account.

On December 1, 1802, Hicks made the move which put

him in a new business and speeded his transition from commission agent to merchant investor: for a syndicate interested in the Russian trade Hicks bought the 396-ton ship *Thames*.[8] This trade became Hicks's major business concern for the next four years.

Patiently, Hicks had worked to assemble the talent and necessary capital for the project he had been contemplating since 1799, the year he and Paddock shared in a venture to St. Petersburg. Since that date Paddock had been enthusiastic about trying another voyage, but both agreed that they lacked the funds to make a success of such an extended enterprise. Moroccan pirates delayed the plans by capturing Captain Judah Paddock and selling him into slavery, an interlude which effectively took him out of circulation for a year.[9] After Paddock's release Hicks tried to interest Samuel Rodman, a New England ship owner, but was unsuccessful. Hicks's luck changed late in 1801 though he did not necessarily realize it at the time. Hicks engineered a partnership between one of his Hudson accounts, Robert Jenkins & Company, and Robert & John Bolton of Savannah for the purpose of owning jointly the ship *General Mercer,* a vessel intended for a New York, Savannah, Liverpool run. By bringing these two firms together Hicks, it turned out, was only one step away from uniting all of the parties for the purpose of his pet project. Jenkins, who already knew and trusted his fellow citizen from Hudson, Judah Paddock, willingly assented to the plan presented by Hicks and Paddock. Finally, in July 1802 the Boltons decided that "should . . . a suitable vessel for that trade" be offered at a reasonable price, they would join. Hicks had assembled his team; the Peace of Amiens depressed the carrying trade sufficiently to make the *Thames* go for the bargain price of $17,000.[10]

The ship was a beauty. Intended as an Indiaman, this two-year-old vessel measured about one hundred tons more than

Letter of February 8, 1803, from Isaac Hicks to Captain Judah Paddock, then in Savannah awaiting the loading of the *Thames* for a voyage to Russia.

The Names of the Stockholders in jericho turnpike

Shares

Lewis S. Newlett — 40
Valentine Hicks — 40
John Titus — 40
Lewis & Charles Newlett 40
Jackson Townsend — 10
Walter Jones — 20
William Jones Major — 20
Benjamin Hicks — 20
Willet Robbins — 40
Foy Willis — 25
William Jones — 60
Arnold Fleet — 20
Billop Seaman — 40
Samuel Jones Jun.r 20
Samuel Titus — 160
Benj.n Platt — 20
Isaac Hicks — 30
William Aldrich — 15
Royal
Townsend Jackson 100
Jacob Willits — 20
Samuel Willis — 20
George Newlett — 20
Charles Willits — 20
Thomas Willis — 10
Jacob Shirby — 10
Obadiah Jackson — 20
Benjamin Rowland 100
Townsend Willis — 10
Israel Wakefield — 20
Matt & Freelove Townsend 40
L. Titus (Deceased) 100

Richard V. Wyck — 12
Saml. Sands (Estate) 20
Gideon Seaman — 10
Timothy S. Williams d. 40
Thomas Tredwell — 10
John Wood — 30
John Ketcham — 10
David Ketcham — 10
Robert Willits — 10

1360

Names of Stockholders
of the Jericho Turnpike
Road — 1818 —

Isaac Hicks and his brother Valentine were among the stockholders in
the Jericho Turnpike Road which still borders Hicks property in Westbury.

the average commercial vessel in the European trade. After two happy voyages as her commander, Paddock used the *Thames* as a standard for comparing the sailing capabilities of other vessels. The owners were impressed by her cargo-carrying capacity.

Risk and managerial responsibility were shared. The Boltons provided half the capital for both the ship and cargo, Jenkins and Paddock an eighth each, and Hicks one quarter. Besides fulfilling an entrepreneurial responsibility for assembling the personnel and capital for the venture, Hicks also acted as "ship's husband," and the seller of the *Thames*'s inbound cargo, a role similar to that played by New York's Oliver Walcott when he organized voyages to China. Paddock, the skipper, was granted wide discretion in disposing of the cargo and in purchasing abroad because of his business experience, particularly in European ports.[11] Having sent their ship, the *Diana,* to Russia in 1798, the Boltons could also claim specific experience with the St. Petersburg run in addition to their broad mercantile knowledge. Their commercial know-how combined with their 50 per cent contribution of capital, of course, earned them a major voice in the councils of this partnership. The politic Hicks urged the Boltons to take nominal direction of the voyage and to write the captain's formal orders. It is doubtful, however, that the formal authority granted the Boltons ever equaled the actual power to control the voyage that Hicks enjoyed through his intimate relation with Friend Judah Paddock.

In early discussion of the route the Boltons favored sending the ship to Savannah to load with "tobacco, rice, and upland cotton, and proceed . . . for Copenhagen, there sell and proceed to Russia. This is the regular route Gray of Salem has . . . followed from this port for several years." Despite Billy Gray's successes with the Copenhagen stop, Hicks preferred a plan which allowed more freedom. The Boltons' instructions to Paddock, as they eventually read, were a token of the influence Hicks's suggestions had in Savannah: "Proceed with the first fair wind for the harbor of Cork in Ireland." There you will "receive letters from merchants to whom both Hicks and ourselves have written—say from London, Havre and after . . . examining them you will adopt such plan as may seem to you most for the advantage of all concerned." [12] The extra stop, though it raised their insurance, enabled the owners to supply the captain with the most up-to-date market reports from European cities.

Hicks's bookkeeping designation of this temporary partnership of Paddock, Jenkins, the Boltons, and Hicks as an "Adventure to Russia" was well chosen. A sense of excitement frequently entered the letters of the participants as they played their parts in this fascinating mercantile venture.

Before the *Thames* was ready to leave New York, the Boltons were urging Hicks to do his part to make the venture a success. "You well know how business is done here by the demand we have on cash. It will not do for the ship to come unprovided, if you wish the cargo to be laid in at the best terms." Then, in the very letter which acknowledged the receipt of $4,000, the Boltons continued their urging: "We learn that the Thames was to sail [in] a few days . . . we feel assured . . . that you will not let the ship come without the needful." [13]

Once Paddock brought the *Thames* up the Savannah River to the town, John Bolton was so impressed by her ample proportions that he immediately upped his estimate of her cargo from a load worth $20,000 to one of $35,000. Even Paddock added his voice to the chorus: Bolton has "done buying for want of the needful." Tongue in cheek, Paddock continued, "You had better charter a small vessel and load with dollars. They don't think much of from $5 to $10,000 a day." Hicks, caught up in the fever of the venture, showed no resentment of the prodding but revealed his own impatience for the success of the project. "I . . . hope the wheels will be kept going," he replied to Paddock. "Surely I have poured in the cash freely since you sailed. Although I had not chartered any vessel to load dollars, I think it best to press forward and load the ship regardless of price and try our fortune." [14]

Lively rapport linked the owner-agent in New York and the shareholding captain of the *Thames*. A spirited man, Paddock did not allow the rigors of the Atlantic or the memory of his recent enslavement "by the Wild Arabs" to quench the excitement of an adventure to Russia. The two chaffed each other more like school boys starting a picnic than a grizzled shipmaster and a grave entrepreneur guiding a $50,000 enterprise. In his first letter teasingly addressed to Master Isaac Hicks, between Post & Russels and Samuel Hicks, New York," Paddock saluted Isaac: "Agreeable to promise, Boss, I write you." [15] Using similar wayward salutations Paddock wrote Hicks an almost daily version of the proceedings.

Unfortunately, the unpredictable mail service played a trick on both men. After receiving no replies from Hicks for almost a month Paddock growled: "When you told me to write every opportunity I expected to have some of the like in return if it's only to let me know you are . . . in the land of the living." Hicks, ironically, was peeved for the same reason and unjustly accused his employee-friend. "I feel almost out of patience with thee for thy paltry negligence in not writing me a single line since thee sailed." Since it was then almost three weeks after the *Thames*'s arrival in Savannah, Hicks stormed on: "Why this obstinate negligence and want of attention?" When the series of letters did come through, neither man apologized to the other but each resumed his earlier tone. "I notice thee had a pleasant voyage of nine days," Hicks chaffed his captain, "which was as short as I expected considering who was the Headman." Paddock next saluted Hicks, "Old Friend and Scolder." [16]

Another sally started when the Quaker captain described John Bolton's plan to buy some of the *Thames*'s cotton in Augusta. "I was to have gone to Augusta today with $6,000 to purchase," Paddock informed the punctiliously religious New Yorker. "John says I must carry pistols which I have no objection to as you armed the ship with cannon. Did you mention we were to carry no other shot but four pound . . . I believe you did not!" Paddock next took a dig at Hicks for his larger share in the venture: "Now suppose a fellow undertakes to rob me and I kill him. I shall bear . . . one eighth of the crime . . . therefore you are shouldered double which makes me quite easy." [17]

Paddock's teasing had found its mark; Hicks did not sanction these apparent deviations from Quakerly pacific appearances. "If thee goes [to] Augusta with the cash, take care of thyself," Hicks wryly counseled, "but carry no pistols, or if so, carry no powder nor balls." As for the "cannon," Hicks fumed; "I wish thee to sell one of thy Signal Guns and make no more ado about them, for I shall take no responsibility of myself." [18] Although this banter was inconsequential in itself it indicated a mutual sensitivity calculated to heighten the chances of a well-coordinated venture.

Even though the Boltons always emphasized how "busy" they had been with the *Thames* it was still ten weeks after the ship's January 6th arrival before she dropped down the river to Four Mile Point to complete her loading in deeper water. Finally, on March 23, 1803, she pulled up anchor and set sail for Cork. Curtis Bolton, the firm's youngest partner, sent Hicks the final tally of her cargo—$8,000 more than John Bolton's revised estimate of her capacity:[19]

415 bales cotton	104,537 lbs.	$16,725.92
611 barrels and half bbls. rice	329,198	16,459.90
— charge for barrels		305.50
132 hogsheads of tobacco	159,326	7,966.30
Charges		640.96
Commissions		1,057.45
	593,061 lbs.	$43,156.03

The "Silent H," as Paddock and Hicks privately dubbed the *Thames,* reached Cork on April 26, "after a cold passage of 33 days, 15 days from Isle Sable, all the rest from Savannah there, with continual head winds." Paddock's account continued with a description of the routine hazards of ocean travel: "Nine days after leaving port . . . both pumps choaked with tar," but fortunately, as the resourceful Paddock explained, "having spirits of Turpentine aboard in two hours got at the water again which flowed six inches an hour the whole passage." [20]

In Cork, Paddock had to make his first important decision: which market would be best for the cargo? Hicks's advice via Harvey, Deaves & Harvey was: "If thee can sell thy cotton in Cork for 14½*d* to 15*d* British sterling . . . I should advise a sale there of at least two-thirds of it and place the funds to draw for." Paddock dropped this suggestion when he learned that cotton "would not have brought 13*d* Irish."

To make his decision Paddock "went to Cork . . . found 13 letters from Mellish & Co., broke them all open and worked upon them with Harvey, Deaves and Harvey some hours." Paddock continued: "We all agreed from what we could gather that Havre was our mark. Mellish," he concluded, "recommends strong for London without advancing what I called good reasoning." [21]

Though the captain had made up his mind, his troubles in

Cork were not over. "We lost three men by the press shame-fully. Last night . . . was boarded by a King's Cutter who took Platt Lawson (he had lost his protection) [and] the Negro I shipped before your door," Paddock lamented. "Platt I expect to get back if the cutter comes in before I sail, if not Harvey, Deaves & Harvey think they will recover him . . . the Negro stands but a bad chance." This was not all: "The commodore's boat came aboard and took James Rose, a Block Island man, by what they called a flaw in his protection. Such a press was never known before, landsmen not exempt from their fury." [22] Nevertheless, Paddock did get two of his men back but the third, the Negro, was held.

After a five-day passage from Cork, Paddock dropped anchor off Le Havre. With the Anglo-French wars in the process of starting again, the cotton found a good market. Paddock sold it quickly to Arthur Spear, agent for the firm of Quenoille, Lanchon, Hanin, Spear & Company at 33 sous a pound. Even though Spear allowed for only 96,028 pounds of cotton, about four tons less than the invoice, the sale after deducting commissions brought $28,000, a nice advance over the first cost of $17,000. [23]

Paddock, however, was in doubt about his next move because the rice and tobacco were not in great demand and his own instructions for their disposal were vague. Should he follow the Boltons' advice of March 7th: "We expect that Copenhagen will be the best market for your Rice and tobacco."? To Hicks Paddock wrote the gloomy report which explained that in the case of their rice and tobacco there was "such a glut at present that no calculation can be made." The disadvantage of the Copenhagen move was that "a consider-able quantity," Paddock wrote, has "gone from here to that place." Furthermore, "large quantities of rice and tobacco have arrived at Cowes within two months and gone on some-where." Copenhagen, Havre, or somewhere else? Paddock had to decide, and quickly, because in two days the last of the cotton would be unloaded. Wistfully he wrote Hicks: "Wish I could have only five minutes' chat with you—would be highly gratifying. I've many times wished that the ship and cargo was positively consigned, that I might be like other Ship Masters: boys sent on errand," he confessed, somewhat out of character. "But as you have placed such confidence in me, shall move on slowly." [24]

Napoleon's decree settled the question. "This day we were to depart the port for Copenhagen when a general embargo took place the tide we were to depart," Paddock informed Hicks. "In consequence of this Stop, I was induced to sell the rice at 36 and some at 37 livres . . . the tobacco will be sold by the Samples when drawn." The results could have been much worse: $20,000 for the rice and something over $12,000 for the tobacco brought several thousand dollars over the Savannah costs. While the second round of unloading proceeded, Paddock had some of the *Thames*'s leaks plugged by the French caulkers, who "work well but tediously slow." [25]

With the outbound cargo sold at a profit, Paddock now had to decide where to place the funds. The Boltons' orders had left the decision open: "Request the House to whom you consign the cotton to open you a credit in Paris, or Amsterdam, or wherever you find is the most favorable rate of Exchange." Operating in a situation in which the "sound of Peace or War . . . is variable daily," Paddock changed his plans several times. "Our calculations were to have our funds partly in London, part in Hamburg, and part in Paris subject to my draughts in Petersburg." This was altered because, "the situation of affairs are such I think to have the whole in Hamburg." Eleven days later Paddock described the final arrangements to Hicks. "Mellish recommends London; Exchange more favorable there [than] the situation on the continent. All which induced me to direct the House here to have the amount of our cargo remitted to J. & W. Mellish subject to my draughts." [26] Paddock considered the matter closed—an unduly optimistic conclusion.

Thanks to the temporary embargo, Paddock picked up "a small brig-load of wine . . . for 200 guineas, to land a part at Elsineur [Helsingör]" where the *Thames* would pay her Sound Dues, "the remains . . . Petersburgh." [27] This small French freight had unforeseen consequences for the venture.

The British Navy provided the first surprise. Without incident the *Thames* sailed past "the British frigate who lay off the harbour's mouth. Soon after spoke [to] an English cutter who hailed us and let us pass. On the 8th off Dungeness," Paddock's luck ran out. "Was brought to by the frigate *Immortalitie,* Captain Owen, who after examining my papers concluded us a good prize. Sent on board two ignorant lieutenants, one foolish midshipman, six lousy marines, and four ragged sailors," Paddock seethed, "and ordered us for the Downs. Brought . . . to off Deal the Lieutenant who held the Papers went off to London." Unwilling to trust fate, Paddock followed the lieutenant. "We rode all night . . . next morning . . . I called on Mellishes and related what had happened. They sent a clerk with me to the frigate's agent who opened the papers at 4 o'clock. When Mellishes demanded damages," Paddock wrote disgustedly, "all we got was 10 guineas and expended about 17 . . . this much for British Humanity." [28] The French wine had been the excuse for the capture.

Paddock's second unpleasant surprise immediately followed the first. Before leaving London on the seven o'clock stage, he used this opportunity to check his credit arrangements with the Mellish firm. He inquired whether the letters of credit had been sent on to Helsingör and St. Petersburg as requested, but received a startling answer: "No. We will open a credit for you no faster than the proceeds comes into our hands." [29]

The directors of the *Thames*'s voyage had taken for granted that the English firm with which Bolton had an established correspondence would open the credit in St. Petersburg before the French merchants finished making all of their remittances. Paddock wrote Hicks that he had queried Chambers, the acting partner of J. & W. Mellish, "if they had any doubt of Quenouille, Lanchon, Hanin, Spear & Company. Their answer, 'No.'" Asked about Perigaux in Paris," Paddock continued; "their answer, 'No.' That they were the first Bankers in Paris and that they had every right to expect Perigaux's remittances regular but they would not trust a Frenchman out of sight and that Buonaparte was so great a rascal he might forbid bankers to remit money to England." [30]

Still not convinced that Chambers was giving the real reason for the firm's uncooperativeness, Paddock "asked them if they had any doubts of Isaac Hicks and Robert and John Bolton—if everything else failed." Once again the answer was "no," but the Mellish firm still argued that "in failure on part of France they should be a year out of their money." Finally the real reason for the refusal came out. "If you had brought the cargo to us that we could have got a £1,000 out of you," Mellish informed Paddock, "we then would open a credit immediately." Paddock concluded his report to Hicks: "from conversation with your Great London friends . . . my opinion of them is Small." [31]

Before catching the stage back to Dover, Paddock wrote a brief note to a firm which had done a good deal of business with Hicks, the Liverpool Quakers, Rathbone, Hughes & Duncan. Paddock appealed to them for advice—obviously he could not wait for a letter from America—and suggested that they forward a reply to Helsingör where the *Thames* had to pause to unload its wine.[32]

When he reached that Danish port at the head of the Sound, Paddock found this gratifying example of Quaker-capitalist cooperation: "We perceive the situation in which you are placed in respect to funds," the Liverpool firm stated. "Feeling anxious for the interest of our respected friends concerned, we shall ourselves today lodge a credit with our bankers, Sir James Esdaile & Company, in London, to an amount not exceeding £13,000."[33] Paddock felt better.

Back in America John Bolton was furious when he heard about the selfish caution of J. & W. Mellish. Summering in New York, Bolton learned from Hicks's letters about the conduct of the firm which the southerner had characterized as "safe as the Bank of England." "In the whole transaction I can see Mr. Chambers," wrote Bolton, who had visited the firm in London, "but we cannot separate the blame. The house is what we look to and not the individuals, though . . . Mr. Mellish is both too honorable and independent to descend to the meanness which is so glaring in the transaction. Taking the whole or separate," Bolton concluded, "I think there is sufficient grounds for both you and me to withdraw *all* confidence . . . in them. For my part I have determined to request a final settlement."[34]

Fortunately, the restrictions on credit imposed by J. & W. Mellish caused no serious embarrassment to the venture. By August 9 the last of the remittances from Paris reached London, and the London house in turn opened the full credit in St. Petersburg for the Owners of the Ship *Thames*. Only the general slowness of business transactions everywhere and the leisurely pace of eighteenth-century vessels kept this close call from being a disaster. Nonetheless, Paddock met with some inconvenience in St. Petersburg because of the arrangements with the Mellishes. "As our funds had not yet reached London before I left . . . but very few houses (not knowing our concern) would be willing to advance on any uncertainty." He was "almost confined" to Cramers Smith & Company, the house to which J. & W. Mellish addressed the ship and lodged the credit. The arrangement also prevented Paddock from selling his own bills of exchange on J. & W. Mellish and saving, according to his own reckoning, "2½ to 3 per cent." [35]

The growing popularity of the Baltic trade with American shippers diminished the possibilities of earning a prodigious profit on this venture. Describing conditions in Russian waters the summer of 1803, Paddock reported: "About sixty Sail in Port and gone of our vessels. Thirty five have cleared which takes with them 2,079 tons of Hemp, 2,472 tons Iron, 17,026 pieces canvas, and 3,620 pieces of Ravens Duck." In consequence prices in the port tended to rise as some goods became scarce. On the bright side, Paddock noted, "Most of the vessels not cleared . . . are small and [with] small capitals, many that don't exceed £3,000, one only $3,000. These small folks," Paddock chuckled, "expected to have made India voyages [not literally but figuratively—that is, to buy valuable goods at a very low price] and now find they will not get a new penny for an old one and promise not to try it again." [36] Paddock's observation suggests the wisdom of Hicks's patient efforts to assemble sufficient capital before launching this extended venture.

After his arrival in St. Petersburg on June 24, 1803, Paddock moved slowly in collaboration with Cramers Smith & Company to buy the quality of goods he wanted at a price he was willing to pay. Not until August 17 did he complete his buying. By July 20, however, he had been able to report that 170 tons of iron and hemp had been laid in the hold and much of the less solid manufactures were on "lighters which with the first wind will be along." [37]

When the *Thames* finally sailed that August Paddock had

spent all but 148 rubles of the £12,000 sterling credit for the cargo, ship repairs, and various charges and commissions. In her hold she carried[38]

100 tons or 2,992 bars of New Sable iron	11,206 rubles
20 tons or 1,122 bars of assorted iron	3,885
140 tons or 141 bundles of clean hemp	41,539
200 pieces of Sail cloth	4,432
100 pieces of Ravens duck	1,527
1,000 pieces of broad diaper	6,546
280 pieces of Flems (sheeting)	6,986

On separate accounts from the main venture, such as Paddock's traditional privilege as captain, the *Thames* also carried featherbeds, cordage, oakum, and fine napkins.

Such was the pace of business in America's early national period that though the *Thames* reached New York in late September 1803, it was not until March 4, 1805, that Hicks closed the account on the "Adventure to St. Petersburg," a venture which had begun December 1, 1802, with the purchase of the ship. After all of his own charges and commissions had been deducted, Hicks's sales in New York came to $56,355, about $6,000 over the invoice value of the cargo. If the New York sales did not go for a very high markup, thanks to the fairly heavy importing from Russia, the net from the sales on the final leg of the voyage represented a comfortable advance over the cost ($43,156) of the initial cargo in Savannah.

Hicks had made a tidy profit on the venture. On his investment of $10,789 in the cargo, Hicks realized a 23 per cent net margin, or $3,299. Hicks earned an additional $1,597 as his fee calculated at 2½ per cent for selling the goods.[39]

Long before the final calculations on the venture were available, the participants decided to try again. The basic pattern of the 1804 venture repeated the first. Changed circumstances—such as the new French law which prohibited a stop at a British port before visiting France—forced some minor alterations in the earlier plan. Desire for greater profits dictated other changes.

On the first leg of the second voyage to Russia Paddock reported his adventures en route to Savannah. "On 15 January while you were in Meeting," the captain taunted the pious entrepreneur, "we cast off from the wharf. On the way down [to Sandy Hook] had the Pleasure of beating the ship *Brothers,* Captain Holman. Not till we were under way did I know there were several wagers laid on the two ships' sailing, which the pilot told me of," and so spoiled Hicks's pleasure in the *Thames*'s speed. To make this leg of the voyage pay for itself Hicks had ballasted the ship with building stone, 10,000 bricks, 100 casks of stone lime, and freighted 30 bundles of hay and 200 bushels of oats in bags. Paddock was thankful for the ballast. Off Hatteras: "Blew heavy. We went off 11 knots under close reef main sail and reef fore sail till 3 a.m. on the 18th, when for fear of losing our canvas, hove to and lay till 8 a.m. . . . same time water freezing on deck." [40]

Although the *Thames* reached Savannah twenty days later on the second voyage than on the first, thanks to more efficient management in Savannah she left sixteen days earlier—an important advantage in beating rivals to the European ports. Half-seriously Paddock wrote Hicks: "Don't know whether we shall be allowed time to deliver the building stone or bricks . . . tobacco is waiting and no store room." Actually Paddock declared himself better pleased "to be hurried this way than to wait as we did last year." [41]

Part of the efficiency resulted from a scheme of Hicks and the Boltons to make some extra profits for themselves. The Boltons had invited Hicks to share equally with them in building a cotton gin in Augusta. They had located Mr.

Samuel Smyth to handle this operation. He "would . . . purchase on the lowest terms to the amount of cash supplied . . . free of commission, and gin and bag for 1/8 or 1/6 as toll for the Gin." Another advantage, according to the Boltons, was that "this plan would insure us the article in time and at a much better rate than by purchasing it already ginned and bagged, besides the certainty of avoiding deceptions which are sometimes so nicely managed to avoid detection." Furthermore, John Bolton arranged "with Mr. Smyth for buying the tobacco that may be wanted for the *Thames,* so that the . . . cotton and tobacco may be in Savannah even before the ship's arrival." Best of all: "this plan will completely hide us from the view of speculators and the coming of the ship will consequently not have that bad effect on the market . . . as was produced last season" when the capacious *Thames* arrived in port. The tobacco arrived early; the cotton was had in abundance; in consequence Hicks and the Boltons shared a profit of $1,145 for their special entrepreneurial efforts.[42]

When the *Thames* cleared Tybie Light bound for Dieppe on March 7, 1804, she carried a more valuable cargo than on her previous trip. Paddock and the Boltons had squeezed on board 200 hogsheads of tobacco, 280 whole and 38 half-barrels of rice, and $24,106 worth of upland cotton, $3,929 worth of it on deck because the quantity exceeded the storage space between decks. The entire cargo was valued at $50,151—some $7,000 more than the cost of the first cargo out of Savannah.[43]

An incident with the French customs illustrates America's newness as a cotton-growing nation. "When we arrived, having more cotton about us than they supposed could [have] been brought from America, it was immediately reported we had been in England"—and thus broken French wartime regulations. "The commissary would have stopped our entry," Paddock explained, "but the American consul came on board, examined the Logbook and reported that we had been no nearer England than four miles, and so the matter ended." [44]

After anchoring at Dieppe on April 14 it took Paddock a little over three weeks to sell and unload the cargo, arrange for credit in St. Petersburg, and ballast the ship. The cargo brought close to $70,000, despite the glut of tobacco and surfeit of vexatious taxes. Paddock arranged the exchange by having "100,000 livres on Amsterdam and the remainder on Paris." [45]

To avoid trouble with the British Navy and "having no desire to visit your *London Friends,*" Paddock wrote Hicks that he "declined taking some small parcels of goods on freight or passengers for Petersburg." Paddock was an optimist. Six days out of Dieppe, "was stopped by the *Lynx,* [British] sloop of war, who detained us three hours. Was very hungry. The thief found nothing to steal," Paddock commented ruefully, "only poor Pat whom he took saying he wanted men and must have them." Having suffered this all too common impressment of a crewman, Paddock allowed himself an unQuakerly reflection: "He was cruising for a French Corvette of 22 guns and 200 men who is on that coast. The *Lynx* has 15 guns and 60 men—it is to be hoped he will fall in with Johnny Patete." [46]

When Paddock reached St. Petersburg on June 3, 1804, he had at his disposal not only the $70,000 in drafts on Paris and Amsterdam bankers but also over $8,000 which he could draw on Sir James Esdaile & Company in London. John Bolton was so optimistic about the return cargo that he bought almost ten tons more of cotton than the *Thames* carried. Shipping it on the *Washington, Cleopatra, Rufus,* and *Daphne,* Bolton consigned it in the name of the "Owners of the ship *Thames* to Rathbone, Hughes & Duncan in Liverpool. Again, Paddock dealt with Cramers Smith & Company in St. Petersburg and bought a valuable cargo worth 121,353 rubles. Over a third of the money he used to purchase 160 tons of hemp, the rest going for Flems, sailcloth, Ravens duck, 10 tons of New Sable iron, a few odd lots of textiles, and 15 featherbeds.[47]

On August 31, the *Thames* was back in New York, and Hicks had the responsibility of selling a cargo invoiced at $77,665. Once again a two-year wait was necessary before he made the final tally, but this time Hicks's operation added almost $22,000 over the invoiced value in New York.

Hicks made himself a handsome profit. He had invested $14,200 in the outbound cargo in Savannah and received as his share of the New York sales, $24,824. To that figure he added his $572 profits from the purchasing and ginning arrangements in Augusta, and his commissions of $2,665 for his service in selling the Russian cargo and in managing the ship.[48] A gross profit of almost $14,000, nearly 100 per cent on his investment in the venture, speaks well for the entrepreneur who engineered these two adventures to Russia for the "Owners of the ship *Thames.*"

Before his career in business was over Hicks initiated two more ventures to Russia, but with different partners and with somewhat less happy results. A natural calamity forced the Bolton firm to withdraw. "The Sea Island cotton crops have been almost destroyed by caterpillars and the late storm, and most of the rice also on the river plantations," the Savannah firm lamented to Hicks. "The losses sustained by the planters . . . and the consequent disappointments we must experience by their failure of payments will oblige us to engage all our resources in preserving our credit [and] continuing our business here."[49] Perhaps unwisely, Hicks speeded the liquidation of the association by selling Paddock's pet, the "Silent H." The *Thames* quickly brought $26,000, or $9,000 more than the owners had paid for this large vessel.

Early in 1805 Hicks organized another Russian venture by adding the capital and services of John Hone, a New York City auctioneer who was the elder brother of Philip Hone, the famous auctioneer and diarist. Hone supplied one third of the capital, Robert Jenkins a third, Hicks the remaining third, while Paddock withdrew as a partner but stayed on as the captain of Robert Jenkins's stodgy ship, the *West Point.* Her first skipper "allowed" that she was "tolerable handsome" and likely to be "full equal to middling clumps in getting forward." [50] Unfortunately the *West Point* made middling clumps seem fast.

On this third venture to Russia Hicks had the *West Point* loaded in New York with $78,000 worth of coffee, sugar, and an assortment of potash, cotton, pepper, logwood, and oil. Sailing February 23, 1805, en route to Nantes, Paddock met up with the Bolton ship *Nixon,* which passed them going "5 feet to our 3—of course was soon out of sight." A storm forced Paddock to order 230 strokes per hour on the pumps and 150 for the rest of the voyage. Paddock dourly observed: "Am now satisfied that until the builders go in their own Ships with but one pump, and that a very bad one, they [the ships] will not be tight." [51]

In Nantes Paddock had even less reason to be happy. His observations confirmed the fact that America was in the process of establishing a new high in the export trade for that year. "I found markets for most of our Exports glutted, particularly sugar and coffee." To make matters worse, "a monstrous additional duty on coffee and pepper [means] that they will not sell at all." Ship after ship had brought "pepper enough to last an age. It seems," mourned Paddock, "as if all America is afloat." [52]

Despite his gloomy foreboding Paddock did not lose money on the cargo he disposed of in Nantes. To speed the departure of the sluggish *West Point* Paddock did not wait for final sales before unloading but consigned unsold portions to Arthur Spear, the agent who had won the trust of the partnership in earlier ventures. Napoleon rewarded this expeditious if uncertain handling of the cargo by decreeing an embargo which kept the *West Point* in the Loire six extra days. Then the *West Point* sailed at such a leisurely pace—an entire month to get from St. Nazaire to Helsingör —that by the time she finally reached St. Petersburg letters awaited Paddock which announced the completion of the sales in Nantes. To make his purchases in Russia, Paddock could draw on $87,000, a reassuring if modest advance over the cost of the goods in New York.

By July 7 Paddock had purchased a cargo worth 132,000 rubles made up of the usual assortment of Russian goods. Two weeks later the loading was finished and Paddock had the ship under way for Helsingör and home. Ambling along, the *West Point* reached New York October 22, 1805. From "Brooklin" Paddock wrote to Hicks in his new Westbury home: "Here I am at last—arrived last evening . . . after a moderately short passage of 92 days." Once off this vessel, Paddock could joke about a "moderately short" passage but this experience decided him against another Russian voyage.[53]

John Hone, who sold the goods brought in on the *West Point,* also declined a share in a projected Russian venture in 1806. All agreed that they wanted no more of the ungainly *West Point.* Despite the adverse implications of the British Admiralty's *Essex* decision, which seemed to threaten America's re-export trade, Hone sold the vessel after advertising her for two months in the *American Citizen.* To everyone's surprise and relief she went for $16,000—$1,500 over her cost.[54]

Although Hicks had retired to the country during 1805 he organized one more voyage to Russia. Robert Jenkins, the Hudson merchant, continued in the partnership and provided half the capital for a modest outbound cargo of $24,491 worth of flour and barrel staves.[55] Jenkins again supplied a Hudson-built ship, the *Robert Bolton,* which had considerably more promise than the unfortunate *West Point.*[56] To replace the dependable Paddock the partners chose John Morris to act as their skipper and agent in foreign ports.

Anxious to avoid detention of the ship by the intensified British blockade of French-controlled ports and intrigued by reports of a crop failure and high prices in Portugal, Hicks decided to send the flour to Lisbon. Because too many other American shippers had the same idea, the price of flour in Lisbon fell to $7 or $8 a barrel, a price which would not even cover the first costs in New York. Hicks's overseas correspondents had sent letters to Captain Morris in Lisbon advising him to bring the flour to a better market in England. Before he could act on his decision to sail for Liverpool, Morris was stopped by a twelve-day quarantine and then by an equally vexatious stretch of eight idle holy days.[57]

In Liverpool Morris quickly sold the staves for a profit of $936, but the flour sales slowed with the result that he left the remainder on consignment with the Liverpool merchants, Rathbone, Hughes & Duncan.[58] After having the *Robert Bolton*'s leaks repaired Morris put to sea on June 6, 1806, bound for St. Petersburg.

Again, Cramers Smith & Company, in the Russian port city, aided the venture by assisting the captain with his purchases. Hicks had arrangements with Rathbone, Hughes & Duncan whereby Morris could draw for considerably more than the value of the cargo the *Robert Bolton* carried from New York. Accordingly, Morris bought a Russian cargo worth 100,137 rubles.[59] When this shipment reached New York on October 8, 1806, and was sold by John Doughty,

Hicks's relative and senior clerk who ran the New York counting house, Isaac Hicks's exciting and profitable adventures to Russia were over.

Since 1803, the year of the *Thames*'s first voyage to St. Petersburg, Hicks had been investing his money in ventures which had no connection with his own business as a commission agent or as an exporter and importer on his own account. Perhaps with his own retirement in mind he made investments, often as a stockholder, in which the active management was out of his hands—a frequent practice of businessmen in this era.

In 1803 Hicks participated in the formation of the Merchants Bank by subscribing to 500 of the bank's $50 shares. This investment made him one of the Merchants Bank's original directors, a position he filled for two-and-a-half years. As a director of this concern, however, he was not free from managerial responsibility, and at the beginning of the *Thames*'s second voyage, for example, he had to make a three-week visit as a lobbyist in Albany to protect the bank's existence. In addition to enjoying handsome dividends on his investment, Hicks occasionally earned additional money by acting as an agent in the sale of the bank's stocks.[60]

Although no John Jacob Astor, Hicks also turned from commerce to real estate speculation. His first venture, a modest 170 acres in Fabius, Onondaga County, New York, he bought in 1803 for $1,300. Two years later he bought a similar parcel of "New Lands" in Vermont through an attorney bidding at a local auction. In 1804 he was persuaded to buy stock and serve as a trustee in a grandiose city development scheme. Anthony Dey formed a New Jersey corporation to sell 3,000 shares of stock at $100 each for the purpose of "erecting a city at Powles Hook." Some of the other trustees, "gentlemen of respectability and Wealth in New York and New Jersey," were Richard

Varick, Jacob Radcliff, Archibald Gracie, Joseph Bloomfield (New Jersey's Governor), and Judge Pennington
(Newark's Mayor).[61] Hicks, who left for Westbury the
next year, appears to have taken no active role in this unsuccessful promotion.

After his move to Westbury in 1805, Hicks put money in
a number of ventures which did not require much active
supervision on his part. In 1806 he did a small amount of
insurance underwriting and in 1811 even became a nominal,
though certainly not active, director of the Commercial
Insurance Company. When Hicks's Hudson friend, Robert
Jenkins, helped to organize a bank to serve his fellow
Republicans in Federalist-minded Columbia County, Hicks
amiably subscribed to 100 of these doomed $50 shares. In
1815 he bought thirty of the Jericho Turnpike's $20 shares,
a project which brought an improved road alongside Isaac's
Westbury farm. From time to time during his retirement
he also loaned small quantities of mortgage money.[62]

Once Hicks became a Westbury farmer the character
of his investing, understandably, became different. Before
this time, when he invested in activities outside of his established commission business, such as in the Russian ventures
or in the Merchants Bank, he gave considerable portions
of his time to their management. But after 1805, despite
some visits to New York where he stayed in rented quarters, Hicks left most of the management to others. Hone
disposed of the 1805 Russian cargo, Doughty of the 1806
cargo. Hicks held his bank stock but resigned as a director.
Heretofore, Hicks had worked to increase the amount of
money he had available for investments; after 1805 he followed the classic pattern of retirement and let his invested
money work for him.

CHAPTER VII

A Life Free from Commercial Cares

A T   F I R S T glance Isaac Hicks's retirement in 1805 would seem to be the most startling decision in his whole life. In his thirty-eighth year, at the apex of his business successes, he left the city and took his family to live a secluded existence on a farm near his Westbury birthplace. He left the hum of the market place and the chance of even greater fortune for the drone of the countryside and a virtual end to material striving.

Perhaps this was a startling decision. John Hone, his partner in the third Russian venture, did not understand it. Commenting on Hicks's letters after six months of retirement, Hone expostulated, recalling a different Hicks: "I cannot account for the gloomy complexion of my friend's letters. It seems incredible that they were written by the lively cheerful *Friend* that so recently related the stories respecting fiddlestrings, perjury, and want of respect for superiors." Unable to picture Hicks a part of staid rural life, Hone prognosticated: "I have before predicted it and I now repeat that you will have to leave Westbury and come back to your old friends. It does not suit your naturally lively turn of mind to be confined in the country amongst a steady set of old Dons who think gravity a virtue and consider it almost as great a crime to smile as to say 'Sirs' or 'Mr. Hicks!' " [1]

Hicks did slip back to his old way of life late in 1805 when he briefly rented quarters in town. There he assisted Hone with the dissolution of the affairs of the *West Point* partnership. But after a few more brief visits to the city in

1806 and 1807 Hicks no longer had any active business concerns to lure him back to New York.

Perhaps after the move Hicks, too, had misgivings. Sixteen years of city living may have given him a different perspective on rural life which made him less fit for this new role. Nevertheless, considerable evidence suggests that this move of Hicks's was exactly what he wanted—deliberately, purposefully, and successfully planned.

If Hicks occasionally left Westbury to tend to business in the city, there were, at the same time, strong reasons for his wanting to spend his time in Westbury. An immediate problem in 1805 was to finish building his house. Between July 19, 1805, and August 16, 1806, Hicks's journal lists over $3,000 in expenses for such things as English paint, 23,000 laths, 16 doors, 22 window frames, brick, stone, timber, lime, plank, and hardware.[2] Besides attending to the house, Hicks was trying to bring the farm into running order.

An even more imperative demand kept Isaac in Westbury. In October of the year he retired, Elizabeth, his first daughter, was born. Unfortunately, in the following January, Sally, his wife, was still "in a very poor state of health."[3] Here were obligations which a man like Hicks was bound to take seriously.

Even before he made the actual move back to Westbury many signs had pointed to this retirement. Three are prominent. In 1802 he had announced plans to withdraw from commission work and had transferred some accounts to his brother Samuel's firm.[4] Further, his announcement on February 15, 1804, of retirement from the commission business, although it did not put an end to all work, established the break with the main part of his business career. Finally, in 1805, once the venture of the *West Point* was well under way, Hicks had made himself free to retire. His retirement, then, was by no means an impulsive or capricious gesture. Over the years he had been arranging his business affairs to make it possible.

Five years before his return to Westbury, Hicks had been busy preparing the way. In March 1800 Isaac and his father selected some farm acreage in Westbury not far from the Meetinghouse. That year he spent only $2,530, but by the end of 1802 his "Estate at Westbury" had been debited with $7,759 in expenditures. A stream of letters and pamphlets on farm subjects testifies to his interests in those years. Frequently absent from his counting house during the summer months from 1800 on, Hicks supervised the planting of over a hundred fruit trees of twenty-three varieties.[5] To the neglect of his city business, Hicks was preparing to make the transition to Westbury life.

A backward glance from 1805 shows that Hicks's way of life had given him some valuable preparation for a life free from commercial cares. Hicks would never have made a good flesh-and-blood illustration of that economists' abstraction, "the economic man." During his business career he often allowed his other interests to interfere with profit-making.

Isaac Hicks's reading was nothing if not serious. Even in 1796, the year he broke away from his partners to form his own firm, his reading list was impressive. One group of books was in the practical category that a man in business might want for reference. He had two dictionaries, *Walker's Gazetteer,* the *Universal Geography,* two volumes of the laws of New York, and a book on surveying.

The rest of the books Hicks listed at that time were less usual on a merchant's shelf—even a Quaker's. Besides such staples of Quaker fare as George Fox's *Journal* and the works of William Penn, Hicks read accounts of the "life and religious labors" of a number of Quaker leaders—John Woolman, Samuel Fothergill, Thomas Chalkley, John Grattan, Sarah Grubb, and Samuel Bownas.

Quaker history also interested this hard-working business man. William Sewel's standard, *History of the Rise, Increase and Progress of the Christian People called Quaker,* and George Bishop's *New England Judged* were in his collection, as was John Rutty's description of Irish Friends. Hicks had Robert Proud's *History of Pennsylvania* and a volume of Rollins' ancient history.

The most impressive work dealing with religious ideas was Robert Barclay's *Apology.* Several Biblical commentaries, an analysis of prophecies, a survey of the evidences of religious truths, and one or two books of sermons by non-Quakers supplemented Barclay.

Only a few items might be considered escapist. Hicks had a few books on travel, and Seneca's works.[6] This last pagan inclusion on the shelves of a pious Friend suggests an interesting glint of nonconformity.

Hicks took his religion seriously. As a Quaker his religious needs were not likely to be satisfied by periodic participation in formalized ritual. Because Quakers lacked both the sacraments of other Christian churches and the assistance of a professional clergy, conscientious laymen were very active in religious and social concerns.

Although Isaac Hicks does not seem to have been one of the outstanding spiritual leaders of the New York Meeting, he was an active, concerned Friend. He received, as a token of the Meeting's esteem, appointment to a number of posts which made use of his business experience. During his busy year, 1796, Hicks acted as the collector of quarterly subscriptions from the members of his Preparative Meeting, a membership which very nearly duplicated the names of local merchants in Hicks's business ledgers. In 1802 he headed a three-man committee to draw up specifications for additional quarters for the New York Meeting and to supervise its construction. Because Friends opposed lawsuits, disputes between members were brought to the Monthly

Meeting for arbitration. Over a four-year period Hicks patiently represented before the New York Overseers the Philadelphian, Henry Drinker, in his dispute with Nathaniel Pearsall.[7]

Dozens of letters from or to business friends further suggest the strength of Hicks's religious interests during his business career. Nantucketer James Barker felt that Hicks was the kind of man who could be trusted to recommend someone for the Quaker school to teach "reading, spelling, writing the Inglish language and arithmetic." He and William Rotch, Jr. of New Bedford exchanged letters lamenting the "affecting . . . instances [which] occur to disgrace our high religious profession." Talking about warnings to businessmen, Rotch added that he wished to "join with thee in belief that more watchfulness and care has become necessary, particularly in early inspection and advice which I think we ought all to be open [to] and candidly receive."[8]

Hicks's own interest is reflected in the many comments Quaker businessmen made in their letters to him about the traveling religious leaders of the period. Samuel and Miers Fisher, for instance, wrote of looking forward to a visit by such weighty Friends as Richard Mott, Daniel Titus, and Hugh Judge. When Hannah Bernard, who was in some ways a precursor of the Hicksite group whose views split the society in 1828, passed through New York, Thomas and Joshua Fisher wrote from Philadelphia: "We understand our beloved Friend Hannah Bernard and Companion have taken their Passage [to England]. If . . . thou hast opportunity our Thomas Fisher would be glad thou would communicate his dear Love and sympathy to them, particularly to H.B." Isaiah Hussey in New Bedford regaled Hicks with his father's letter from England: "He says," wrote Isaiah, "it is a very busy time with him as it is now (he says) 'Our Yearly Meeting, and you must suppose me very much engaged.' By his manner of expression one would think he considered himself quite a Londoner. He talks of . . . spending Evenings with David Sands, Hannah Bernard, and E. Cogshall." William Rotch, Jr. understood Hicks's interests when he commented on his patriarchal father's projected visit to New York: "I expect thou will soon have an opportunity of seeing my father. I hope you will have a feast of fat things in the Spiritual œconomy." [9]

In some instances Hicks put the "Spiritual œconomy" ahead of the material, at least in his affairs with fellow Quakers. To Samuel & Miers Fisher, Hicks wrote only a line to describe a business matter and explained his brevity as a "consequence of our Yearly Meeting and the attention it demands from me. Your message to Thomas Rotch and wife," he added, "shall meet attention as they are both here and in health." Cropper & Benson, an important English connection, was similarly put off with the announcement: "Our Yearly Meeting is now beginning which causes my being much taken up." [10] Whether his correspondents did or did not sympathize with his preference for Quaker concerns to those of business, the important fact remains that by his own admission Hicks was willing during his business career to put religious duties over money-making.

As a direct result of his Quaker training and associations, Hicks had a deep concern about slavery and for Negro welfare. An early abolitionist, Hicks was a member of an organization which included such prominent Friends and non-Friends as Caesar Rodney of Delaware, Walter Franklin, Benjamin Rush, William Rawle, and Thomas Cope of Pennsylvania, Joseph Bloomfield of New Jersey, Thomas Tillinghast of Rhode Island, and Alexander Hamilton of New York. In convention this group had declared as one of its objects the preparation of "the minds of our unfortunate African brethren for that condition of freedom and

rank in society to which they must, sooner or later, arrive—
to disseminate among them useful instruction on moral and
religious subjects, and to . . . have schools established for
the purpose of teaching them to read and write." [11]

Hicks was a fund-raiser in New York for the African
Free School, a local project of this group. In 1797, to help
keep this "seminary" for about 150 students running, Hicks
collected $257.90, which included $100 from a surprising
source, Robert Bolton of Savannah. At the end of the 1800
campaign Hicks had raised another $250, this time $25 from
his own pocket. Hicks also dunned his New England
Quaker correspondents. William Rotch responded with a
$50 contribution. Thomas Hazard, Jr. and Abraham Barker
gave sizable aid.[12]

As a member of the New York Manumission Society,
Hicks was much interested in the campaign to change state
laws on slavery, to apprehend slave-runners, and to prevent
"the disgraceful and inhuman practice of kidnapping
(which it appears from several attempts lately detected is
carried to a considerable extent)." Hicks's and Paddock's
letters tell how they worked to gather affidavits in southern
ports about captains involved in the kidnapping of northern
Negroes.[13]

Besides this legal work and lobbying, members of the
New York Manumission Society often tried to solve special
instances of the slavery problem by purchasing the victim's
freedom. Odd notations in Hicks's papers record his part
in these transactions, such as his ten pounds "to pay for
Charles." [14]

If these interests can be viewed as distractions from his
business career, these same "distractions" during his retirement filled his existence. When Hicks left his counting
house for his farm he was not a man under sentence to lay
down everything that had given life zest and meaning. A

rather young man at his retirement, Isaac Hicks also had well-developed interests which after 1805 could enjoy new leeway.

Hicks continued his reading and expanded his library. Bliss Forbush, the biographer of Elias Hicks, notes: "After 1806, Elias Hicks had free access to the splendid library of his cousin Isaac Hicks . . . which numbered several hundred volumes, including the current English historical and religious books." [15]

Once the house and farm were in shape Hicks had more time for the Meeting than he had had in New York. Again, his appointments by the Meeting are indicative of his activity and interest. As a man of substance who had been capable of disciplining sea captains, Hicks found himself employed to deal with wayward Friends. In 1807 Hicks and four others were appointed by the Meeting to investigate the case of John Searing who "hath failed in the payment of his debts." [16] This was a serious matter, not just for Searing, but for the Society which feared its reputation might be jeopardized.

One year later Hicks served on a similar committee to deal with the cardinal sin of that period. "James Peters has gone out in Marriage to one not a member, which was accomplished by a Magistrate," ran the Meeting minute. "Friends on considering the matter conclude he ought to be disowned. Daniel Titus and Isaac Hicks are appointed to inform him thereof." Daniel Pearsall's mixed marriage won a similar fate with Hicks acting as the grim messenger. Somewhat different was the case of Caleb Powell who had "widely deviated from plainness in Dress and Address . . . married one not in Membership with us . . . by a Methodist minister." He was disowned "until he from a sense of error condemned the same to the satisfaction of this Meeting." Isaac Hicks and Stephen Rushmore were appointed to show

Powell "a copy of this minute," and "inform him of his right of appeal." [17]

Much more pleasant were Isaac's assignments to building committees. When Cowneck Friends could not decide where to build their meetinghouse in 1808, a committee from the Westbury Monthly Meeting, including Hicks, offered their judgment. Later, Hicks served to "plan the house, provide materials, and superintend the building." The Monthly Meeting gave him similar assignments to aid Oyster Bay and Bethpage Meetings. In 1810 Hicks faced a struggle with the members of his own Westbury Meeting. To avoid the expense of erecting adequate horse sheds, one faction earnestly "referred to the good meetings of former days when the trees were the only shelter." Isaac, who well understood the inventiveness of delinquent debtors, parried by suggesting that "if better meetings would come of it, the better way might be to pull down the old sheds," although he "could not but be apprehensive that . . . his meditation would be seriously broken in upon during cold or storm to know that his horses were without other protection than the trees." Hicks's name led the list of appointments on a committee "to have some more shelter for Horses at this place." [18]

As he approached his fiftieth year Hicks received the highest post his Meeting had to offer. Only one year after his appointment to the powerful body of Overseers, Hicks in 1816 was nominated Clerk of the Meeting. The clerk's function was particularly important because of the Society's mystical conception of a direct relationship between men and God, and the absence of a clergy in the usual sense. To transact its corporate business the Meeting held regular sessions as a committee of the whole. Operating without a chairman or the guidance of parliamentary mechanics, these monthly meetings reached decisions in an unusual fashion.

Because almost unlimited individual expression was tolerated and no vote was taken, the clerk required acute sensitivity to determine the nature of "weighty Friends' " judgment and then, if possible, to state "the sense of the Meeting." The response of the Meeting indicated whether the clerk's statement represented a consensus. Isaac served in this capacity until his death.[19]

By the time the Westbury Monthly Meeting first nominated Hicks as Clerk, he had already distinguished himself in Quaker circles beyond the Meeting. This came through his association with his cousin, Elias Hicks, who was one of the most prominent Quakers in American history.

Elias Hicks dominated the history of American Quakerism for five decades after the Revolutionary War because of his inspired gift for preaching. Individuals possessing a talent for preaching had the tradition of "Traveling Friends" in which to exercise this talent. Like George Fox himself, they visited the scattered groups of Friends throughout the country and on occasion brought the "Precious Truth" to gatherings of non-Friends.[20] If the "truth" of the traveling Friend was well received, the various Meetings wrote minutes of acceptance to the preacher's home Meeting which had authorized the journey.

Elias's memorable eloquence had explosive consequences for the Society of Friends in America because of changes which had taken place within it. As city Friends gradually increased in wealth and amenability, they tended to lose the more rigorous aspects of their Quaker heritage. At the same time these capable, urbane members of the Society gravitated naturally to the positions of power in the Yearly Meetings. Country Friends, almost automatically conservative by training, had been far less exposed to the popular tides in Protestant theology which swept through the cities. A tension developed between the two groups, in part because the less

sophisticated felt patronized and excluded from the administration of affairs and in part because of doctrinal differences.
In this situation, not of his own making, Elias Hicks
exhorted Friends to accept the original vision of Quakerism.
The country Friends had a champion; many city Friends
saw in Hicks's primitive mysticism an unbridled individualism dangerous to their comfortably established order. By
constantly emphasizing the primacy of the individual religious experience, he gave offense to those who held such un-
Quakerly but conventional dogmas as the Trinity, atonement,
and the Bible as indivisible divine revelation. In 1827 as the
Orthodox grew more rigid, a bitter schism tore the once
united Quakers into two wrangling factions. Even though
Elias took no part in their organization, the opponents of
the Orthodox were given the name "Hicksites." [21]

Elias Hicks called his cousin Isaac his "armour bearer." [22]
When traveling Friends, particularly older ones, set off on
long expeditions, arrangements were always made with the
home Meeting to have a companion assist the preacher.
Isaac's role as aide to Elias, though it involved no preaching, could be arduous in the extreme. In the second decade
of the nineteenth century thousand-mile journeys over
American roads were in themselves strenuous. Elias was nine-
teen years older than his cousin and suffered from a suscepti-
bility to colds, stomach trouble, and other more mysterious
complaints, and ministering to them increased Isaac's burden.
But actually no definition of "armour bearer" is complete
without a suggestion of the psychological demands of the
position. In his messages to outlying meetings, speaking once
every day and sometimes even more frequently, Elias seldom
felt the Inner Light grow dim after a mere hour's message.
From all accounts he experienced deep emotion every time
he felt the call to speak. As an intimate traveling companion

of Elias, Isaac's main role was to provide emotional support and sympathy for the crusading preacher.

A journey into "upper Canada," one of the longest made by the pair, Elias Hicks dismissed with a single sentence in his usually detailed journal.[23] Starting in early June of 1810, Elias and Isaac traveled up the Hudson River valley and stopped off at Quaker Meetings until they reached Albany. Turning west the pair continued to attend Meetings as far as Niagara. Near there they took a sloop to York and visited Queenstown and other Canadian villages where Quakers were to be found before turning around for a similar trip back home. Slow transportation and many stops meant that they did not return to Long Island until late September or early October.[24]

A southern journey begun "seventh, day 8th of 5 month, 1813," took Elias and Isaac as far as Alexandria, Virginia. "First day," according to the *Journal* of Elias, "attended Friends' meetings . . . in the morning at Pearl Street, and in the afternoon at Liberty Street." Outside New York they attended appointed meetings in Newark, Elizabethtown, Plainfield, Rahway, and New Brunswick. Each week was filled with meetings in New Jersey, Pennsylvania, Delaware, and Maryland, until they reached Washington on July 17. On their return they crisscrossed these states and arrived back on August 3 to complete a three-month journey.[25]

Three years later Elias "called on my kind kinsman Isaac Hicks . . . to go with me as a companion." This time the pair set off for Bridgeport, New Haven, Hartford, Leicester, Lynn, Seabrook, Dover, Portland, Falmouth, Durham, Newton Center, New Bedford, and so round about the towns in Massachusetts and Rhode Island where Friends were to be found. Unsatisfied, Elias turned west to Amawalk, Peekskill, and then stopped at a number of other Westchester Meetings before returning to Long Island on March 30, 1816. Elias and Isaac were away from home "nearly three months on this journey, traveled upwards of one-thousand miles, and attended fifty-nine particular, three monthly, and two quarterly meetings." [26]

Isaac made his last big trip in the autumn of 1818, not with Elias but with several aged Long Island Friends bent on attending the Meetings between New York and Washington. Sick for about a week on this trip, he was nursed at the home of his former business associate, Samuel R. Fisher. Perhaps it was the knowledge of his own poor health and the rigors of travel that forced him to make this journey his last one for the cause; at least he declined to go with Elias on his visit to the Ohio Meeting in 1819.[27]

Although Isaac's role as the "armour bearer" was humble, even menial, Elias and other leaders accepted him as a fellow-worker. Over the years Isaac had more than ever come to share their religious point of view, their goals, even their way of speech. His service as companion was symbolic of his unity with this movement.

Even before Isaac's retirement Elias wrote him long accounts of his religious labors and frequently referred to their "real friendship." After Isaac had a heart attack early in 1819 Elias wrote his cousin a rather long exposition of his religious views which were intended to suit the occasion. Near the end he interrupted his sermon with this revealing remark: "But why need I mention these things to thee, seeing thou know them as well or better than myself . . . let them suffice as a manifestation of sympathy felt for each other." [28]

John Comly of Philadelphia, a noted traveling Friend and staunch supporter of Elias Hicks, knew Isaac and respected him as a valuable co-worker. "Need I tell you it was grateful to be thus remembered by you?" Comly wrote to Hicks in 1815. "The precious unity of spirit that was mutually felt when together (and very often since) was revived, renewed, and afresh quickened by the lively interest you have felt and expressed in this important concern in which your poor brother John Comly was engaged—your counsel and encouragement—was truly cordial." [29]

In 1817 Comly wanted to know: "How are you employed in the Blessed Cause of truth? How does the principle of Peace on earth and good will to men appear to be gaining ground in the *bays, coves, harbours, towns, brush,* and *more favoured parts* of your Island? Thou hast known enough of my mind to anticipate the job, the satisfaction, the encouragement and consolation that 'good news from a far country' . . . produces in such a mind. For if I mistake not," Comly conjectured, "some similarity exists between our natural and spiritual temperament of thought—a congeniality of feeling and a brotherhood in our exercises." [30]

The similarity of thought shared by Isaac, his cousin, and John Comly was a belief in a distinctive form of quietism found in certain sections of the Society of Friends in that period. For men like Elias Hicks all truth was the product of an inner experience. God's will manifested itself through an "Inner Light," a "Seed." In contrast "external experience," "creaturely activity," or "worldly works" were suspected of being at variance with this inner "Truth." Elias seemed convinced that "corruption is associated with whatever is institutional or external. Therefore we must guide people to a complete dependence upon the inner witness." Even the Bible itself was cautiously appraised as "the cause of fourfold more harm than good to Christendom since the apostles' days." [31]

Isaac's intimate letters to his wife reveal how much of this position he held. "I . . . hope thee will have a reward from the great Master by being permitted to partake of the hidden manna," he wrote Sarah from Hudson on one of his journeys.

"It is needful for us all to be on the watch against the intrusions of self-love and self-will that we may not be doing our own will instead of that of our great Lord and Master." Humbly Isaac acknowledged: "I've been deceived in this way too often." On a Canadan trip with Elias, Isaac wrote Sarah that he had experienced "that sensation," and, as a result, "my mind has been tendered and made to see my own inability to do anything for the cause of true religion unless aided by the great Master, and that all our acts of devotion are in vain unless we experience them blest with his presence." [32]

"Dwell deep," "center down," and other peculiar turns of speech used by this group were Isaac's. "Above all I earnestly wish that we both seek the right fountain," he wrote Sarah, "whence flows all true and substantial joy, that inexhaustible Source of light, life, and heavenly consolation." This mystical afflatus was "only to be enjoyed when the mind is humbled under a sense of its own nothingness, its own unworthiness, and deep abasement of its Self." Isaac felt that "when the World and all its tumults are laid low and of no repute . . . then it is we are sometimes permitted to taste of the Heavenly Manna." The well-read, successful businessman then gently admonished: "Be always on guard against action . . . without first feeling Self utterly reduced. Oh, my dear Sally, let us dwell deep and seek to the author and finisher . . . who will not fail in his own time . . . to bestow suitable food to the truly hungry and thirsty soul." [33]

Paradoxically, Isaac Hicks, Elias, and others who urged men to close out the world's distractions and turn inward, often were the most active in trying to change the very world they disparaged. They were the most zealous among contemporary Friends in trying to do away with slavery. [34] They were staunch in their opposition to war. [35] These same Quakers who did not trust prepared messages or worldly knowledge did try to establish schools for the "guarded education" of Friends. This is particularly surprising in the light of the avowed anti-intellectualism of a man like Elias Hicks.[36]

The educational concerns of Isaac and his friends ranged from colleges to lower schools. Elias favored the parochial education which would give a "guarded education to youth." To that end, "proper schools might be established . . . under the care of pious tutors, that . . . Friends' children, while getting the necessary school learning, might be religiously instructed, and preserved from evil example . . . by which their tender minds might be wounded and led from the simplicity of truth." Elias was appointed by his Quarterly Meeting to "stir up Friends to this concern." Comly followed intently his Philadelphia Yearly Meeting's abortive plans for a college.[37] Practical Isaac shared all his friends' interests and in addition served on the board of trustees of the school founded by his Westbury Meeting.

A central tenet of this group was a belief in "plainness." This belief relates closely to their rejection of "worldliness," and to their suspicion of "vain creaturely demands." Proper plainness in dress and address was supposed to encourage inward spiritual experiences by guarding the mind against the intrusion of temporal vanities.

In true physiocratic fashion they described one aspect of plainness as a life lived close to the soil. Thomas Jefferson and John Taylor could not be more opposed than Elias Hicks to city life. "Most of our capable, well-looking young men are running into cities and populous towns," bemoaned Elias, "to engage in merchandise or some other calling by which they live by their wits, being unwilling to labour with their hands: although it is the most sure way marked out by divine wisdom for our truest comfort and peace here, and a right preparation for eternal joy hereafter." [38]

Comly worried about the same thing: "My mind has been much exercised . . . respecting the state of our society as it regards our pursuit of worldly concerns. The numerous failures that have occurred . . . are proof that society has lost ground on this noble testimony," Comly stated in 1818. "Speculation and making *haste* to be rich have caused many to fall into snares and into many . . . hurtful lusts. Banks have been multiplied. Public confidence in Quakers," lamented this author, "is much lost. If our society slumbers on a while . . . bankruptcy will hardly be reckoned a subject for monthly meeting labor." [39]

How did "the rich Isaac Hicks" [40] fare in Comly's eye? The Quaker from Byberry, Pennsylvania, was particularly critical of wealthy retired Quakers whose ostentatious life and "city manners are not profitable to country Friends." On the other hand, "our valued friend, Isaac Hicks, although very wealthy, is very much an exception to these remarks," Comly stated in his *Journal:* "It is all due to his example . . . that much plainness and simplicity and moderation appear in his house, furniture, carriage, and deportment, and especially in the dress and education and employment of his children." [41]

Isaac's will, abounding in admonitions to "be thou plain," instructed his wife on the upbringing of their children. "My dear Sarah, let me encourage thee . . . to nurture and train up our dear Children not failing . . . to be firm against the vain fashions of the world and the vain amusements . . . keeping plainness steady in views." In another part of the document he cautioned his unmarried son, Benjamin, "not to allow thyself any liberty to look out of Society [of Friends] for a Companion. Seek one who," he counseled, "with Modesty and Sobriety is endowed with Spiritual and Inward Graces more than the outward polish and . . . used to temperance and Industry and Country Education, not much attached to Company or City habits." [42]

Though Isaac failed to induce his second son, Robert, to follow John, the firstborn, in a career of farming, he made a strenuous effort. Most revealing is a letter Anne Mott wrote to her daughter Mary, Robert's wife: "I see no remedy in the present situation. Robert's mind has got a bias one way and his father's another." Anne Mott, however, really favored Isaac's point of view: "I should very sincerely rejoice," she wrote, "if Robert could be satisfied with a farm, not only because . . . he would be more comfortable than he imagines, but because . . . much is due to an affectionate parent, willing to make his children comfortable, but naturally wishing to do it in the way which his observation and experience has led him to believe is the best." Nonetheless, by the end of 1815 Isaac relented and helped to establish Robert as a ship chandler. Two years later Robert had received from Isaac sums amounting to over $10,000.[43]

Besides laboring to preserve plainness in his own immediate family, Isaac must be credited with another victory for the cause. Prompted by John Comly, Isaac helped to save his cousin, Edward Hicks, from a most distressing lapse from plainness.

Early nineteenth-century Quakers recognized Edward Hicks as a gifted traveling preacher; later Americans know Edward Hicks, painter of "The Peaceable Kingdom," as one of the most appealing of America's early primitive artists. But painting had the same odious name as music or fancy dress among early Friends who abominated these and all other "vain amusements."

"Much discouraged on account of his temporal concerns," Edward Hicks, according to Comly's letter to Isaac in 1817, "concluded to apply himself industriously to painting . . . in order to extricate himself from his difficulties." Unhappy man.

"From the time he gave up to the heavenly vision," Comly explained, "[Edward] felt conviction in his mind on the subject of ornamental painting. For some years past, he declined to indulge what is called his native genius for such paintings—a genius," Comly speculated, "which if the Divine Law had not prohibited, might have rivalled Peale or West—but as the indulgence of it appeared to him to feed a vain mind and promote superfluity," Comly continued, "and having a testimony given him to bear in favor of Christian simplicity, he clearly saw the contradiction and inconsistency of such a calling."

Alas, Edward's debt had driven him "to return with . . . application as often keeps him up till near twelve o'clock at night painting pictures. To make things more glaring," a dismayed Comly wrote, Edward had "advertised in the Bucks County papers 'to execute coach signs and ornamental painting of all descriptions in the neatest and handsomest manner,' with his name annexed. He has resorted to the forbidden tree to retrieve himself . . . even at the expense of his own peace . . . hoping to clear $1,200 a year by it—a delusive dream!!"

Painting was bad enough in itself but Comly was more distressed by the loss of Edward as a preacher. Before being distracted by his creditors, Edward had received a minute from his Meeting to travel and preach. "I endeavored," Comly reported, "to encourage him to set out, but . . . am apprehensive . . . all his prospect will vanish." [44]

Comly's appeal to Isaac brought results. Edward was hauled out of the "deep mire of the paint" by virtue of $500 sent by Isaac and a matching check from his brother Samuel. On May 23, 1818, Comly happily reported that Edward "having been plucked as a brand out of the burning fire . . .

is again engaged in appointing Meetings on First Day after-
noons in villages and obscure places . . . and *we* have the
satisfaction of seeing . . . that the precious gift bestowed on
him is yet on the candle stick." [45]

Important though religious concerns were to Isaac Hicks
in his retirement, his attachment to his wife and family was
not something he overlooked or took for granted. Almost
every letter written to "dear Sally" contained some unusual
remark or salutation reflecting their close agreement and
their deep mutual affection.

During one of his trips with Elias, Isaac revealed his feeling for his wife: "Dear Sally, I wrote three letters yesterday
to thee and in them complained of having no letters from
thee, but in the evening I received two from thee and one
from John, which was a feast and much the more so as by
them I found thee and our dear little ones in health," the
grateful husband wrote, "and particularly that thee gave
such encouragement for keeping patient until the sight of my
returning home." The pleasure of hearing from home did
not make Hicks reluctant to see his duty through but "much
encouraged my mind to go forward." [46]

In 1811 their roles were reversed. Isaac stayed home with
the children while Sarah took advantage of the opportunities
open to her sex in the Society of Friends. Sarah, who had
received local encouragement to "develop her gift" for
speaking in Meeting, felt the call to make a religious journey
to the Meetings in the Hudson River valley. Although Isaac
encouraged her in her labors he chided her for not writing
more often. "It begins to be time, I think, that I heard from
thee. I've heard nothing since thy 3rd letter . . . written at
Judah Paddock's and that is now 10 or 11 days ago." Considering Isaac provided her with an excuse for not writing
by assuming that "thee could not so well find opportunities
as thee might wish." Something else did trouble him: "My

letters have been so numerous that I wish thee to omit letting thy company know how many thee has got, least they think," Isaac explained, "I'm so poorly a Love Sick or Hypped that I am almost constantly writing thee. With much love and affection I'm thy loving Husband." [47]

The letter Isaac wrote to his "Beloved Wife," when he was ill during his trip to the South in 1818, has the same eager tone as earlier letters. "I have waited for several days with strong expectation of hearing from home, but to my great disappointment I've received no letter." Happily the fifty-one-year-old spouse could report that his cold and sore throat were on the mend, and that soon he would be able to leave Friend Fisher's. "On thee, my dear wife, my love and affection is . . . placed, and I hope and trust I shall embrace thee in my arms before many more days. Thy affectionate Partner." [48]

A few months after his return from this last lengthy religious journey, Isaac made an unsuccessful pilgrimage for his health to Saratoga Springs. Judah Paddock, deeply concerned about the report that Isaac felt "weaker though the same as to the complaint in the brest," implored his friend to try the Spa's curative powers once again, with himself as companion.[49] Perhaps suspecting that he had but a short time to live—in reality four months—Isaac chose to spend the remainder with his family and in that service which had helped to give meaning to his life in retirement. Once more he accompanied Elias Hicks, this time on a short journey.

On December 22, 1819, Elias, his wife Jemima, and "my kinsman Isaac Hicks" set off on a five-day visit to "the inhabitants in the compass of our quarterly meeting." After this circuit, Elias and Isaac stayed in Westbury and Jericho for about a week until, as Elias explained, "feeling my mind drawn to attend the monthly meeting of Friends in New York . . . left home again" in Isaac's company. A not entirely peaceful session, "the Meeting for worship and that for discipline continued upwards of six hours." Still not satisfied, the pair "left the city soon after the close of this long meeting and passed over the river to Brooklyn where . . . we had a meeting that evening composed of the different professions of the inhabitants . . . very few Friends residing there." Unstinting of their own energies, they "next day . . . proceeded to Flushing and attended their Monthly Meeting. We also had an appointed meeting in the evening for the inhabitants of the town, which, according to Elias, "was large and solemn." Next day at Newtown the two followed a similar schedule, before they rode wearily home on January 8, 1820.[50]

This was the last time Isaac saw his cousin. "On second-day morning [January 10, 1820,] I was informed that my kinsman and kind fellow-traveler, Isaac Hicks, was taken with a severe illness about ten o'clock," Elias wrote in his *Journal,* "and lay at the point of death." Hearing the news, Elias "hastened to see him and found him breathing his last. It was a sudden and unexpected trial to me to be thus almost instantaneously separated from such a kind and valued friend." [51]

The manner in which a man expends his life provides a strong indication of the values by which he lives. Once his heart attacks had started, Isaac probably suspected that he did not have much more time to live. And yet he gave himself unstintingly to the cause which inspired him. His death, at fifty-two, interrupted not an idler who planned at some future time to do the things close to his heart's desire, but an active man who chose to be steadfast in the pursuit of those values which had given meaning to his entire life.

CHAPTER VIII

Capitalist and Quaker Reconsidered

A MAN'S life poses certain questions. If Isaac Hicks was a country-bred Quaker and a city businessman, a man devoted to his family and an actively concerned member of the Society of Friends, how harmonious were these parts of his existence? Did the values he lived by reinforce or war with each other?

One of the safest conclusions about the relationship of these parts to one another is the assumption that Hicks's wife, Sarah, shared her husband's beliefs and goals. Home and office probably lived in substantial harmony. Sarah cooked for apprentices and entertained visiting merchants and sea captains. Isaac's profits bought her a fine city house and female servants.[1] Moreover, Sarah was no country lass uprooted from her familiar environment by an ambitious husband, nor was she a lady of elegant birth forced to tolerate a tradesman. Born a Quaker, Sarah was the daughter of a prosperous butcher who owned a shop in the Fly Market.[2] Her religious upbringing should have disposed her to look with favor upon her husband's industry and his observance of Quaker business ethics; her social expectations must have been gratified by his success.

The evidence is positive that Sarah approved of Isaac's later dedication to religious causes. If he left her for months at a time with the full responsibilities for farm and children, she must have understood his promptings because she also went on journeys and left him at home. And indeed it was a part of her tradition to share the fate of Jemima Hicks and other grass widows of the Quaker "Saints."[3] Meeting and marriage were in fruitful alliance. It seems clear, then, that Sarah reinforced Hicks's efforts as a businessman and as a concerned Friend.

The whole story of Isaac's accomplishments is at the least a denial of any notion that a rural Quaker upbringing might prejudice his success in business. Indeed, there is much to suggest that the connection was positive. Country Friends had the reputation of fostering in their young sobriety, diligence, and orderliness. Hicks was orderly; Hicks followed his earthly calling with both zeal and caution and was reckoned austere in his expenditure of the profits from this calling. These business-oriented virtues were attributable in part to his upbringing.

More tangible and easier to substantiate was the existence of a preference group which worked in Hicks's favor simply because he was known to be a Quaker. Quaker merchants sought one another's trade. Though they were only a small fraction of the general population their frequent choice of business as a profession made them a significant minority. The scattering of Quaker names throughout the narrative of Hicks's business career is indicative of the fact that he did at least one third of his business with other Quakers.[4] The existence of this preference group meant simply that it was easier for Hicks to break into the business world and to increase the volume of his transactions than for an individual not a member of such a group.

Hicks benefited not only from ready access to Quaker trade but also from occasional special favors granted to him by Quaker houses. In 1794 Harvey & Lecky, a firm of Irish Quakers, handling a shipment made by Hicks, paid the purchaser the difference between Hicks's invoice and the actual count and saved Hicks from a serious loss. By their own admission the Irish Quakers covered Hicks's inadvertent error and exposed their own firm simply because the New

Yorkers were Quakers, and would honor the obligation to Harvey & Lecky. At another time, Rathbone, Hughes & Duncan extended a £13,000 sterling credit to Hicks and his associates after they had been disappointed by J. & W. Mellish. When Cropper & Benson refused to accept Harvey & Deaves drafts made out to Hicks, the English firm offered to pay Hicks anyway and added: "as to the risk, we should not hesitate one moment if the amount was ten times as heavy." [5] This willingness to trust other Quakers can be explained in part by the fact that they expected at the very least scrupulous honesty on the part of the individual Quaker given the assistance. Hicks's records indicate that on several key occasions he demonstrated unflinching honesty.

Along with other Quaker merchants, Hicks benefited from the fact that even non-Quakers sometimes preferred to do business with members of the Society despite the demonstrable business clannishness of this group. When the Boltons wanted a new correspondent in Philadelphia they asked Hicks if he had any recommendations: "a plain-dealing friend, as near like yourself as possible . . . a Quaker would be preferred." Hicks gained a customer when Thomas Willitts wrote about his selection of Hicks as an agent, "as your being a Quaker was sufficient recommendation." [6] Being a Quaker had its advantages for a businessman; Hicks's upbringing seemed to be in harmony with his adult ambitions for material success.

There is, however, another way of looking at the question. Perhaps Hicks profited both from his early training and from the external advantages of being recognized as a member of the Society of Friends, but did he find his business congenial to his adult religious professions? This reverses the relationship and asks the question: how harmonious were his strivings as a capitalist with his beliefs as a Quaker?

Did Hicks, the businessman, live up to Friends' testimonies

on the subject of honesty and prudence, slavery, the sale of
spiritous beverages, the use of law, and devotion to one's
spiritual calling? These were six items of Quaker belief
which applied to businessmen. Hicks's business behavior at
these points provides some specific evidence to test the con-
gruence which is assumed by theorists like Max Weber between the regimen of Quakerism and the demands of capitalism.[7] At many points these forces appear to have worked
in harmony, but at other points these same forces produced
discord.

Hicks's honesty in handling the property of others has
been described. Here there was no conflict for him. Capitalist
rationalization of business and Quaker councils of caution
and honesty were highly compatible. Weber observes that
"capitalism cannot make use of . . . the businessman who
seems absolutely unscrupulous in his dealings with others." [8]
The Quaker stand against dishonesty or overextending one's
self in trade carried into the business world the very ethical
codes needed to rationalize that world. For his honesty Hicks
could hope to improve his profits and to remain a happy
Quaker.

A brief review of the facts shows that Hicks prudently
guarded against overextending his trade—a virtue allied to
the Quaker testimony on honesty. In 1789 he started on a
small scale. Until he had acquired business experience he
stayed within the relative safety of partnerships. When he
was in a position to make decisions on his own, he chose a
line of business which presented the least risk to his still
limited capital. He shifted from importing dry goods with
the firm's own capital to commission work, which meant
serving the investments of others. Never in his business
career did he overextend himself for the sake of a big profit.
When he invested on his own account, he first did so on a
modest level until he had proportionately more capital to

risk. Even after 1803, in his major speculations, though involved in large single projects, Hicks undertook them with the risk spread among partners. At the end of his career his investing followed the sound principle of the "mixed portfolio." He was a good capitalist and a good Quaker.

On the score of slavery, capitalism and the Quaker religion did not necessarily lead a merchant to the same conclusion. Capitalism is neutral on this subject; Quakerism is not. Logically, a doctrinaire capitalist, as a capitalist, should be willing to sell his own family into slavery if a profit were in the offing. If he chose not to make such a sale, however, this does not prove that in capitalism there is an objection to slavery on principle. As a good capitalist he might have refrained from this profitable but outrageous business so as not to imperil his greater gain. Public opinion might turn against him and endanger his other business. On the other hand, if a businessman refused profits from dealing with slavery when the community condoned them, then, presumably, his motivation was other than economic. The Quaker objection was simple because it was a moral absolute. Considerations of profit did not enter the decision. By Hicks's day the buying or selling of another human being, though accepted by most of the public, constituted a serious breach of the Quaker Discipline.[9]

Judged even by the standards set by fellow-Quakers, Hicks's record stands out. He risked his biggest single source of profits when he propagandized the Savannah Boltons about the evils of slavery. He took legal steps to apprehend and punish slave-runners. He worked with the abolitionist movement at a time when few Quakers could match his activism.

Still Hicks made some compromises with commerce. As a commission merchant and as a speculator he made substantial profits from slave-raised cotton, tobacco, rice, and sugar.

Even though no official statement by the Meetings condemned this indirect association with slavery, no late eighteenth-century Quaker could regard such business as beyond moral questioning. John Woolman and Anthony Benezet had already pointed the way to the absolutist's position. It is more than probable that Hicks knew the substance of Woolman's *Journal:* "Some years ago I retailed rum, sugar . . . and fruits of the labour of slaves . . . but of late years being further informed respecting the oppression . . . I have felt an increasing concern to be wholly given up to the leadings of the Holy Spirit." In Woolman's new view: "To trade freely with oppressors without labouring to dissuade them from such unkind treatment, and to seek gain by such traffic, I believe tends to make them more easy respecting their conduct. I have for some years past declined to gratify my palate with those sugars." [10] Even one of Hicks's own customers had requested a barrel of "free"—non-slave-raised—rice.

Perhaps an uneasiness in his own position made Isaac feel defensive when he criticized the absolutist stand Elias Hicks took on slavery. It is interesting that in the eyes of a sympathetic nineteenth-century family historian, Isaac's "inconsistency" and "half-way position" with regard to handling slave products was the one part of Hicks's life held up to mild censure.[11] Still, to give a balanced and fair impression about Hicks's conduct it must be recognized that this discussion is referring to a very advanced standard of behavior. After all, James Mott, Jr., who received considerable praise in Quaker circles for shifting on moral grounds from the cotton to the wool commission business, did so in 1830 and only after repeated entreaties in the 1820's by his parents and by Elias Hicks.[12] Had Isaac made the same decision thirty years earlier he would have anticipated all but a handful of radical Quaker "Saints."

Quaker testimony on the immoderate use or sale of alcoholic drink grew increasingly strong during Hicks's business career. "The Preparative Meeting of New York informs that the Overseers," ran a minute in Hicks's own Meeting, "Having visited a few amongst us who continue a commerce in distilled spirits." Optimistically this 1790 minute concluded: "We shall in a short time be quite clear of trafficking in that article." [13] This pressure continued unabated.

In theory, business would make no distinction between the sale of one product and another except on the basis of its ability to produce a profit. Again, as in the case of slavery, a businessman might refrain from handling a product because adverse public reaction might threaten other more important profits. It is worth noting, though, that almost no businessman is so single-minded that he makes the profit his sole criterion. [14] He is a man susceptible to all of the pulls in society which may influence him in his business decisions to do some things that are indifferent, if not harmless, to his profits.

On the score of strong drink, Hicks was caught between conflicting loyalties. For most of his business career he followed the lead of the rest of the business community and sold wholesale quantities of Hudson and imported rum, French brandy, and Geneva gin. But in 1803 Isaac changed his mind and turned over his consignments of strong drink to a non-Friend to manage. Hicks was in no danger of losing larger profits by continuing to deal in alcoholic beverages; the brandy shipments that he turned away had been offered by a Quaker firm! [15] Hicks's belated decision was a moral one; his stand was taken in disregard of what was accepted in his community as good business sense.

The oldest Query in a Friends *Discipline* dated in 1682 reads: "Are love and unity maintained amongst you?" [16] Quakers developed a tradition that members must not resort to law to settle differences but were supposed to arbitrate them before the Meeting. By the middle of the eighteenth century, however, as the Society adjusted to the demands of commercial rather than agrarian life, this testimony against the use of law was relaxed. "There may be some Cases wherein the . . . wholesome order . . . cannot be Complyed with . . . such as parties absconding . . . with Design to Defraud their Creditors," reads a minute of the New York Yearly Meeting, "That going [to] the Meeting (by the time it must necessarily take up) Be a manifest . . . damage to the creditor." [17]

If no absolute injunction restrained Friends from taking legal measures, the difference between the behavior of Quaker businessmen and restrained non-Quaker businessmen was slight. Hicks's conduct, far from litigious, was distinctly satisfactory by Friends' relaxed standards, or, for that matter, by the standards of sensible businessmen. But Hicks was human. When goaded by the repeated delinquencies of the former Westbury Quaker, Cornelius Wing, he exploded: "I have ordered her," Hicks wrote Wing about his ship *Franklin,* "attached to secure my demand. I shall follow her . . . until I get my pay, even to Europe if I don't succeed in this country." [18]

With regard to the Quaker testimony on war, Hicks is a better Quaker than he is a businessman. For the businessman thinking only of profits, the question of the use of armed force, or the sale of war goods or prize goods, is simply one of comparative economic advantage. During the Napoleonic era a hard-headed businessman might decide that the risk to his cargoes was less in an unarmed ship. For the Quaker an absolute ethic said "no" to any taint of war regardless of the economic merits of the position.

Hicks appears to have been scrupulous without the slightest taint of hypocritical evasion. In his personal life he was too young for the Revolutionary War, took no part in the

War of 1812, and suffered confiscations rather than pay taxes for war preparedness. In his business Hicks did sell goods—no munitions, of course—to belligerents, but standards which might be applied today to such sales by diplomatic, let alone religious guides, were not conceived of in those days before the advent of "total war." With a free conscience Hicks sold cotton, wheat, flour, and other staples to either belligerent with no intention of helping or harming either. Far from indifferent to arming his ships, Hicks laid down the law when twitted by Paddock about the *Thames*'s signal guns.[19] Hicks can not be called indifferent to all save profit.

The question of retirement provides the crucial test for the two forces contending for Hicks's loyalty. Would the quest for profits capture and hold his imagination or would he prefer a life free "from commercial cares"[20] in which he could dedicate more time to the things of the spirit? To have the capitalist mentality, according to Max Weber's possibly extreme definition, one must accept as the "*summum bonum* ... the earning of more and more money." Man, shaped by the norms of this system, "is dominated by the making of money, by acquisiiton as the ultimate purpose of his life." In fact the duty of the individual to increase his capital "is assumed as an end in itself."[21]

Weber's definition, although intended as a theoretical model for understanding an event rather than as a description of real men, does seem to fit many historic instances. The aged and very rich Jacob Fugger, when asked about retirement, "thought ... he wanted to make money as long as he could."[22] Examples abound in nineteenth-century America of men like John Jacob Astor, Commodore Vanderbilt, or Jay Gould, who found the challenge of business far more exciting than a life of retired ease. In fact a commonplace dread of retirement has haunted businessmen to this day and sometimes makes them seem to want to be at their desks when they die. For the sake of historical accuracy, however, it must be recognized that a number of non-Quaker businessmen in Hicks's day retired at a conspicuously early point in their careers. Nevertheless, whatever their reasons may have been, these men who retired early do not appear to constitute anything close to a majority.

The Quaker ethic and tradition offered Hicks another direction from that followed by most of his non-Quaker business contemporaries. Although Quakerism shared capitalism's respect for the profit motive, it also set up contradictory tensions. The Quaker businessman owed a loyalty to both "temporal affairs" and "spiritual affairs," to the "inner plantation" and to the "outer." Unmistakable though the urging was to be diligent in a material occupation, the warning against overemphasis in this direction was clear and ever-present. The earthly calling though proper was not an end in itself; it was the spiritual calling that should receive priority. "The manifestation of the spirit of truth . . . lead out of bondage to the spirit of this world, but the inordinate love and pursuit of worldly riches," read the *Discipline* in Hicks's Meeting, "often lead those who are captivated . . . into . . . dangers and obstructs the work of religion in the heart. They who will be rich," this strongly worded warning concludes, "fall into temptation and a snare and . . . 'pierce themselves through with many sorrows.' "[23]

Personal example gave force to this precept. John Woolman noted in his *Journal:* "The increase in business became my burden; for though my natural inclination was toward merchandise, yet I believed truth required me to live more free from outward cumbers." Daniel Wheeler, another Friend, makes the break complete. "As I have . . . endeavored to dwell near . . . the calming influence of His power . . . I believe that it will be most conducive to my present peace . . .

entirely to give up the trade I am at present engaged in."
Isaac's cousin Elias progressively gave up one material concern after another and begrudged the time he still spent on
his farm. "How true is the saying, 'No man can serve two
masters,'" Elias recorded in his Journal, "O, how hard a
master the world is; and from whose servitude I often feel
strong desires to be fully redeemed: so that all my time may
be more fully dedicated to the service of my heavenly
master." [24]

Especially for the quietist branch of Quakerism, this
struggle was not simply for more hours during the day but
for the mind of man. The quest for profits was subversive
to the state of mind for those who yearned to "center down"
and "reach for the deep spring." Their goal was a mystical
relation with God. It was this particular strain of Quakerism
that had the greatest influence on Isaac Hicks.

Hicks's decision to retire must be understood against the
background of these polar attractions. By deliberately choosing retirement in his thirty-eighth year, after only sixteen
active years in business, Hicks would seem to have yielded
to the pull of his religion rather than to the magnet of profits.
This explanation becomes more compelling when alternative
explanations for his retirement are examined. Finally, it
must be remembered that after Hicks did retire he devoted
a conspicuous amount of time and energy to religious concerns.

What alternatives can be offered to the "either or" of
capitalism versus Quakerism? If a reason for Hicks's retirement can be found which is independent of the tug of war
between these two opposing values, then the force of this
action which appears to be capitalism's loss and Quakerism's
gain is turned aside and diminished.

Perhaps as a clever businessman Isaac Hicks foresaw all

the trouble American merchants would be in for after 1807. American shippers did not really get back on their feet until after the War of 1812.[25] Perhaps he withdrew because he had the prescience to avoid this conflict, not because he was dissatisfied with profit-making.

Without a doubt Hicks's withdrawal from business was fortuitously timed, even though there is no indication that he was aware of any special diplomatic or economic reasons for quitting. Since the beginning of 1793 Hicks had carried on his business in a world almost continuously at war. Excursions and alarms, including an undeclared war with France, were a normal part of his business day. Hindsight can suggest that the *Essex* judgment in 1805 of a British prize court which threatened the re-export trade signaled the beginning of real trouble for America's commercial fortunes. After this decision things went from bad to worse. Might Hicks, in his retirement year, have distinguished this important 1805 action from all of the previous false alarms? The timing is wrong. Hicks had been signaling his intention several years before his actual move to the country; furthermore, the *Essex* award came on July 23, *after* Hicks and his family had moved back to Westbury.

Perhaps a plausible case could be made that Hicks felt that he had enough money and wanted to get away from all the vexations of business. If he was not exactly a merchant prince, he was regarded by the standards of his day as a rich man. At the same time he was in a highly competitive business in which one slip might lose a customer to some other commission agent. More than once he had had the bad luck to insure a client's ship with underwriters who defaulted, or to sell a consignment of goods to an incipient bankrupt. Keeping abreast of the ever-changing commercial regulation of belligerent and neutral countries must by itself have produced constant tension in Hicks. From this one could argue that Hicks had enough money, and wanted to relax and enjoy life.

For all its surface appeal this description of Hicks's motivation does not fit well. If it is true that Hicks felt that he had "enough" money, then this is a direct denial of the capitalist spirit. In its pure form this is not a game that can be won by amassing a fixed number of points—the game's the thing. A primitive harvest worker may stay on the job only long enough to collect a preconceived sum, but his mentality is a world apart from that of a man brought up in a society where the incentive of the profit motive is taken for granted. If Hicks could hold the values of the business world at arm's length, this is not to say that this Westbury-born merchant was truly a primitive. The rejection was on other terms.

The second part of this alternative explanation offers a "tired" hypothesis—after all, Hicks did sicken and die when he was still rather young. There are two clear difficulties with this arugment. Fatigue is irrelevant. When a man is trapped by the gambling spirit he visits the tables in a wheel chair; when a capitalist is obsessed by making money, he disregards the doctor's advice in order to continue the most exciting quest he knows. Besides, the thirty-eight-year-old Hicks did not lack energy. In Westbury he threw himself into a round of house-building, farming, Meeting matters, and long enervating trips with Elias Hicks.

No alternative explanation seems capable of weakening the first hypothesis. Hicks found his earthly calling in direct conflict with his spiritual calling and resigned one in favor of the other. On the score of retirement, loyalty to Quaker values won out over capitalist values.

Retirement is such a crucial issue that a reassessment of the relationship between Quakerism and capitalism seems warranted. First, the doctrine of the earthly calling and its corollary propositions offered substantial reinforcement to the psychological make-up necessary for successful capitalist endeavor. Second, other Quaker testimonies which impinge on business activity, such as the adjurations to be honest, have no connection with slavery, war, strong beverages, and the avoidance of lawsuits, do not vitally affect a businessman's chances for success except in extreme cases. Such testimonies as honesty and moderation in the use of law probably increase the likelihood of good business fortune. Refusal to sell certain goods or to rely on armed force might be regarded as quixotic in the business community, but hardly constituted a frequent or severe menace to business success. Finally, the testimony on the dual callings, the injunction to accept the material occupation with sufficient restraint to allow room for religious pursuits, puts in a new light all of the former testimonies which appear as aids to capitalism.

Was the Quaker businessman likely to have any advantage over his competitor who was not a Quaker or not a member of one of the sects singled out by Weber? For as long as he stayed in business he may have benefited considerably, not only from the favorable business reputation enjoyed by Friends but also from the additional conditioning for capitalist success provided by Quaker upbringing and beliefs. Perhaps the long-run effect of Quakerism on capitalism was subversive. In remaining a steadfast Quaker the individual seems, under constant pressure from his religion, to have loosened or dropped his ties with business.

This force also worked in reverse. Many Quaker businessmen died at their desks, but by so doing made a choice that denied a central part of their Quakerism. Others, more consistent, continued to enjoy the challenge of their business and its fruits but dropped their Quakerism for a more permissive religion.[26] Isaac's former clerk, Jacob Barker, did not lack in piety as a youth, but in the course of pursuing business into his eightieth year shuffled off his Quakerism to become a "non-Weberian" Episcopalian. Isaac Hicks followed a different course: a successful short-lived capitalist, he remained a good Quaker.

BIBLIOGRAPHY
NOTES · INDEX

BIBLIOGRAPHY

MANUSCRIPT SOURCES

M O S T information about Isaac Hicks came from his own carefully preserved records (H.P.), a rich collection of over 10,000 letters received, letter books, ledgers, journals, bankbooks, and thousands of other business documents. Marietta Hicks of Westbury presented this collection to the New York Historical Society in 1958. Information about Hicks's Westbury Meeting of the Society of Friends can be found in the records (W.R.) under the care of the Meeting Recorder, Westbury. The Record Room of the New York Yearly Meeting of Friends in Friends Seminary, New York City, has a fuller collection (N.Y.R.) of contemporaneous Meeting material, including Hicks's New York Monthly Meeting. More Meeting records and correspondence of Elias Hicks to Isaac's business associates are in the Friends Historical Library of Swarthmore College. The New York Public Library and the New York Historical Society have manuscript holdings of Hicks's fellow New York businessmen.

ARTICLES, CHAPTERS, AND NEWSPAPERS

Albion, Robert G., "Foreign Trade in the Era of Wooden Ships," chap. viii in *The Growth of the American Economy,* Harold F. Williamson, ed., New York: 1946, pp. 156–171.

——— "Maritime Adventures of New York in the Napoleonic Era," *Essays in Modern English History in Honor of Wilbur Cortez Abbott,* D. K. Clark and others, Cambridge, Massachusetts, 1941, pp. 315–344.

——— "New York Port and the New Republic, 1783–1793," *New York History,* 38:388–403 (October 1940).

——— "New York and Its Disappointed Rivals, 1813–1860," *Journal of Economic and Business History,* 3:602–629 (August 1931).

——— "Yankee Domination of New York Port, 1820–1865," *New England Quarterly,* 5:665–698 (October 1932).

Baxter, W. T., "Credit, Bills, and Bookkeeping in a Simple Economy," *The Accounting Review,* 21:154–166 (April 1946).

Bell, Herbert C., "The West Indian Trade before the American Revolution," *American Historical Review,* 31:272–287 (July 1916).

Bowen, Harold R., "Ethics and Economics," John C. Bennett and others, *Christian Values and Economic Life,* New York, 1954, pp. 183–200.

Bruchey, Stuart, "Success and Failure Factors: American Merchants in Foreign Trade in the Eighteenth and Early Nineteenth Centuries," *Business History Review,* 32:272–292 (Autumn 1958).

Cadbury, Henry J., "Intercolonial Solidarity of American Quakerism," *Pennsylvania Magazine of History and Biography,* 60:352–374 (October 1936).

Carosso, Vincent, "Werner Sombart's Contribution to Business History," *Bulletin of the Business History Society,* 26:27–49 (March 1952).

Cole, Arthur H., "Evolution of the Foreign Exchange Market of the United States," *Journal of Economic and Business History,* 1:384–421 (May 1929).

Daniels, George W., "Cotton Trade under the Embargo and Nonintercourse Acts," *American Historical Riveiew,* 21:276–287 (January 1916).

Fayle, C. Ernest, "The Employment of British Shipping," *The Trade Winds. A Study of British Overseas Trade during the French' Wars, 1793–1815,* C. Northcote Parkinson, ed., London, 1948.

Fischoff, Ephraim, "The Protestant Ethic and the Spirit of Capitalism: The History of a Controversy," *Social Research,* 11:53–77 (February 1944).

Forbush, Bliss, "Elias Hicks, Prophet of an Era," *Bulletin of the Friends Historical Association,* 38:11–19 (Spring 1949).

Griswold, A. Whitney, "Three Puritans on Prosperity," *New England Quarterly,* 7:475–493 (September 1934).

Hancock, Harold B. and Norman B. Wilkinson, "The Gilpins and Their Endless Papermaking Machine," *Pennsylvania Magazine of History and Biography,* 81:391–405 (October 1957).

Hidy, Muriel, "The Capital Markets, 1789–1860," chap. xiv in *The Growth of the American Economy,* Harold F. Williamson, ed., New York: 1946, pp. 282–302.

Hidy, Ralph, "The Organization and Functions of the Anglo-American Merchant Bankers, 1815–1860," *Journal of Economic and Business History Supplement* (December 1941), pp. 53–66.

Jones, Rufus M., "Elias Hicks," *Dictionary of American Biography,* New York, 1932, IX, 6–7.

Luke, Myron, "Some Characteristics of the New York Business

Community, 1800–1810," *New York History*, 49:393–405 (October 1953).

Monaghan, Frank, "The Results of the Revolution," chap. x in *History of the State of New York*, Alexander C. Flick, ed., New York, 1933, pp. 323–362.

New York Daily Advertiser,

Parsons, Talcott, "Capitalism in Recent German Literature: Sombart and Weber," *Journal of Political Economy*, 36:641–666 (December 1928), 37:31–51 (February 1929).

—— "H. M. Robertson on Max Weber and His School," *Journal of Political Economy*, 47:688–696 (October 1935).

Redlich, Fritz, "Some Remarks on the Business of a New York Chandler in the 1800's," *Bulletin of the Business History Society*, 16:92–98 (November 1942).

Reinoehl, John, "Post-Embargo Trade and Merchant Prosperity: Experiences of the Crowninshield Family, 1809–1812," *Mississippi Valley Historical Review*, 42:236–246 (September 1955).

Stone, A. H., "The Cotton Factorage System of the Southern States," *American Historical Review*, 20:557–565 (April 1915).

Tawney, R. H., "Studies in Bibliography II: Modern Capitalism," *Economic History Review*, 4:336–356 (October 1933).

Tolles, Frederick B., "Benjamin Franklin's Business Mentors: The Philadelphia Quakers," *William and Mary Quarterly*, 4:60–69 (January 1947).

—— "Quietism vs. Enthusiasm, the Philadelphia Quakers and the Great Awakening," *The Pennsylvania Magazine of History and Biography*, 69:26–49 (January 1945).

Trueblood, D. Elton, "Elias Hicks," in *Byways in Quaker History*, Howard Brinton, ed., Pendle Hill, 1944, pp. 77–93.

Volke, Albert F., "Accounting Methods of Colonial Merchants in Virginia," *Journal of Accountancy*, 42:1–11 (July 1926).

BOOKS

Albion, Robert G., *The Rise of the Port of New York*, New York, 1939.

—— and Jennie B. Pope, *Sea Lanes in Wartime*, New York, 1942.

—— *Square Riggers on Schedule*, Princeton, 1938.

Alexander, James W., *The Merchant's Clerk Cheered and Counselled*, New York, 1856.

Andrews, Charles C., *The History of the New York African Free Schools, from . . . 1787 to the Present*, New York, 1930.

Ashley, Clifford, *The Yankee Whaler,* Boston, 1926.

Ashton, Thomas S., *An Economic History of England in the Eighteenth Century,* London, 1955.

Atherton, Lewis E., *The Southern General Store, 1800–1860,* Baton Rouge, 1949.

Barker, Jacob, *Incidents from the Life of Jacob Barker of New Orleans,* Washington, 1855.

Barnard, Chester, *The Functions of the Executive,* Cambridge, Massachusetts, 1938.

Barrett, Walter, pseud. [Joseph A. Scoville], *The Old Merchants of New York,* 4 vols., New York, 1863–66.

Baxter, W. T., *The House of Hancock,* Cambridge, Massachusetts, 1945.

Bemis, Samuel, *Jay's Treaty, a Study in Commerce and Diplomacy,* New York, 1923.

Bennett, John C., and others, *Christian Values and Economic Life,* New York, 1954.

Bishop, Joseph A., *A Chronicle of One Hundred and Fifty Years: The Chamber of Commerce of the State of New York, 1768–1918,* New York, 1918.

Blodget, Samuel, *Economica: A Statistical Manual for the United States of America,* Washington, 1810.

Boulding, Kenneth, *The Organizational Revolution: A Study of the Ethics of Economic Organization,* New York, 1953.

Bradbury, Anna R., *History of the City of Hudson, New York,* Hudson, 1908.

Braithwaite, William C., *Beginnings of Quakerism,* London, 1912.

—— *Second Period of Quakerism,* London, 1919.

Brayshaw, Alfred N., *The Personality of George Fox,* London, 1933.

Bridenbaugh, Carl, *Cities in the Wilderness,* New York, 1938.

Brinton, Howard, ed., *Byways in Quaker History,* Pendle Hill, 1944.

—— Quaker Education in Theory and Practice, Wallingford, 1940.

—— *Friends for 300 Years,* New York, 1952.

Brooks, George S., *Friend Anthony Benezet,* Philadelphia, 1937.

Brown, John C., *A Hundred Years of Merchant Banking,* New York, 1909.

Bruchey, Stuart W., *Robert Oliver, Merchant of Baltimore, 1783–1819,* Baltimore, 1956.

Buck, Norman S., *The Development of the Organization of Anglo-American Trade, 1800–1850,* New Haven, 1925.

Carmer, Carl, *The Hudson,* New York, 1939.

Carson, Gerald, *The Old Country Store,* New York, 1954.

Clauder, Anna C., *American Commerce as Affected by the Wars of the French Revolution and Napoleon,* Philadelphia, 1932.

Cochran, Thomas C., *New York in the Confederation,* Philadelphia, 1932.

Comly, John, *Journal of the Life and Religious Labors of John Comly,* Philadelphia, 1853.

Cooper, William A., *The Attitude of the Society of Friends Toward Slavery,* Camden, 1929.

Cornell, Thomas C., *Adam and Anne Mott: Their Ancestors and Descendants,* Poughkeepsie, 1890.

Cox, John, Jr., *Catalog of the Records in Possession, or Relating to the Two New York Yearly Meetings and Subordinate Meetings,* New York, 1938.

—— *New York City and Long Island,* vol. III of *Encyclopedia of American Quaker Genealogy,* ed. by William Hinshaw, Ann Arbor, 1940.

—— *Quakerism in the City of New York, 1657–1930,* New York, 1930.

Dewey, Davis R., *Financial History of the United States,* New York, 1928.

Domett, Henry W., *A History of the Bank of New York, 1784–1884,* New York, 1884.

Dorfman, Joseph, *The Economic Mind in American Civilization, 1606–1865,* vol. I, New York, 1946.

East, Robert, *Business Enterprise in the American Revolutionary Era,* New York, 1938.

Eaton, Clement, *History of the Old South,* New York, 1945.

Federal Writers Project, *New Jersey: A Guide to Its Present and Past,* New York, 1939.

Flint, Martha B., *Early Long Island, A Colonial Study,* New York, 1896.

Forbes, John D., *Israel Thorndike,* New York, 1953.

Forbush, Bliss, *Elias Hicks, Quaker Liberal,* New York, 1956.

Fox, Dixon R., *The Decline of Aristocracy in the Politics of New York,* New York, 1918.

Fox, George, *The Journal of George Fox,* revised by Norman Penny, London and Toronto, 1924.

Gabriel, Ralph H., *The Evolution of Long Island,* New York, 1924.

176   *Bibliography*

Gill, Conrad, *The Rise of the Irish Linen Industry*, Oxford, 1925.

Gottesman, Rita, *The Arts and Crafts in New York, 1777–1799: Advertisements and News Items from New York City Newspapers*, New York, 1954.

Gras, N. S. B., *Business and Capitalism, An Introduction to Business History*, New York, 1939.

——— and Henrietta Larson, *Casebook in American Business History*, New York, 1939.

Hall, David, *An Epistle of Love and Caution*, London, 1750.

Hall, Thomas C., *Religious Background of American Culture*, Boston, 1930.

Hallowell, Anna D., *James and Lucretia Mott: Life and Letters*, Boston, 1884.

Hammond, Bray, *Banks and Politics in America from the Revolution to the Civil War*, Princeton, 1957.

Harden, William, *Savannah and South Georgia*, Chicago, 1913.

Harrington, Virginia, *New York Merchants on the Eve of the Revolution*, New York, 1935.

Hawes, Charles B., *Whaling*, Garden City, 1924.

Hedges, James B., *The Browns of Providence Plantation: Colonial Years*, Cambridge, Massachusetts, 1952.

Hedges, Joseph E., *Commercial Banking and the Stock Market Before 1863*, Baltimore, 1938.

Heilbroner, Robert L., *The Quest for Wealth: A Study of the Acquisitive Man*, New York, 1956.

Hicks, Elias, *Journal of the Life and Religious Labours of Elias Hicks, Written by Himself*, New York, 1832.

Hidy, Ralph, *The House of Baring in American Trade and Finance: English Merchant Bankers at Work, 1763–1861*, Cambridge, Massachusetts, 1949.

Hobhouse, Stephen H., *William Law and Eighteenth Century Quakerism*, London, 1927.

Hodge, Allen, and Campbell, *New York Directory and Register for the Year 1789*, New York, 1789.

Hodgson, William, *The Society of Friends in the Nineteenth Century. A Historical View of . . . That Period*, Philadelphia, 1875.

Hubert, Philip G., *The Merchants National Bank of the City of New York*, New York, 1903.

Huebner, Solomon, *Marine Insurance in the United States*, reprint from *Annals* of American Academy of Political and Social Science, vol. 26, September 1905.

Hunt, Freeman, *Lives of American Merchants*, New York, 1858.

Hutchins, John G. B., *The American Maritime Industries and Public Policy, 1789–1914*, Cambridge, Massachusetts, 1941.

Irwin, Ray W., *Diplomatic Relations of the United States with the Barbary Powers, 1776–1816*, Chapel Hill, 1931.

James, Marquis, *Biography of a Business*, New York, 1942.

James, Sydney V., *A People among Peoples: Quaker Benevolence in Eighteenth-Century America*, Cambridge, Massachusetts, 1963.

Janney, Samuel, *The Life of George Fox*, Philadelphia, 1855.

Jenks, Leland H., *The Migration of British Capital to 1875*, New York, 1938.

Jensen, Merril, *The New Nation: A History of the United States during the Confederacy, 1781–1789*, New York, 1950.

Johnson, Emory R., and others, *History of the Domestic and Foreign Commerce of the United States*, Washington, 1915.

Jones, Fred M., *Middlemen in the Domestic Trade of the United States, 1800–1850*, Urbana, 1937.

Jones, Rufus M., *Faith and Practice of the Quakers*, London, 1927.

—— *George Fox, Seeker and Friend*, New York, 1930.

—— *Later Periods of Quakerism*, London, 1921.

—— *Quakers in the American Colonies*, London, 1911.

Kalb, John H., and Edmund de Brunner, *A Study of Rural Society*, Boston, 1940.

Katona, George, *Psychological Analysis of Economic Behavior*, New York, 1951.

Keiler, Hans, *American Shipping, Its Historic and Economic Conditions*, Jena, 1913.

King, Rachel H., *George Fox and the Light Within*, Philadelphia, 1940.

Larson, Henrietta, *Guide to Business History: Materials for the Study of American Business History and Suggestions for Their Use*, Cambridge, Massachusetts, 1948.

Lauterbach, Albert, *Men, Motives, and Money, Psychological Frontiers of Economics*, Ithaca, 1954.

Lloyd, Arnold, *Quaker Social History, 1669–1738*, London, 1950.

Luke, Myron, *The Port of New York, 1800–1810: The Foreign Trade and Business Community*, New York, 1953.

McNeill, John T., *The History and Character of Calvinism*, New York, 1954.

Macy, Obed, *History of Nantucket*, Boston, 1835.

Marriner, Sheila, *Rathbones of Liverpool, 1845–1873*, Liverpool, 1961.

Mathias, Peter, *The Brewing Industry in England, 1700–1830*, Cambridge, England, 1959.

Miller, Perry, *The New England Mind: From Colony to Province*, Cambridge, Massachusetts, 1953.

Miller, Stephen B., *Historical Sketches of Hudson*, Hudson, 1862.

Morison, Samuel E., *The Builders of the Bay Colony*, Boston, 1930.

—— *The Maritime History of Massachusetts, 1783–1860*, Boston, 1941.

Myers, Margaret C., *The New York Money Market: Origins and Development*, vol. I, New York, 1931.

Nelson, Benjamin N., *The Idea of Usury: From Tribal Brotherhood to Universal Otherhood*, Princeton, 1949.

Nevins, Allen, *The American States during and after the Revolution, 1775–1789*, New York, 1924.

—— *The History of the Bank of New York and Trust Company, 1784–1934*, New York, 1934.

Niebuhr, H. Richard, *Social Sources of Denominationalism*, New York, 1929.

Noble, Vernon, *The Man in Leather Breeches*, New York, 1953.

Norwood, Frederick A., *The Development of Modern Christianity Since 1500*, New York, 1956.

Nussbaum, Frederick L., *A History of the Economic Institutions of Modern Europe*, New York, 1933.

Nuttall, Geoffrey, *The Holy Spirit in Puritan Faith and Experience*, Oxford, 1946.

Onderdonk, Henry, Jr., *The Annals of Hempstead, 1643 to 1832 also, The Rise of the Society of Friends on Long Island and New York, 1657 to 1826*, Hempstead, 1878.

[Hempstead Seceders], *A View of the Testimony, Issued by the Orthodox Seceders of Westbury and Jericho*, New York, 1829.

Overton, Jacqueline, *Long Island's Story*, New York, 1929.

Parsons, Talcott, *The Structure of Social Action*, Glencoe, 1949.

Penn, William, *Fruits of a Father's Love: Being the Advice of William Penn to His Children Relating to their Civil and Religious Conduct*, Dublin, 1727.

Pitkin, Timothy, *A Statistical View of the Commerce of the United States of America*, New York, 1817.

Pomerantz, Sidney I., *New York: An American City, 1783–1803*, New York, 1938.

Porter, Kenneth W., *The Jacksons and Lees: Two Generations of*

Massachusetts Merchants, 1765–1844, Cambridge, Massachusetts, 1937.

—— *John Jacob Astor, Business Man,* Cambridge, Massachusetts, 1931.

Raistrick, Arthur, *Quakers in Science and Industry Before 1800,* London, 1930.

Rigge, Ambrose, *A Brief and Serious Warning to Such as are Concerned in Commerce and Trading, 1678.*

Robertson, H. M., *Aspects of the Rise of Economic Individualism: A Criticism of Max Weber and His School,* Cambridge, England, 1926.

de Roover, Raymond, *The Medici Bank: Its Organization, Management, Operations, and Decline,* New York, 1948.

Ross, Peter, *A History of Long Island,* New York, 1902.

Rotch, William, *Memorandum Written by William Rotch in the Eighteenth Year of His Age,* Boston, 1916.

Russell, Elbert, *History of Quakerism,* New York, 1943.

—— *The Separations after a Century,* Philadelphia, 1928.

Schlatter, Richard B., *The Social Ideas of Religious Leaders, 1660–1688,* London, 1940.

Setser, Vernon G., *The Commercial Reciprocity Policy of the United States, 1774–1829,* Philadelphia, 1937.

Seybert, Adam, *Statistical Annals of the United States of America,* vol. I, Philadelphia, 1818.

Smith, Walter B., and Arthur H. Cole, *Fluctuations in American Business, 1790–1860,* Cambridge, Massachusetts, 1935.

Sombart, Werner, *The Jews and Modern Capitalism,* trans. M. Epstein, London, 1913.

—— *The Quintessence of Capitalism,* trans. M. Epstein, New York, 1915.

Spaulding, E. Wilder, *New York in the Critical Period,* New York, 1932.

Starbuck, Alexander, *History of American Whale Fishery,* Waltham, 1878.

Stiles, Henry B., *A History of the City of Brooklyn,* vol. II, Brooklyn, 1869.

Still, Bayrd, *Mirror for Gotham: New York as Seen by Contemporaries from Dutch Days to the Present,* New York, 1956.

Tawney, R. H., *The Acquisitive Society,* London, 1952.

—— *Religion and the Rise of Capitalism,* New York, 1926.

Thompson, Benjamin, *History of Long Island,* 3 vols., New York, 1919.

Tolles, Frederick B., *Meeting House and Counting House: The Quaker Merchants of Colonial Philadelphia, 1682–1763,* Chapel Hill, 1948.

Tooker, Elva, *Nathan Trotter, Philadelphia Merchant, 1787–1853,* Cambridge, Massachusetts, 1955.

Tower, Walter, *A History of the American Whale Industry,* Philadelphia, 1907.

Troeltsch, Ernst, *The Social Teaching of the Christian Churches,* trans. Olive Wyon, vol. II, London, 1931.

United States Bureau of the Census, *Historical Statistics of the United States, Colonial Times to 1957,* Washington, 1960.

Weber, Max, *The Protestant Ethic and the Spirit of Capitalism,* trans. Talcott Parsons, London, 1930.

Wecter, Dixon, *The Saga of American Society,* New York, 1937.

Wertenbaker, Thomas J., *Father Knickerbocker Rebels: New York City during the Revolution,* New York, 1948.

White, Philip L., *The Beekmans of New York in Politics and Commerce, 1647–1877,* New York, 1956.

Wilbur, Henry W., *The Life and Labors of Elias Hicks,* Philadelphia, 1910.

Wilson, Warren H., *Quaker Hill, A Sociological Study,* New York, 1907.

Woolman, John, *The Journal of John Woolman,* Boston, 1886.

NOTES

Chapter I: Isaac Hicks's Advantages in 1789

1. Kenneth W. Porter, *John Jacob Astor, Business Man* (Cambridge, 1931), I, 20. Stuart Bruchey, *Robert Oliver, Merchant of Baltimore, 1783–1819* (Baltimore, 1956), pp. 52–76. Freeman Hunt, *Lives of American Merchants* (New York, 1858), I, 108. Elva Tooker, *Nathan Trotter, Philadelphia Merchant, 1787–1853* (Cambridge, 1955), pp. 3, 4, 220.

2. Samuel E. Morison, *The Maritime History of Massachusetts 1783–1860* (Boston, 1941), p. 178.

3. *Ibid.*, p. 166.

4. Bray Hammond, *Banks and Politics in America, from the Revolution to the Civil War* (Princeton, 1957), pp. 144–145.

5. "By thus pooling their funds the merchants were better able to do what they had previously accomplished by informal arrangement." (Joseph E. Hedges, *Commercial Banking and the Stock Market Before 1863*, Baltimore, 1938, p. 15.) Hammond quotes Robert Troup's concern that the chartering of the Manhattan Company "will contribute powerfully to increase the bloated state of credit" (*Banks and Politics*, p. 153). See also, Bruchey, *Robert Oliver*, pp. 115–20.

6. John C. Brown, *A Hundred Years of Merchant Banking* (New York, 1909), p. 19.

7. Hammond, *Banks and Politics*, p. 193. A. H. Cole states that bills on London were not quoted with any regularity in American periodicals until after 1795. Arthur H. Cole, "Evolution of the Foreign Exchange Market of the United States," *Journal of Economic and Business History*, 1:386 (May 1929).

8. Solomon Huebner, *Marine Insurance in the United States,* Reprint from *Annals* of American Academy of Political and Social Science, 6:254 (September 1905).

9. Joseph B. Bishop, *A Chronicle of One Hundred and Fifty Years, The Chamber of Commerce of the State of New York, 1768–1918* (New York, 1918), p. 39.

10. John G. B. Hutchins, *The American Maritime Industries and Public Policy, 1789–1914* (Cambridge, 1941), p. 173.

11. *Ibid.*, p. 175.

12. Thomas S. Ashton, *An Economic History of England in the Eighteenth Century* (London, 1955), pp. 46, 147. C. Ernest Fayle, "The Employment of British Shipping," in C. Northcote Parkinson, ed., *The Trade Winds. A Study of British Overseas Trade during the French Wars, 1793–1815* (London, 1948), p. 84.

13. United States Bureau of the Census, *Historical Statistics of the United States, 1789–1945* (Washington, 1949), p. 245.

14. See: Jacqueline Overton, *Long Island's Story* (New York, 1929), p. 166.

15. Thomas C. Cornell, *Adams and Anne Mott: Their Ancestors and Their Descendants* (Poughkeepsie, 1890), p. 375. A note in Isaac Hicks's business records indicates that in May of 1802 his father lent him $1,000.

16. Robert Bolton to Isaac Hicks, December 13, 1800, Hicks Papers. The Hicks Papers, hereafter "H.P.," are now with the New York Historical Society.

17. It is difficult to authenticate the accounts of Isaac Hicks's life in Westbury before 1789. Marietta Hicks, a dedicated compiler of family records, showed me her unpublished notes and supplied me with family anecdotes. In 1887 the elderly Richard Mott wrote his recollections from childhood of Isaac Hicks. (Richard Mott to John Hicks, July 21, 1887, H.P.) All of these accounts of Hicks's early years are in essential agreement.

18. Cornell, *Adam and Anne Mott,* p. 374; Richard Mott to J. D. Hicks, July 21, 1887, H.P.

19. Book B, 2, A Transcript of the Monthly Meeting of Westbury, July 31, 1765, pp. 79, 80, 84. These minutes and other records in the possession of the Westbury Monthly Meeting will be referred to as Westbury Records, "W.R."

20. "James Titus and Henry Post reported that they had attended the Marriage of Samuel Hicks and . . . [noted] disorderly exerciseing and playing ball." *Ibid.,* p. 84.

21. Book C, Westbury Minutes, Feb. 23, 1773, pp. 104–05, W.R. The conclusion of this affair, which the Meeting condemned as "having a tendency to lay waste the order of Friends," was that Titus returned the slave and Hicks gave back £38 of the purchase price, and the Meeting recorded "their affair settled according to the Judgment of last Monthly Meeting." *Ibid.,* pp. 106, 112.

22. Volume 3, April 27, 1780, W.R.

23. Frederick B. Tolles, "Benjamin Franklin's Business Mentors: The Philadelphia Quakers," *William and Mary Quarterly,* 55:61 (January 1947).

24. "An Additional Extract from Other of George Fox's Epistles," Works, VII, 345, as quoted by Frederick B. Tolles, *Meeting House and Counting House: The Quaker Merchants of Colonial Philadelphia, 1682–1763* (Chapel Hill, 1948), p. 55. Thomas Chalkley, *A Journal . . . of . . . Thomas Chalkley in A Collection of the Works of Thomas Chalkley,* pp. 97–98 as quoted by Tolles, *Meeting House and Counting House,* p. 58. Tolles writes, "Friends regarded diligence in a warrantable calling as a religious duty," *Ibid.,* p. 57.

25. William Penn, *The Advice of William Penn to His Children in*

Works, I, 908–909, as quoted by Tolles, *Meeting House and Counting House,* p. 45.

26. Isaac Norris I to Joseph (?) Norris, April, 1719, Norris Letter Book, 1716–1730, pp. 183–184, as quoted by Tolles, *Meeting House and Counting House,* p. 58. See also, Howard Brinton, *Friends for 300 Years* (New York, 1952), pp. 134–143.

27. "The process of sanctifying life could thus almost take on the character of a business enterprise. A thoroughgoing Christianization of the whole of life was the consequence of this methodical quality of ethical conduct into which Calvinism as distinct from Lutheranism forced men. That this rationality was decisive in its influence on practical life must always be borne in mind in order rightly to understand the influence of Calvinism" (Max Weber, *The Protestant Ethic and the Spirit of Capitalism,* London, 1930, pp. 124–125). "The converted Christian could never take a single action, nor think a single thought, without a purpose to glorify his God" (Richard B. Schlatter, *The Social Ideas of Religious Leaders, 1660–1688,* London, 1940, p. 188).

28. Jean Pierre Brissot de Warville, *Nouveau voyage dans les Etats-unis de l'Amerique septentrionale,* II, 187, as quoted in Tolles, *Meeting House and Counting House,* p. 61.

29. William Penn, *Fruits of a Father's Love: Being the Advice of William Penn to His Children Relating to their Civil and Religious Conduct* (Dublin, 1727), p. 36.

30. An extract from the New York Yearly Meeting was read in Hicks's Monthly Meeting in New York on July, 1790, cautioning businessmen. "Divers by unguardedly extending . . . business have endangered the Testimony, the Peace, and Welfare of their Families, and some instances have occurred where they have been unable to render justice to their creditors. And many lively and pertinent remarks were made to quicken Friends to their duty . . . and to encourage them to Watch over one another for good and timely to advise and caution such as may be in danger, and that overseers be vigilant in their care." Book 1012, July 5, 1790, New York Yearly Meeting Records, hereafter, "N.Y.R." These records are housed in the Record Room of the New York Yearly Meeting, 121 E. 15th Street, New York, N. Y. These instructions are not idle exhortations. This same book includes an entry from "The Preparative Meeting of Flushing [which] informs Rodman Field has been treated with for neglect in the payment of his Debts." Two months later a brief entry noted that Field had been disowned. *Ibid.,* April 6, 1791, June 1, 1791, N.Y.R. See also, Tolles, *Meeting House and Counting House,* pp. 58–59.

31. Tolles, *Meeting House and Counting House,* p. 59. Raistrick, *Quakers in Science and Industry,* p. 48.

32. Tolles, *Meeting House and Counting House,* pp. 234–243. William

Hodgson, *The Society of Friends in the Nineteenth Century. A Historical View . . . of that . . . Period* (Philadelphia, 1875), p. 14.

33. Raistrick, *Quakers in Science and Industry,* pp. 341–342.

34. Carl Bridenbaugh, *Cities in the Wilderness* (New York, 1938), p. 415.

35. Elbert Russell, *History of Quakerism* (New York, 1943), p. 225. See also, Rufus M. Jones, *Later Periods of Quakerism* (London, 1921), pp. 57–103. Sydney V. James, *A People among Peoples; Quaker Benevolence in Eighteenth-Century America* (Cambridge, Massachusetts, 1963), p. 170, chs. X–XVI.

36. Volume I, p. 1, W.R. Friends in unity were expected to conform to the following section of the Discipline: "Our object is to let decency, simplicity, and utility be our objectives. We . . . tenderly exhort all to consider seriously the plainness and simplicity which the gospel enjoins; and to manifest it in their dress, speech, furniture of their houses, manner of living, and general deportment" (Vol. 41A, p. 64, W.R.).

37. Volume 2, pp. 338–339, W.R.

38. William C. Braithwaite. *Beginnings of Quakerism* (London, 1912), p. 131.

39. Tolles, *Meeting House and Counting House,* pp. 234–243. Fox said: "The least member in the Church hath an office and is servicable and every member hath need one of another" (Arnold Lloyd, *Quaker Social History, 1669–1738,* London, 1950, p. 175). "One natural result of this extensive itinerancy was the eventual prevalence of a single type of Quakerism throughout the far-sundered communities that composed the Society. Wherever . . . Friends maintained a group life . . . there was among them a similarity in ideas, in phrases, in conscientious scruples, in emotional tones, in spiritual perspective and emphasis, in garb and manner, in facial expression and voice modulation" (Stephen H. Hobhouse, *William Law and Eighteenth Century Quakerism,* London, 1927, p. 190).

40. "The importance of family connection in the business of New York cannot be overestimated. The merchant . . . about to take on a new apprentice chose first his sons and then looked among his promising nephews. If there were no available relatives, then, and then only, he applied to a friend" (Virginia Harrington, *New York Merchants on the Eve of the Revolution,* New York, 1935, pp. 51–52). See also Kenneth W. Porter, *The Jacksons and the Lees, Two Generations of Massachusetts Merchants 1765–1844* (Cambridge, 1937), I, 46.

41. Peter Mathias, *The Brewing Industry in England, 1700–1830* (Cambridge, England, 1959), pp. 271–275, 286–291.

Chapter II: From Grocer to Dry Goods "Specialist": 1789–1794

1. Volume 1012, April 7, May 6, 1790, N.Y.R.

2. Porter, in *The Jacksons and the Lees,* calls "the Massachusetts mer-

cantile group . . . pretty much of a closed corporation. One does not encounter barefooted farm boys, who come to Boston, secure a warehouse job, study nights, get promoted to the countinghouse, become junior partners, and make their fortunes. It was not . . . impossible for a poor boy to work himself up to the position of an independent merchant, but his route would be by way of the fo'c'sle and quarter deck" (I, 97).

3. On May 1, 1802, Samuel was able to lend his son $1,000 for 60 days at 6%. MS notes, 1802, H.P.

4. Hodge, Allen and Campbell, *New York Directory and Register for the Year 1789* (New York, 1789), p. 61.

5. Harrington, *New York Merchants,* p. 61.

6. 1790 Journal, H.P.

7. *Ibid.,* p. 23.

8. *Ibid.,* p. 13 and *passim.* The symbol "£" stands for New York pounds, the currency of account used by Hicks until 1796. Merchants calculated the New York pound at exactly $2.50. British Pounds Sterling will be written "£___ Sterling." The official value of sterling at this time was $4.44.

9. Richard Mott to John D. Hicks, July 21, 1887, H.P.

10. Porter, *Astor,* I, 27, 114.

11. Harrington, *New York Merchants,* pp. 57-59.

12. "A young merchant might . . . make the most of his slender capital by inducing some other promising beginner to form a partnership with him" (Porter, *Jacksons and Lees,* I, 45-46).

13. *New York Directory 1790,* p. 50.

14. 1790 Journal, pp. 4, 16, H.P.

15. Robert G. Albion, *Square Riggers on Schedule* (Princeton, 1938), pp. 118-119.

16. Volume 288, Record of Certificates Received, p. 200, May 19, 1790, N.Y.R.

17. Names from the 1790 Journal were checked against Meeting records and the names listed in William W. Hinshaw, *Encyclopedia of Quaker Genealogy* (Ann Arbor, 1940).

18. Russell, *History of Quakerism,* p. 202.

19. Porter, *Astor,* I, 26. *New York Directory,* 1789; 1790.

20. Ackers & Wilson, Nathaniel and Faulkner Phillips, Peel Ainsworth, and Peel Yates—all in Manchester; John & Jeremy Naylor in Wakefield and John Warder & Company in London. Alsop & Hicks's Blotter, 1791, records payments to these firms in behalf of Loines, Alsop & Company, H.P.

21. Bill of sale, Frederick Jenkins, John Alsop, and Richard Barker to William Loines, John Alsop, Isaac Hicks, and Richard Loines, Nov. 10, 1790, for sloop *Hudson Packet.* £500. H.P.

22. "The number concerned therein and the many inconveniences con-

sequent thereon, led to a belief that a separation would be best," was part of the guarded announcement made by the successor firm, Alsop & Hicks. Letter Order Book, 1791, p. 1, H.P.

23. Two versions of the dissolution statement exist: one on a separate statement and one in the 1790 Journal, the latter showing somewhat smaller amounts. The figures in the text are taken from the separate statement. H.P

24. Baxter, *House of Hancock,* p. 224.

25. *New York Directory* 1792.

26. H.P. and *New York Directory* 1793.

27. Alsop & Hicks to Waldo, Francis & Waldo, Oct. 10, 1791, Letter Order Book, H.P.

28. Although the firm announced in a number of letters that it was in the dry goods line it never chose to give itself this special listing in the New York Directory. In 1789, when some 33 firms listed themselves as dry goods houses, the number that chose the term "merchant" was far in the lead of other business categories. Out of approximately 4,000 entries there were 232 merchants listed as against 132 grocers. In 1794, rather than finding more firms choosing a specialized title, one finds fewer. Only four chose to be listed as dry goods firms, but of the 7,000-odd entries, 654 said "merchant," 380 "grocer." Of course a large number of the "merchants" handled dry goods and many probably considered them the principal business of the firm.

29. Norman S. Buck, *The Development of the Organization of Anglo-American Trade, 1800–1850* (New Haven, 1925), pp. 99ff.

30. The Quaker house of Robert Bowne sold the firm 1,225 yards of Irish linen worth $207. Pearsall & Bowne let them have 21½ pieces of coatings valued at $277: A $236 purchase from William Morewood gave Alsop & Hicks 198 yds. of denim and 134 yds. of velveteen. Unbound bills, H.P.

31. Generous British credits were the order of the day. See Muriel Hidy, "Capital Markets, 1789–1860," in chap. xiv, Harold F. Williamson, ed., *The Growth of the American Economy* (New York, 1946), p. 289, and Margaret C. Myers, *The New York Money Market* (New York, 1921), I, 58. This was a continuation of pre-Revolutionary practice (see Harrington, *New York Merchants,* pp. 101–102).

32. "The firm of Nathaniel and Faulkner Phillips & Company of Manchester, kept an agent in America. He was an Englishman, and was paid a regular salary, and not paid on a commission basis" (Buck, *Anglo-American Trade,* p. 106). John Travis wrote Alsop & Hicks: "My partners, Nathaniel and Faulkner Phillips." John Travis to Alsop & Hicks, May 26, 1794, H.P. Robert Oliver, the Baltimore merchant, bought bills from John Travis (Bruchey, *Robert Oliver,* p. 118).

33. Alsop & Hicks to John Warder, Aug. 17, 1791; to Philip Nicklin, Aug. 17, 1791; to John Travis, Aug. 25, 1791, Letter Order Book, H.P.

34. Alsop & Hicks to Waldo, Francis and Waldo, Oct. 10, 1791, *Ibid.*

35. Benjamin Chase to Alsop & Hicks, Sept. 8, 1792; Alsop & Hicks to Sylvannus Hussey, May 14, 1793, Country Letter Book; Jonathan Mix to Alsop & Hicks, account current, May 1794; John Reynolds to Alsop & Hicks, Aug. 4, 1792; Alsop & Hicks Blotter, May 19, 1792, H.P.

36. The Quaker firms of Willet Seaman, Kirby & Parsons, Willet and Mott Hicks, led the rest in these barter sales. Sometimes they were as frequent as three in one week with one firm. Unbound bills, 1791, 1792, 1793, 1794, H.P.

37. Alsop and Hicks Invoice Book, Nathaniel and Faulkner Phillips & Company, Feb. 11, 1793, H.P.

38. Fred M. Jones, *Middlemen in the Domestic Trade of the United States, 1800–1860* (Urbana, 1937), pp. 9–10.

39. Still, everything is relative, for Philip L. White in *The Beekmans of New York* claims that specialization of function had advanced considerably in pre-Revolutionary New York thanks to the "greater abundance and wider distribution of money" and to the concentration of merchants in one port area, unlike the scattered merchants on New England's smaller ports. *The Beekmans of New York in Politics and Commerce 1647–1877* (New York, 1956), pp. 545–547.

40. Baxter, in *The House of Hancock,* notes this pattern in pre-Revolutionary days, pp. 185–187.

41. Alsop & Hicks to Robert Bolton, Nov. 29, 1792; to William Lamb, Dec. 6, 1792, Country Letter Book; Alsop & Hicks Blotter, pp. 1–77, H.P.

42. "As we have an overstock of woolens," the firm wrote George Kelly, a Norfolk merchant, "thou will dispose of them at public sale on our account" (Alsop & Hicks to George Kelly, Dec. 12, 1791). The firm sent a similar consignment to a Savannah merchant (Alsop & Hicks to Alexander Leslie, Jan. 1, 1792, Country Letter Book, H.P.).

43. Eli Whitney to Alsop & Hicks, Oct. 27, 1791; Shadrack Sill to Alsop & Hicks, Nov. 26, 1791; Alsop & Hicks to Peel Yates, Feb. 24, 1794, Letter Order Book, H.P.

44. William Mitchell to John Alsop, April 3, 1792; Alsop & Hicks to Thomas Howland, Nov. 2, 1793, Country Letter Book; William Lamb to Alsop & Hicks, Jan. 8, 1792. H.P.

45. Bruchey, *Robert Oliver,* p. 42; Porter, *Jacksons and Lees,* p. 78; Harrington, *New York Merchants,* pp. 64–65; Baxter, *House of Hancock,* pp. 16-28. Myron Luke comments that the merchant was at the mercy of his country debtors. Luke, "The Port of New York, 1800–1810; The Foreign Trade and Business Community," unpub. diss., New York University, 1950, p. 219.

46. Alexander Leslie to Alsop & Hicks, Oct. 8 to Oct. 22, 1792; Isaac Hicks memorandum of trip, 1792; Jonas Morgan to Alsop & Hicks, Jan.

14, 1794; Robert Perrigo, Jr. to Alsop & Hicks, May 6, 1794, H.P.
  47. John Chapman to Alsop & Hicks, Aug. 30, 1794, H.P.
  48. Statement of John Hutchinson, Feb. 4, 1794, H.P.
  49. Baxter, *House of Hancock*, p. 34.
  50. Robert Perrigo to Alsop & Hicks, March 6, 1794, H.P. Two other upstate customers, Job Whipple and Benjamin Stratton, paid the firm by sending lumber for dry goods (H.P.). A few doors from Alsop & Hicks's Water Street address Thomas Clarke advertised his dry goods with the concluding remark: "All which he will sell on reasonable terms; lumber will be received in payment" (*New York Daily Advertiser*, Sept. 12, 1794). This kind of barter worked both ways in Hicks's day. Some New York merchants advertised, "Dry Goods will be taken in barter for oak, square timber and plank by Johnson & Ogden, No. 32 Queen Street" (Aug. 24, 1786, *The New York Packet*). See also *ibid.*, May 29, 1786, cited by Rita S. Gottesman, *The Arts and Crafts in New York, 1777–1799: Advertisements and News Items from New York City Newspapers* (New York, 1954), IV, 135, 245. Before the Revolution, merchants like the Browns accepted payment in kind for their dry goods, even a mortgage on a farm. James B. Hedges, *The Browns of Providence Plantation: Colonial Years* (Cambridge. 1952), p. 186.
  51. *New York Daily Advertiser*, Sept. 22, 1794.
  52. The mechanism of exchange is discussed in the following: Harrington, *New York Merchants*, p. 115; Walter B. Smith and Arthur H. Cole, *Fluctuations in American Business 1790–1860* (Cambridge, 1935), p. 6; Arthur H. Cole, "Evolution of the Foreign Exchange Market of the United States," *Journal of Economic and Business History*, 1:384–386 (May, 1929); Bruchey, *Robert Oliver*, p. 45. The following transaction of Alsop & Hicks illustrates the use of the foreign bill of exchange. On June 6, 1792, the firm paid Daniel Mason in New York £102/10/0 stg. for a bill drawn against Spencer Mason of London for £100 stg., a 2½% advance. Alsop & Hicks sent the bill directly to the firm's creditor, John Warder & Company of London, who could present it to Mason or turn it over to a bill broker for collection (Alsop & Hicks Blotter, June 6, 1792, H.P.).
  53. "Month-to-month variability was due in part to the smallness of the bill market. Had there been more dealers in exchange, and had there been more willingness on the part of American merchants to invest in foreign drafts, undoubtedly the rate would have been more steady. A small market for bills arising from a commodity trade in which there were wide swings" (Smith and Cole, *Fluctuations in American Business*, p. 24). See Bruchey, *Robert Oliver*, p. 164; Cole, "Evolution of Exchange," *Journal of Economic and Business History*, p. 386.
  54. Myers, *Money Market*, I, 69; see also Hammond, *Banks and Politics*, p. 293.

55. Alsop & Hicks to Peel Yates, Aug. 13, 1793; Alsop & Hicks to John and Thomas Watson, Nov. 15, 1793, Letter Order Book, H.P.

56. Smith and Cole, *Fluctuations in American Business,* pp. 13–15.

57. Alsop & Hicks to Peel Yates, May 24, March 24, 1792, Letter Order Book, H.P.

58. John Warder (Philadelphia) to Alsop & Hicks, Oct. 24, 1792, Jan. 14, 1794; note on Alsop & Hicks in favor of Edmund Prior drawn by John Warder, Jan. 14, 1794, H.P.

59. Alsop & Hicks to Philip Nicklin & Co., Aug. 13, 1793; Alsop & Hicks to Peel Yates, Aug. 13, 1793, Letter Order Book, H.P.

60. Alsop & Hicks to Joseph Anthony & Sons, May 22, 1794; Alsop & Hicks to John Travis, May 22, 1794; Alsop & Hicks to Philip Nicklin, May 22, 1794, Letter Order Book. Nicklin had demanded an advance of 6½ per cent. "We are sorry we cannot say with you that exchange is falling. Bills now bring 8 or 9 per cent. We will, however, venture to receive your amount at 6½ per cent." (Philip Nicklin to Alsop & Hicks, May 21, 1794, H.P.).

Buck's findings, especially his evidence from the Parliamentary Papers, indicate that this method of using the agent to make the remittances became common:

" 'What is the mode of payment?'

'By notes or by cash to an agent in America, which agent purchases bills with those notes and cash.'

'You mean that the agent in America collects the debts due to houses, and receives the money in American bank notes, or in specie, and buys bills with that property?'

'Not in bank notes, notes that are negotiable, that are issued there.' " (From Parliamentary Papers *Evidence of Merchants,* 1808, p. 13, as quoted in Buck, *Anglo-American Trade,* p. 118).

61. Cole quotes Alexander Brown of Baltimore: "We think if Exchange keeps as high as at present . . . dry goods men will remit in Cotton in preference to giving 175 per cent for bills." Cole, "Evolution of Exchange," *Journal of Economic and Business History,* p. 387.

62. Alsop & Hicks to Caspar Voght, Feb. 28, 1794, Letter Order Book, H.P. "Our object in the present shipment being as a remittance . . . we propose to draw in favor of:

Bowerbank Monkhouse & Company, London.	£150/0/0
John Warder & Company, London.	£275 (about)
James & Thomas Watson, Nottingham.	£134/18/9
William Rawson & Company, Halifax.	£100/0/0."

63. It would be interesting to know whether the dry goods merchant used the goods he accepted as barter payments for overseas payments. Robert Weir, a New York dry goods importer contemporaneous with Hicks,

shipped to England the same kind of commodities that dry goods merchants had been accepting as barter: beeswax, flaxseed, ashes, tar, barrel staves, tobacco, cotton. R. Weir Account Book, New York Public Library.

64. Alsop & Hicks Blotter, Sept. 17 to Feb. 10, 1792, H.P.

65. Alsop & Hicks to John Banks, Nov. 22, 1792; to Theophilus Breed, May 14, 1793, Country Letter Book; Samuel Coates to Alsop & Hicks, Oct. 23, 1794; Alsop & Hicks to Samuel Coates, Oct. 25, 1794, Country Letter Book, H.P.

66. Sales Account of B. H. Phillips, Curaçao, Dec. 1, 1792; Statement of Tiddeman Hull, 1793; Alsop & Hicks to Harvey & Lecky, Sept. 29, 1794; Alsop & Hicks to Edward Forbes, Dec. 1794, Letter Order Book; Charter Party for the ship *Peggy,* Thomas Clarke and Alsop & Hicks, Sept. 30, 1794; Harvey & Lecky to Alsop & Hicks, March 1, 1796; Alsop & Hicks to Lydia Bunker, March 28, 1796, Country Letter Book, H.P.

67. Alsop & Hicks Blotter, Sept. 24, 1791; Thomas Jenkins to Alsop & Hicks, March 5, 1792, April 14, 1792; Alsop & Hicks Blotter, April 16, 1792; Alsop & Hicks to B. H. Phillips, July 14, 1792, Letter Order Book; Sloop *Hudson Packet* in account current with William Bunker, Dec. 20, 1792, H.P.

68. N. S. B. Gras, *Business and Capitalism* (New York, 1939), p. 145.

69. W. T. Baxter, "Credit, Bills and Bookkeeping in a Simple Economy," *The Accounting Review,* no. 21 (April 1946), p. 161.

70. Henry and John Hull draft on Alsop & Hicks, Nov. 24, 1793, H.P.

71. Thomas Jenkins draft on Alsop & Hicks, Nov. 22, 1792, H.P.

72. "A month here or there meant nothing in that easygoing society" (Baxter, "Credit, Bills and Bookkeeping," *Accounting Review,* p. 162).

73. Drafts on Alsop & Hicks, 1791-1794; Judah Paddock draft on Alsop & Hicks, June 22, 1794, H.P.

74. Thomas Jenkins draft on Alsop & Hicks, Nov. 22, 1792, H.P.

75. Raymond de Roover, *The Medici Bank; Its Organization, Management, Operations and Decline* (New York, 1948), p. 29. Tooker, *Nathan Trotter,* p. 153. Hammond, *Banks and Politics,* pp. 165, 193.

76. Drafts on Alsop & Hicks, 1791 through 1794, H.P.

77. Alsop & Hicks Blotter, Sept. 1, 1791, to Jan. 1792, H.P. One missing page throws this calculation off by an indeterminable amount.

78. Alsop & Hicks to Robert Bolton, Nov. 29, 1792, H.P.

79. Alsop & Hicks Invoice Book; Alsop & Hicks Blotter, H.P.

80. Porter, *Jacksons and Lees,* I, 25. Minturn and Champlin, which had operated as a competitor of Alsop & Hicks in the dry goods trade in New York, failed in 1815 with the introduction of British dumping of dry goods on the auction market (Myers, *Money Market,* I, 63).

Chapter III: "We Are in the Shipping and Commission Line"

1. This announcement to an Irish Commission House, Harvey & Lecky

(Sept. 29, 1794, Letter Order Book, H.P.) was similar to others going to English and Irish Merchants.

2. Some commission merchants guaranteed the reliability of purchasers' notes and charged a higher commission, *del credere,* to their principal. Porter, *Jacksons and Lees,* p. 75. See also Bruchey, *Robert Oliver,* p. 64. Apparently Alsop & Hicks did not follow this practice.

3. During the Revolution Jenkins impeached William Rotch and four other Quakers for "high treason." Without the consent of the Massachusetts government Rotch visited a British port in order to plead the case of Nantucket. Jenkins also accused Rotch of being responsible for the loss of Jenkins' property, which was seized during the Revolution (Obed Macy, *History of Nantucket,* Boston, 1835; William Rotch, *Memorandum,* pp. 16–23, 82–89.

4. Elias Hicks to Thomas Rotch, Dec. 19, 1794; Elias Hicks to Samuel R. Fisher, Feb. 19, 1798; Elias Hicks to Henry Drinker, May 10, 1779, in Friends Historical Library, Swarthmore, Pa. See also Bliss Forbush, *Elias Hicks: Quaker Liberal* (New York, 1956), pp. 42-43, 88, 99.

5. Anna R. Bradbury. *History of the City of Hudson* (Hudson, 1908), pp. 16-20; Dixon R. Fox, *The Decline of Aristocracy in the Politics of New York* (New York, 1918), pp. 39-40; Stephen B. Miller, *Historical Sketches of Hudson* (Hudson, 1862). Cornell, *Adam and Anne Mott,* p. 210.

6. Cornell, *Adam and Anne Mott,* p. 210. See also Book B, "A Record of Certificates Given," May 29, 1771, W. R. Alsop & Hicks Blotter, Oct. 24, 1791, Mar. 19, 1792; Alsop & Hicks to Falconer and Blackiston, Country Letter Book, Jan. 23, 1796, H.P.

7. Accounts Current, Alsop & Hicks with Isaac Hicks, July 11, 1800, to July 6, 1802; Alsop & Hicks with John Alsop, May 20, 1794, to Aug. 17, 1801; Alsop & Hicks with John Dickinson [attorney for the firm] Feb. 27, 1804, H.P.

8. Sidney I. Pomerantz, *New York: An American City, 1783–1803* (New York, 1938), p. 158.

9. Jones, *Middlemen in Domestic Trade,* p. 10; Gras, *Business and Capitalism,* pp. 168, 197; Buck, *Anglo-American Trade,* p. 6; Robert East, *Business Enterprise in the American Revolutionary Era* (New York, 1938), pp. 322–323.

10. Commercial-minded Hudson wangled a Customs House after independence and had more ships registered than New York City at the end of the Revolution. Bradbury, *History of Hudson,* pp. 25, 47; Carl Carmer, *The Hudson* (New York, 1939), p. 159. Virginia Harrington notes that even the larger city of Albany shared Hudson's limitations. "Merchants at Albany had regular correspondents in New York who performed all the services of factor or agent in selling and shipping goods, filling orders, insuring ships or cargoes, and even acting in some instances as middlemen

between them and the English Wholesalers." Harrington, *New York Merchants,* p. 237.

11. *New York Daily Advertiser,* May 10, 1792.

12. Thomas Jenkins & Sons to Alsop & Hicks, April 30, 1792, H.P.

13. *Ibid.,* Oct. 14, 1794, Oct. 17, 1794, April 13, 1796, Sept. 23, 1794; Rush to Alsop & Hicks, May 18, 1795. From Southampton Hunting wrote despairing of completing his assignment: "My Indians . . . have gone off that I intended for the Brig. They are all very unwilling to go a skinning." Benjamin Hunting to Alsop & Hicks, Oct. 17, 1794, H.P.

14. Alsop & Hicks to James Ansdale, Michael Walton, Samuel Newton, Ackers & Wilson, George Green, Nathaniel & Faulkner Phillips, John & Jeremiah Naylor, and Peel Yates, May 24, 1792, Letter Order Book, H.P., Albion, *Square Riggers on Schedule,* p. 20.

15. In 1795 Thomas Jenkins formed a partnership with Alsop & Hicks, Thomas Jenkins & Company, to underwrite insurance. (Agreement with Thomas Jenkins, Jan. 29, 1795, H.P.) Jenkins furnished half the capital and Hicks in New York did the actual contracting. A number of shipping agents of that period also acted as insurers: Armstrong & Barnwall, Knox & Briggs, John Ferrers, Lawrence & Seton (*New York Daily Advertiser,* 1794, 1795, and 1796). By the end of 1795 the firm had collected $13,182 in premiums and was responsible for $217,121 of marine insurance. Though a number of the brokers' books are missing, the record with nine brokers indicates that the losses exceeded the gains by about $2,000 on the transactions indicated.

16. William Rotch, Jr. to Alsop & Hicks, Oct. 30, 1794; Alsop & Hicks to William Rotch, Jr., Nov. 10, 1794, Country Letter Book, H.P.

17. Alsop & Hicks to Isaiah Hussey, Jan. 27, 1795; Alsop & Hicks to William Rotch, Jr., Feb. 1, 1796, Country Letter Book, H.P.

18. David Starbuck to Alsop & Hicks, Aug. 29, 1795; Alsop & Hicks to Joseph Hussey and William Mackey, Jr., July 16, 1795; Alsop & Hicks to Shubael Coffin, April 16, 1796, Country Letter Book, H.P.

19. Alsop & Hicks to Francis Macy, March 5, 1706, Country Letter Book, H.P.

20. *Ibid.,* March 19 and April 16, 1796.

21. *Ibid.,* April 16, 1796. The English firm replied: "It is . . . our object to divide our influence with respect to freight as equally, and . . . impartially, as we can," Rathbone, Benson & Co. to Hicks & Doughty, June 27, 1796, H.P.

22. Alsop & Hicks to Francis Macy, April 26, 1796, Country Letter Book, H.P.

23. Francis Macy to Alsop & Hicks, June 3, 1796, H.P.

24. Orders to Captain Cartwright, Country Letter Book, H.P.

25. Alsop & Hicks to Rathbone, Benson & Co., May 10, 1796, Letter Order Book, H.P.

26. Joseph Cartwright to Hicks & Doughty, June 18, 1796, H.P.

27. Bird, Savage & Bird to Alsop & Hicks, July 13, 1796, H.P.

28. Ralph W. Hidy, *The House of Baring in American Trade and Finance: English Merchant Bankers at Work, 1763–1861* (Cambridge, 1949), p. 32.

29. Account current, Ship *Ann* with Philip Sansom, August 1796; Thaddeus Coffin to Isaac Hicks, May 13, 1797; Francis Macy to Isaac Hicks, June 23, 1797, H.P.

30. Francis Macy to Isaac Hicks, Oct. 10, 1796, H.P.

31. *New York Daily Advertiser,* 1794, 1795, 1796.

32. Alsop & Hicks Blotter, Nov. 23, 1791, to June 11, 1792; Alsop & Hicks to Robert Bolton, Nov. 29, 1792, Country Letter Book. The firm made a similar proposal to an Albany merchant. John Jauncey to Alsop & Hicks, Dec. 26, 1792, H.P.

33. "At the instance of our mutual friends Seth Jenkins & Sons, we now take the liberty to address thee with a small consignment of lamp oil" (Alsop & Hicks to Edward Forbes, December 1794, Letter Order Book, H.P.).

34. *Ibid.,* April 28, 1795.

35. *Ibid.,* June 1, 1795.

36. Harrington, *New York Merchants,* p. 70; Alsop & Hicks to Edward Forbes, June 1, 1795 *et seq.;* 1796, Letter Order Book; Edward Forbes to Alsop & Hicks, 1795, 1796, H.P.

37. Alsop & Hicks to Edward Forbes, June 9, 1795, Letter Order Book, H.P.

38. Edward Forbes to Alsop & Hicks, May 21, 1796, H.P.

39. Joseph Coolidge to Alsop & Hicks, June 17, 1795; Alsop & Hicks Invoice Book, Aug. 27, 1795, H.P.

40. Alsop & Hicks to George McConnell, Dec. 15, 1795, Letter Order Book, H.P. Conrad Gill, *The Rise of the Irish Linen Industry* (Oxford, 1925), p. 177.

41. Alsop & Hicks to George McConnell, March 24, 1795, Letter Order Book, H.P.

42. George McConnell to Alsop & Hicks, May 19, 1795, H.P.

43. *Ibid.*

44. Harvey & Lecky to Alsop & Hicks, March 1, 1796, H.P.

45. James Holmes & Co. to Alsop & Hicks, March 12, 1796, H.P.

46. Alsop & Hicks to George Pennock, Jan. 11, 1796, Country Letter Book; Daniel Crommelin & Sons to Alsop & Hicks, July 22, 1796; Hicks & Doughty Waste Book, June 14, 1796, H.P.

47. Harvey & Lecky to Alsop & Hicks, Dec. 1, 1794, H.P.
48. John Alsop to Isaac Hicks, April 20, 1796; Isaac Hicks to John Alsop [copy], April 26, 1796, H.P.

Chapter IV: Oil, Candles, and Ships, 1796 to 1800

1. *New York Daily Advertiser,* Aug. 22, 1796.
2. Francis Joy to Alsop & Hicks, Jan. 1, 1794, H.P.
3. William Rotch & Sons to Alsop & Hicks, July 17, 1795, H.P.
4. Alsop & Hicks to Abraham Barker, Feb. 2, 1796; Alsop & Hicks to Micajah Coffin, Feb. 1, 1796, Country Letter Book, H.P.
5. Alsop & Hicks to William Rotch, Jr., Feb. 16, 1796; Alsop & Hicks to William Rotch & Sons, Feb. 29, 1796, March 7, 1796, Country Letter Book, H.P.
6. Alsop & Hicks to Thomas Hazard, Jr., April 4, 1796, Country Letter Book, H.P.
7. Gardner and Mitchell to Isaac Hicks, June 11, 1799; Jonathan Jenkins to Isaac Hicks, Sept. 17, 1796; Alsop & Hicks to Micajah Coffin, Nov. 23, 1794, Country Letter Book, H.P. Baxter, in *The House of Hancock,* describes attempts to achieve a monopoly of oil exports to London, pp. 168–176, 226–232.
8. Alsop & Hicks to William Rotch, Jr., Feb. 1, 1796, Country Letter Book, H.P.
9. In 1798, for example, the New York City Common Council bought more oil from Hicks than from anybody else. Hicks received $4961.45 in warrants; all the rest totaled $5086.70. Some of the warrants recorded in the names of other firms and individuals such as Latham Bunker and Thomas Jenkins & Sons, both of them Hicks's customers, may have been on sales arranged by Hicks. *Minutes of the Common Council for the City of New York, 1784–1831* (New York, 1917), II, 434, 440.
10. Hedges, *The Browns of Providence Plantation,* p. 95. See also Alexander Starbuck, *History of American Whale Fishery* (Waltham, 1878), p. 151.
11. Alsop & Hicks to William Rotch, Dec. 30, 1795; Alsop & Hicks to Abraham Barker, Dec. 30, 1795, Country Letter Book, H.P.
12. Alsop & Hicks to Cotton Gelston, March 17, 1796, Country Letter Book, H.P.
13. A barrel of oil averaged thirty gallons. Alsop & Hicks to William Rotch & Sons, May 5, 1796, Country Letter Book. H.P.
14. Alsop & Hicks to Jonathan Jenkins, March 18, 1796, Country Letter Book, H.P.
15. Alsop & Hicks to William Rotch, Jr., Feb. 26, 1796, Country Letter Book, H.P.
16. These are almost exclusively domestic sales. On rare occasions Hicks

shipped oil to a better market in Philadelphia, but he did this only when calculations on the New York market did not work out. Hicks did not ship the New Englanders' oil to foreign markets because they did this for themselves. "On February 3, 1783, the ship *Bedford* owned by William Rotch of Nantucket and flying the Stars and Stripes, arrived at the Downs with a cargo of 487 butts of whale oil" (Charles B. Hawes, *Whaling,* Garden City, 1924, p. 87). Though fully prepared to handle the shipping of their oil and to combine these deliveries with return voyages of European goods, men like Rotch would write to their busy New York factor to ask for the latest reports on foreign markets. See also Starbuck, *American Whale Fishery,* p. 700.

17. Tower, *American Whale Fishery,* p. 105; Starbuck, *American Whale Fishery,* pp. 194–197.

18. Samuel Rodman to Isaac Hicks, Aug. 1, 1799, Aug. 14, 1799, H.P.

19. Hawes, *Whaling,* p. 92. When Alsop & Hicks tried to sell the ship *Swan,* the firm described her as "being of too great a draft of water for the Nantucket whaling business, her tonnage, 318 tons . . . built at Newbury . . . by six master builders and calculated for an Indiaman." Alsop & Hicks to Thomas Jenkins, Feb. 17, 1796, Country Letter Book, H.P.

20. Jonathan Jenkins to Isaac Hicks, April 6, 1799; Richard, Obed, Aaron, and Jethro Mitchell to Isaac Hicks, May 15, 1799, H.P.

21. "I observe thou mentions that the stream of business seems to be turning from thy own into other channels," Thomas Hazard, Jr. wrote Hicks. "The painful sensations arising from the loss, I think cannot be wholly unmixed with pleasure at seeing the coffers of thy pupils in so flourishing a condition" (Thomas Hazard, Jr. to Isaac Hicks, Dec. 11, 1800, H.P.); Samuel Rodman to Isaac Hicks, June 6, 1800, H.P.

22. Joseph A. Scoville (Walter Barrett, Clerk, pseud.), *The Old Merchants of New York City* (New York, 1870), Second Series, p. 302. See also W. J. Ghent," Jacob Barker," *Dictionary of American Biography* (New York, 1929), I, 602–603.

23. William Rotch, Jr. to Isaac Hicks, Dec. 3, 1799, H.P. Hicks probably had more information than Rotch about the general slump in commodity prices that took place toward the end of that year. Smith and Cole, *Fluctuations in American Business,* p. 15.

24. William Rotch, Jr. to Isaac Hicks, May 8, 1800, H.P.

25. *Ibid.*

26. Obed & Aaron Mitchell to Isaac Hicks, March 24, 1800, H.P. There seems to have been a mercurial strain in Hicks. His former clerk, Jacob Barker, describes one scene with him in the following fashion: "Mr. Hicks replied in his rapid manner 'Take it, take it, I am tired of the sight of it.' " Jacob Barker, *Incidents from the Life of Jacob Barker of New Orleans* (Washington, 1855), p. 1.

27. Insurance policies, H.P.

28. Isaac Hicks Ledger Book B, folios 201, 271, 212, 268, 394, 451, 468, 556, 648. The *Sarah* was not an isolated case; the *General Mercer* account showed expenditures of $6,215 in 1800, $17,357 in 1801, and over $10,000 in 1802. *Ibid.,* folios 341, 451, 529, 543, 599, 647.

29. Pennock was not Hicks's only link to the Fishers. In true Quaker fashion the Fishers were related to two of Hicks's correspondents in New Bedford, the Quaker Rodmans and Rotches. In addition, Samuel Fisher was a good friend of Isaac's cousin, Elias Hicks. "'Tis our intention thou should have the sale of this wine, thy commission as heretofore, to be 2½ per cent." Samuel & Miers Fisher to Isaac Hicks, Feb. 9, 1801, H.P.

30. John Howland to Isaac Hicks, June 24, 1799; Jonathan Jenkins to Isaac Hicks, May 7, 1799; William Rotch, Jr. to Isaac Hicks, May 24, 1800; Samuel Rodman to Isaac Hicks, Sept. 24, 1797, H.P.

31. James Cropper to Isaac Hicks, Feb. 1, 1797; Benson, Cropper & Benson to Isaac Hicks, Dec. 15, 1802; Isaac Hicks Ledger Book B, H.P.

32. John Robinson & Sons to Isaac Hicks, Feb. 21, 1799; Isaac Hicks Invoice Books 1 and 2, H.P.

33. Miers Fisher to Isaac Hicks, April 19, 1798; Robert Bines to Isaac Hicks, June 6, 1798, H.P. See Harold B. Hancock and Norman B. Wilkinson, "The Gilpins and Their Endless Papermaking Machine," *Pennsylvania Magazine of History and Biography,* 81:391–405 (1957).

34. Morgan & Douglas to Isaac Hicks, April 21, 1797; Isaac Hicks Invoice Book 2; Morgan Douglas to Isaac Hicks, Aug. 1, 1802, H.P.

35. Isaac Hicks Ledgers A and B, Day Book No. 9, H.P.

Chapter V: Isaac Hicks Serves the South

1. Robert & John Bolton to Alsop & Hicks, April 26, 1794, H.P.; Adam Seybert, *Statistical Annals of the United States* (Philadelphia, 1818), I, 94–95; Isaac Hicks Invoice Books 1 and 2, H.P.

2. Robert G. Albion, "Foreign Trade in the Era of Wooden Ships," *Growth of the American Economy,* ed. Harold F. Williamson (New York, 1946), p. 164. See also Albion, *Square Riggers,* pp. 50–53; Clement Eaton, *History of the Old South* (New York, 1945), p. 404. Eaton, however, notes that some cotton was sent directly from the South to Europe. Advertisements for cotton in New York certainly were not very numerous in 1799. In an issue of the *Daily Advertiser,* Jan. 1, 1799, of 100 commodity advertisements, only one mentioned cotton—23 bales; and on Oct. 22, 1799, cotton was mentioned only three times in 125 commodity advertisements.

3. In 1799 the Boltons directed their brig *Rachel* from Savannah to Lisbon with rice and staves and asked Hicks to make insurance for them (Nov. 4, 1799, H.P.). Then the *Nixon* made several voyages from Savannah to Corunna and other Spanish ports, to France, and to Rotterdam, loaded

with cargoes of cotton, tobacco, and rice (Captain John Bolton to Isaac Hicks, May 20, 1800). The Boltons' largest ship, the *Elizabeth,* sailed directly from Savannah to Liverpool and back (Rathbone, Hughes & Duncan to Isaac Hicks, Mar. 19, 1798). When a friend of the Boltons bought a British brig captured by privateers, he sent her from Savannah with Sea Island cotton to Bordeaux and brought back wine and brandy to Savannah (R. & J. Bolton to Isaac Hicks, Nov. 27, 1802, H.P.).

4. "As we expect a large supply of goods," the Boltons wrote Hicks before one of their vessels arrived from Europe, "we shan't want any quantity from your city" (R. & J. Bolton to Isaac Hicks, Aug. 25, 1798). Depending upon the goods acquired and the state of the American markets, the Boltons ordered their inbound ships to New York or to Savannah. "We rather suspect she [the *Nixon*] will be ordered for New York as the tobacco will probably be bartered [in Europe] for articles unsaleable in their market" (R. & J. Bolton to Isaac Hicks, July 1, 1800, H.P.).

5. R. & J. Bolton to Isaac Hicks, April 7, 1801, H.P. See also Nov. 4, 1799, Nov. 29, 1799, Jan. 11, 1800, Aug. 5, 1800.

6. *Ibid.,* March 2, 1798.

7. *Ibid.,* Oct. 8, 1798; Oct. 29, 1799.

8. *Ibid.,* Jan. 3, 1801; Rathbone, Hughes & Duncan to Isaac Hicks, March 25, 1800, H.P.

9. Drafts on Isaac Hicks, 1797 to 1802, H.P.

10. R. & J. Bolton to Isaac Hicks, Jan. 6, 1803; Alexander Halliday to Isaac Hicks, April 28, 1801. Levi Coit, another New York merchant, made a similar statement to his English correspondent in 1810. "As cotton cannot be purchased without cash," Coit wrote, "I . . . have occasion to raise the money for remitting to Savannah" (Levi Coit to Martin, Hope & Thornley, Aug. 30, 1810, Levi Coit Letter Book II, N.Y.P.L.). Coit, incidentally, corresponded with the Boltons after Hicks left business. Coit to Bolton, Jan. 16, 1808, *Ibid.*

11. R. & J. Bolton to Isaac Hicks, Dec. 23, 1797, Dec. 13, 1800, H.P.

12. *Ibid.,* March 19, 1799. The Boltons failed in their attempt to have the Bank of the United States act as a clearing house. Late in 1801 the southern firm proposed to Hicks that he draw on Rathbone, Hughes & Duncan for £2,000 stg. Hicks was to use the money from this bill to cover the Bolton's draft on him: "We shall draw on you in about ten days for $5,000 or $6,000 . . . payable in Philadelphia at 60 days after date, by which means we can take the money in [the] Charleston Bank without even a risk from thence" (R. & J. Bolton to Isaac Hicks, Dec. 10, 1801). Unfortunately, the Charleston branch of the Bank of the United States must have changed its mind about participating because the Boltons wrote a few months later that the "Bank declines doing any thing in that way for the present" (*ibid.,* Feb. 6, 1802). Surprisingly, the Boltons did not favor the establishment of a branch of

the Bank of the United States in Savannah, anticipating "little favor and considerable inconvenience from its unequal operation." They did, however, approve of an independent bank and wrote Hicks, "As we are almost wholly ignorant of the banking system" would he please give them his "opinion of a bank on the Manhattan plan" (*ibid.*, March 9, 1802). After the Savannah merchants formed a bank with John Bolton as one of its directors, the southern firm still had serious problems with receiving funds. In 1803 the firm wrote: "Pray, send no more post notes. Our bank is about to determine on receiving other branch notes as deposits only and to be paid out in same notes, not in its notes or specie" (*ibid.*, March 10, 1803). Such a policy did not help the Boltons much.

13. R. & J. Bolton to Isaac Hicks, Dec. 10, 1801.

14. *Ibid.*, Nov. 5, 1801, March 9, 1802, Mar. 12, 1798. As they put it, even "gold and silver can be refused" (*ibid.*, March 10, 1803, Dec. 11, 1801).

15. *Ibid.*, Dec. 23, 1797, Apr. 9, 1798. Between Oct. 25, 1799, and Jan. 9, 1800, while the French "War" made coastal shipping somewhat dangerous Hicks used the means of shipment shown in the table.

	Date	Shipment by	Amount
October	25	post	$ 500
	29	post	500
	29	*Huntress*	2,000
	31	*Shepherdess*	3,000
	31	post	5,000
	31	*Bellona*	3,000
November	14	post	500
	15	post	500
	15	*Debby*	2,000
	15	Mr. Dekenann	3,000
	22, 23, 25, 26, 27	post	4,000
	28, 30	post	2,000
December	7	*Apollo*	3,000
	2, 3	post	2,000
	5, 7, 9, 10	post	4,750
	26	post	1,000
	30	John Bolton	5,000
January	9	*Shepherdess*	2,000
		TOTAL	$42,250

This recapitulation was in a letter from the Boltons, Jan. 11, 1800, H.P.

16. John Bolton to Isaac Hicks, May 23, 1803, H.P.

17. R. & J. Bolton to Isaac Hicks, Oct. 31, 1798, H.P.

18. *Ibid.,* May 2, 1800; Rathbone, Hughes & Duncan to Isaac Hicks, January 1800, H.P.

19. A. H. Stone, "The Cotton Factorage System of the Southern States," *American Historical Review,* 20:557–560 (April 1915).

20. Isaac Hicks, "Sketch of my Voyage to Savannah and the Proceedings There," undated [1792]; Robert Bolton to Isaac Hicks, Nov. 13, 1797; John Bolton to Isaac Hicks, Sept. 13, 1799, Aug. 31, 1803, H.P.

21. R. & J. Bolton to Isaac Hicks, Dec. 24, 1798, H.P.

22. *Ibid.,* March 28, 1799; Sept. 9, 1800; Nov. 12, 1802.

23. *Ibid.,* Oct. 10, 1800.

24. *Ibid.* Bolton added a delicate hint at the bottom of one letter: "The buckwheat cakes will eat nicely, when they arrive, especially if the Butter should be good" (*ibid.,* Nov. 14, 1801).

25. *Ibid.,* Dec. 16, 1798; April 12, 1800; John Bolton to Isaac Hicks, Oct. 8, 1801; R. & J. Bolton to Isaac Hicks, April 11, 1800, H.P.

26. Robert Bolton to Isaac Hicks, Feb. 25, 1799; Dec. 17, 1798; John Bolton to Isaac Hicks, Oct. 28, 1802, H.P.

27. Robert Bolton to Isaac Hicks, May 7, 1802; R. & J. Bolton to Isaac Hicks, Dec. 20, 1799, H.P.

28. R. & J. Bolton to Isaac Hicks, Mar. 31, 1803. The Savannah merchants formed a joint stock company in 1799 to build a cotton exchange known as the City Exchange. From the beginning the city had been a stockholder and in 1806 formed a committee of the city council to undertake the complete purchase of outstanding shares. This was finished by 1812, after the merchants had ceased to use it as an exchange (William Harden, *Savannah and South Georgia,* Chicago, 1913, I, 267). R. & J. Bolton to Isaac Hicks, Apr. 13, 1799, H.P.

29. Robert Bolton to Isaac Hicks, Aug. 8, 1801, H.P.

30. *Ibid.,* Feb. 23, 1798.

31. *Ibid.,* June 11, 1802.

32. R. & J. Bolton to Isaac Hicks, Nov. 1, 1800, H.P.

33. Robert Bolton to Isaac Hicks, Feb. 16, 1799, H.P.

34. John Bolton to Isaac Hicks, Jan. 12, 1805, H.P.

35. Ledgers A and B., Day Book No. 9; John Robinson & Sons to Isaac Hicks, July 9, 1804. See also Richard Blow to Isaac Hicks, May 5, 1804; Cropper, Benson & Co. to Isaac Hicks, May 17, 1804, H.P.

36. Day Book No. 9; Hicks had made occasional declarations to his customers that he refrained from speculating in the commodities which he handled as a commission agent for his various principals. From 1795 until 1804 his operation was closer to the textbook definition of the "commission agent" than to the "commission merchant," but this was only a matter of degree.

Chapter VI: Isaac Hicks Invests on His Own Account

1. Between 1797 and 1802 Hicks's revenues from commissions were:

1797	$ 7,559
1798	8,006
1799	12,570
1800	15,743
1801	24,780
1802	11,407
TOTAL	$80,065

During these years he earned $23,804 from other than commissions and had apparent expenses of $15,696 for the period. Ledger Books A and B, H.P.

2. On the 1804 venture to Russia, Hicks earned $13,861, a figure which exceeds his commission income for any one year except in his two best years, 1800 and 1801.

3. Commission Income, 1797–1802	$80,065
Other Income	23,804
TOTAL	103,869
Less Expenses	15,696
EARNINGS, 1797–1802	$88,173

4. Ledger A., folio 136, H.P.

5. *Ibid.* See also John Delano to Isaac Hicks, July 4, 1798, H.P.

6. Ledger B, folios 151, 172, 202, 312, 307, 337, 448. When Hicks started his new ledger in 1799, Ledger B, he shifted his money of account from New York Pounds to dollars. This accounts for the different method of expressing profits. New York Pounds may be converted to dollars by multiplying by 2.5. Invoices. Beeldemaker & Co. to Isaac Hicks, Aug. 24, 1799; Ledger B, folio 312; Bills of Sale for Adventure to St. Petersburg with Judah Paddock, H.P.

7. Freeman Hunt, *Lives of American Merchants* (New York, 1858), II, 52.

8. Statement of Ownership of Ship *Thames,* Dec. 1, 1802, H.P.

9. Judah Paddock to Rathbone, Hughes & Duncan, June 5, 1800 (copy sent to Isaac Hicks); Judah Paddock to Isaac Hicks, July 5, 1800, H. P. See also Carl Carmer, *The Hudson* (New York, 1939), pp. 51–53.

10. Statement of Ownership of Ship *General Mercer,* Dec. 31, 1801; R. & J. Bolton to Isaac Hicks, July 2, 1802; Ownership agreement for Ship *Thames.* It is interesting to note that John Jacob Astor, Hicks's contemporary, waited until 1800 before becoming the principal owner of a ship (N. S. B. Gras and Henrietta Larson, *Casebook in American History,* New York, 1939, p. 83).

11. Bradbury, *History of Hudson,* p. 50.

12. R. & J. Bolton to Isaac Hicks, Nov. 1, 1802; R. & J. Bolton to Judah Paddock, March 22, 1803, H.P.

13. R. & J. Bolton to Isaac Hicks, Dec. 10, 1802; Dec. 23, 1802, H.P.

14. *Ibid.,* Nov. 1, 1802; Judah Paddock to Isaac Hicks, Jan. 19, 1803; Isaac Hicks to Judah Paddock, Jan. 29, 1803, H.P.

15. Judah Paddock to Isaac Hicks, Jan. 6, 1803, H.P.

16. *Ibid.,* Feb. 5, 1803; Isaac Hicks to Judah Paddock, Jan. 20, 1803, Jan. 24, 1803; Judah Paddock to Isaac Hicks, Feb. 13, 1803, H.P.

17. Judah Paddock to Isaac Hicks, Jan. 6, 1803, H.P.

18. Isaac Hicks to Judah Paddock, Jan. 24, 1803, H.P.

19. R. & J. Bolton to Isaac Hicks, March 23, 1803, H.P.

20. Judah Paddock to Isaac Hicks, April 26, 1803, H.P.

21. Isaac Hicks to Judah Paddock, March 24, 1803; Judah Paddock to Isaac Hicks, May 4, 1803, April 26, 1803, H.P.

22. Judah Paddock to Isaac Hicks, April 26, 1803, H.P. Unable to staff the Navy with volunteers the British Government had for centuries filled naval quotas by roving "press" gangs which conscripted men on the spot.

23. Quenouille, Lanchon, Hanin, Spear & Co. Account of Sales to Owners of Ship *Thames,* May 13, 1803, H.P.

24. R. & J. Bolton to Captain Judah Paddock, March 22, 1803; Judah Paddock to Isaac Hicks, May 14, 1803, H.P.

25. Judah Paddock to Isaac Hicks, May 17, 1803; Quenouille, Lanchon, Hanin, Spear & Co. Accounts of Sales of the Owners of the Ship *Thames,* June 3, 1803; Judah Paddock to Isaac Hicks, May 17, 1803, H.P.

26. R. & J. Bolton orders to Captain Paddock, March 22, 1803; Judah Paddock to Isaac Hicks, May 14, 1803; Judah Paddock to R. & J. Bolton, May 25, 1803; Judah Paddock to Isaac Hicks, June 5, 1803, H.P.

27. Judah Paddock to Isaac Hicks, May 22, 1803, H.P.

28. *Ibid.,* June 13, 1803.

29. *Ibid.*

30. *Ibid.*

31. *Ibid.*

32. Judah Paddock to Rathbone, Hughes & Duncan (copy sent to Isaac Hicks), June 10, 1803, H.P.

33. Rathbone, Hughes & Duncan to Judah Paddock, June 14, 1803, H.P.

34. John Bolton to Isaac Hicks, Aug. 31, 1803, H.P.

35. Judah Paddock to Isaac Hicks, July 20, 1803, H.P.

36. *Ibid.,* July 6, 1803.

37. *Ibid.,* July 20, 1803.

38. Cramers Smith & Co. account current with Owners of the Ship *Thames,* Aug. 17, 1803, H.P.

39. Day Book No. 9, March 4, 1805, H.P.

40. Judah Paddock to Isaac Hicks, Jan. 26, 1804; R. & J. Bolton to Isaac

Hicks, Nov. 30, 1803; Judah Paddock to Isaac Hicks, Jan. 26, 1804, H.P.

41. Judah Paddock to Isaac Hicks, Jan. 30, 1804, H.P.

42. John Bolton to Isaac Hicks, May 23, 1803; R. & J. Bolton in Account Current with Isaac Hicks, June 15, 1804, H.P.

43. Invoice of Ship *Thames,* Feb. 29, 1804, H.P.

44. Judah Paddock to Isaac Hicks, April 18, 1804, H.P.

45. *Ibid.,* April 26, 1804.

46. *Ibid.,* April 26, 1804 and May 26, 1804.

47. Bill of R. & J. Bolton to Owners of the Ship *Thames,* June 15, 1804; Cramers Smith & Co. in account current with Owners of the Ship *Thames,* June 16, 1804, H.P.

48. Day Book No. 9. May 1, 1806, H.P.

49. R. & J. Bolton to Isaac Hicks, Oct. 4, 1805, H.P.

50. Judah Paddock to Isaac Hicks, Oct. 4, 1804, H.P.

51. Day Book No. 9, March 11, 1805; Judah Paddock to Isaac Hicks, April 4, 1805, H.P.

52. Judah Paddock to Isaac Hicks, April 11, 1805, H.P.

53. Cramers Smith & Co. in account current with Isaac Hicks, John Hone, and Robert Jenkins & Co., July 7, 1805; Judah Paddock, Oct. 22, 1805, Dec. 12, 1805, H.P.

54. Ship *West Point* in account current with Robert Jenkins & Co., Dec. 31, 1805; Day Book No. 9, Dec. 20, 1805, H.P.

55. Outbound Invoice Book, Feb. 14, 1806, H.P.

56. Paddock turned down the offer to be master of the *Robert Bolton* with the comment that she was "the most pleasing one I ever had an opportunity to command except the *Thames.*" Judah Paddock to Isaac Hicks, Dec. 12, 1805, H.P.

57. John Morris to Isaac Hicks, March 24, April 12, 1806, H.P.

58. *Ibid.,* May 1, June 2, 1806.

59. Rathbone, Hughes & Duncan in account current with Isaac Hicks, Nov. 14, 1806; John Morris bill to the Ship *Robert Bolton,* Oct. 8, 1806, H.P.

60. Isaac Hicks to Judah Paddock, March 14, 1804; Day Book No. 9 records dividends to Hicks of $500 on June 21, $1,000 on June 22, 1805, and $813 on June 3, 1806. Thomas Rotch to Isaac Hicks, Dec. 27, 1805; Day Book No. 9, Dec. 19, 1805, H.P.

61. Deed, John Alsop to Isaac Hicks, May 17, 1803; Day Book No. 9. March 15, 1805, May 29, 1805; Subscription Book for Powles Hook Shares, H.P. "The real estate boom was anything but resounding. Although a red brick tavern was built and a few small industries arose, the political domination of the Associates hindered growth. New York's claim to riparian rights . . . hindered the building of piers" (Federal Writers Project, *New Jersey: A Guide to its Present and Past,* New York, 1939, p. 274).

62. Day Book No. 9, May 29, 1805; Bank of Hudson receipts for payment

toward shares, H.P. Partly as a result of the War of 1812 the bank failed in 1819. Bradbury, *History of Hudson,* p. 49. 1790 Journal, rear pages. Oct. 1815; Mortgages of Laban and Deborah Bunker to Isaac Hicks, Sept. 17, 1814; Mortgage of John and Sarah Powell to Isaac Hicks, May 13, 1817, H.P.

Chapter VII: A Life Free from Commercial Cares

1. John Hone to Isaac Hicks, Nov. 22, 1805, H.P.
2. Day Book No. 9, July 19, 1805 to Aug. 16, 1806, H.P.
3. Mark Coffin to Isaac Hicks, Jan. 5, 1806, H.P.
4. "We . . . note thy prospects of retiring from commercial cares and resigning thy affairs to thy Brother, Samuel Hicks" (Benson, Cropper & Benson, June 30, 1802, H.P.).
5. Ledger Book, folios 395, 703. Notebook entry, July 2, 1800. Besides the list of trees, many bills for seeds and other farm supplies are noted in this period from 1800 to 1805:

10 Russetings	5 Vandeveers
10 Rhode Island Greenings	16 Pear
5 Fall Pippins	25 Newton Pippins
2 Harvest Apples	2 /Swar/ Apples
1 Pear Tree	5 Pelton Apples
5 Pierce's Sweeting	10 Esopus Spitzenburgs
2 Hog Island Sweeting	4 Vandine
1 Black Apple	2 Fall Apples
1 Green Apple	4 flatt Apples
2 Prior Sweeting	2 Clay grafts
1 Yellow Coat Pippin	20 not grafted

6. This list of books appears in an unpublished history of the Hicks family by Marietta Hicks. She described her source as a "small leather book marked 1796." I failed to locate this book.
7. Quarterly Subscription Book for the Preparative Meeting held in New York, August 1796; Hicks check stubs, 1796; Henry Drinker to Isaac Hicks, Nov. 5, 1799; Documents of New York Overseers regarding Henry Drinker, Isaac Hicks, Bowne & Pearsall, May 16, 1803, H.P.
8. James Barker to Isaac Hicks, March 2, 1797; William Rotch, Jr. to Isaac Hicks, July 9, 1803, H.P.
9. Samuel & Miers Fisher to Isaac Hicks, Sept. 4, 1801; Thomas & Joshua Fisher to Isaac Hicks, June 18, 1798; Isaiah Hussey to Isaac Hicks, July 9, 1800; William Rotch, Jr. to Isaac Hicks, May 6, 1803. H.P.
10. Isaac Hicks to Samuel & Miers Fisher, May 26, 1801, Letter Order Book No. 4; Isaac Hicks to Cropper & Benson, May 25, 1801, *ibid.*
11. Before Hicks left Westbury, all members of the Meeting manumitted their slaves. Among the Hicks papers is an Epistle from the important London Yearly Meeting on the subject of slavery. "The increasing solicitude

for the suppression of the slave trade which appears among all ranks . . . is cause of thankfulness . . . and encourages us to hope that the time is approaching when this nation will be cleansed from this defilement. Let us in meantime, continue with unabated ardour to be intercessors for the greatly injured Africans" (Epistle from the Yearly Meeting Held in London, May 12, 1788, H.P.). See *Minutes of Abolition Societies,* 1798, pp. 17, 18, H.P.

12. African Free School Subscription Book; William Rotch to Isaac Hicks, Feb. 15, 1800; Thomas Hazard, Jr. to Isaac Hicks, Feb. 25, 1800; Abraham Barker to Isaac Hicks, Feb. 17, 1800, H.P.

13. *Minutes of Abolitionist Societies,* 1803, p. 13; Paddock wrote from Charleston in 1802: "If your Manumission Society were as assiduous here as at home you would find business enough. The fore part of this winter a Ship and Schooner landed their cargoes of slaves between here and Savannah. Such things are become so common very little notice is taken of it to the great Shame of the Government" (Judah Paddock to Isaac Hicks, March 24, 1802). Earlier in this port, Paddock had told of seeing "the captain who brought said Negro, He delivered him up to his master. He is not the man the Negro said his master was but a Lawyer here in town who no doubt knows I am here as we have been reported" (*ibid.,* Feb. 21, 1802). Paddock persisted and by mid-March "got John Dillon to swear to the Negro Business." One part of the information was the names of the New Yorkers involved in the sale of free northern Negroes to southerners (*ibid.,* March 10, 1802). The next year Paddock wrote from Savannah that "Captain H. and myself have been some days trying to get John Dillon . . . to give his oath to the Sale of the other Negro girl. After some difficulty he appeared before a Justice of the Peace." Once the man swore, Paddock reckoned, this would "fix Sally and Tom . . . This much for the Manumission Society" (*ibid.,* March 8, 1803, H.P.).

14. Preparative Meeting Subscription Book, H.P.

15. Bliss Forbush, *Elias Hicks, Quaker Liberal* (New York, 1956), p. 308.

16. Book F, June 18, 1806, W.R.

17. *Ibid.,* Feb. 17, 1808, May 18, 1808.

18. *Ibid.,* June 26, 1808, March 18, 1812, May 20, 1812, Jan. 18, 1809, March 14, 1810, W. R. Richard Mott to John D. Hicks, March 1887, H.P.

19. Book G, June 14, 1815, June 19, 1816, W.R.

20. "There was much traveling by the leading Friends, some of whom were so continuously engaged in religious service that they were seldom at home for any length of time" (Brinton, *Friends for 300 Years,* p. 186).

21. Forbush, *Elias Hicks,* p. 252.

22. John Comly, another traveling Friend, wrote of Isaac, "It seems as if thou art the man to be armourbearer for Elias in this journey" (John Comly to Isaac Hicks, August 1817, H.P.).

23. Elias Hicks, *Journal of the Life and Religious Labours of Elias Hicks, Written by Himself* (New York, 1832), p. 129.

24. Isaac Hicks to Sarah Hicks, June 13, June 15, Aug. 12, Aug. 19, Sept. 8, 1810, H.P.

25. Elias Hicks, *Journal,* pp. 138–150.

26. *Ibid.,* pp. 253, 266.

27. Isaac Hicks to Sarah Hicks, Nov. 1, 1818, H.P.

28. Elias Hicks to Isaac Hicks, Feb. 20, 1819, N.Y.R.

29. John Comly to Isaac Hicks, Nov. 14, 1815, H.P.

30. *Ibid.,* Feb. 12, 1817.

31. Elias Hicks to Phoebe Willis, as quoted in D. Elton Trueblood, "Elias Hicks," in Howard Brinton, ed. *Byways in Quaker History* (Pendle Hill, 1944), p. 83. See Forbush, *Elias Hicks,* p. 136.

32. Isaac Hicks to Sarah Hicks, "Second Day Morning" [1811?], H.P. Note the similarity of Isaac's comments to the thought and language of Elias's recollections of messages he had delivered: "Although men in ignorance . . . strive . . . to live quietly in the gratification of their own wills and creaturely appetites . . . they never can fully come to this" (p. 102). "I was led forth in these meetings to show wherein real Christianity consists . . . although the people of Christendom had the name Christians, yet so long as they lived in the gratification of their own wills and carnal lusts . . . they were only heathen in disguise. For true Christianity is nothing else than a real and complete mortification of our own wills, and a full and final annihilation of all self-exaltation. None are any further Christians than as they come to experience the self-denial, meekness, humility, and gentleness of Christ ruling them" (p. 103). "Self-love and self-will lie shrouded under a mask of doing good" (Elias Hicks, *Journal,* p. 104; Isaac Hicks to Sarah Hicks, Aug. 15, 1810, H.P.).

33. Isaac Hicks to Sarah Hicks, Oct. 14, 1811. Comly wrote Isaac about "the need of depth in religious exercise." True religious experience comes to those who "know their own spirits subjected, and move *only* in the fresh openings of the living Spring." John Comly to Isaac Hicks, May 9, 1819, H.P.

34. In 1811 Elias published a pamphlet, *Observations on the Slavery of the Africans* (New York, 1811), which "was probably one of the first publications in the nineteenth century actually advocating the abolition of slavery" (Henry W. Wilbur, *The Life and Labors of Elias Hicks,* Philadelphia, 1910, p. 93). Though Isaac himself took a very advanced position on the slavery issue, he boggled at the absolute quality of Elias's views. "He uses too strong terms and calls too hard names," Isaac wrote to Sarah Hicks, July 8, 1813 (H.P.).

35. During the Revolutionary War, Elias was true to his principles (Forbush, *Elias Hicks,* pp. 32–35). In 1804 Isaac refused to pay a military

tax and had some of his goods seized by the collector (Day Book No. 9, April 18, 1806, H.P.). Elias expressed himself eloquently on this topic in his *Journal:* "My mind was . . . interrupted by the unChristian commotions and din of war, which are at present mightily prevailing in our land, and by the frequent reports of blood and slaughter, witnessed among professed human rational beings; but alas! how inhuman and irrational do they prove and proclaim themselves to be who can deliberately inbrue their hands in each other's blood for this world's honors and profits" (*Journal,* p. 190).

36. Trueblood, "Career of Elias Hicks," in Brinton, *Byways.* "If the Lord had intended there should be internal waterways," Elias wrote of the planned Erie Canal, "He would have placed them there, and there would have been a river flowing through central New York." As quoted by Forbush, *Elias Hicks,* pp. 280–281.

37. Elias Hicks, *Journal,* pp. 279–280; John Comly to Isaac Hicks, Apr. 21, 1816, H.P.

38. Elias Hicks, *Journal,* pp. 276–277.

39. John Comly to Isaac Hicks, Feb. 11, 1818, H.P.

40. Sidney I. Pomerantz, *New York: An American City 1783–1803* (New York, 1938), p. 160.

41. John Comly, *Journal of the Life and Religious Labors of John Comly* (Philadelphia, 1853), pp. 163–164.

42. Preamble to his will, April 5, 1816, copy in Hicks papers, probated in Queens County Court House.

43. Anne Mott to Mary Mott Hicks, Aug. 3, 1815, in Cornell, *Adam and Anne Mott,* p. 95; 1790 Journal (rear pages), Nov. 15, 1817, H.P.

44. John Comly to Isaac Hicks, June 15, 1817, H.P.

45. *Ibid.,* March 10, May 23, July 7, 1818.

46. Isaac Hicks to Sarah Hicks, June 15, 1810, H.P.

47. *Ibid.,* Nov. 1, 1811.

48. *Ibid.,* Nov. 1, 1818.

49. Judah Paddock to Isaac Hicks, Aug. 16, 1819, H.P.

50. Elias Hicks, *Journal,* pp. 386–387.

51. *Ibid.,* pp. 387–388.

Chapter VIII: Capitalist and Quaker Reconsidered

1. Indenture of Sarah Ryerson to Isaac Hicks, Apr. 9, 1792, H.P.

2. Richard Mott to John D. Hicks, July 21, 1887, H.P.

3. Forbush, *Elias Hicks,* pp. 40–41, 108–109, 311.

4. Of approximately 10,000 letters in the Hicks collection over one third were written in plain speech. Although this characteristic identifies the writer as a Quaker, not all Friends used this form. Judah Paddock does not write "thee" or "thou" until 1818.

5. Harvey & Lecky to Alsop & Hicks, Dec. 1, 1794. In 1801 Rathbone, Hughes & Duncan received a bill Hicks had endorsed, but for which the firm drawing the bill had no funds. Instead of suing Hicks as it had a legal right to do, the English firm took up and paid the amount "for the honor and account of Isaac Hicks." Bill of exchange by Anthony & Pleasants on Rathbone, Hughes & Duncan, April 23, 1801; See Chapter VI, p. 120; Cropper & Benson to Isaac Hicks, June 15, 1801, H.P.

6. R. & J. Bolton to Isaac Hicks, Feb. 12, 1802; Thomas Willitts to Isaac Hicks, Jan. 5, 1802, H.P.

7. Talcott Parsons. *The Structure of Social Action* (Glencoe, 1949), pp. 511, 529.

8. Weber, *Protestant Ethic,* p. 57.

9. It was a disownable offense by 1715. Tolles, *Meeting House and Counting House,* p. 88.

10. John Woolman, *Journal of John Woolman* (Boston, 1886), pp. 229–231. See also James, *A People among Peoples,* pp. 132–140.

11. See notes 12, 13, Chapter VII; Richard Mott to John D. Hicks, July 21, 1887, H.P.

12. Anna D. Hallowell, *James and Lucretia Mott: Life and Letters* (Boston, 1884), pp. 70, 86, 87.

13. Volume 1020, April 7, 1790, N.Y.R.

14. "While expected profit is usually the most immediate and conspicuous incentive for business activity, it is not necessarily the ultimate determinant of such activity in the psychological sense" (Albert Lauterbach, *Men, Motives, and Money, Psychological Frontiers of Economics,* Ithaca, 1954, p. 231; see also pp. xi, 2, 18). Chester Barnard, *The Functions of the Executive* (Cambridge, Massachusetts, 1938), pp. 146–147; George Katona, *Psychological Analysis of Economic Behavior* (New York, 1951), p. 201.

15. Jonathan Jenkins to Isaac Hicks, Feb. 19, 1803; Jonathan Jenkins to Preserved Fish, March 12, 1803, H.P.

16. Brinton, *Friends for 300 Years,* p. 130.

17. *1762 Discipline,* vol. 40, p. 25, W.R.

18. Isaac Hicks to Cornelius Wing, Dec. 16, 1800, Letter Book No. 4, H.P.

19. If the *Thames* had carried more than signal guns, Hicks could have anticipated trouble from the Meeting. Several New York Friends had been forced to sell their share in an armed vessel (vol. 1012, Mar. 7, 1792, N.Y.R.).

20. Benson, Cropper & Benson to Isaac Hicks, June 30, 1802, H.P.

21. Weber, *Protestant Ethic,* p. 53; *ibid.,* p. 51.

22. *Ibid.,* p. 51.

23. Book of Discipline, vol. 41A, pp. 73, 77, W.R.

24. Woolman, *Journal,* p. 91; Brinton, *Friends for 300 Years,* p. 138; Elias Hicks, *Journal,* p. 133.

25. Even after the repeal of the Embargo permitted some trade, American merchants found that the remaining American restrictions and the desperation of the two belligerents made profitable trade unlikely. Levi Coit was one New York merchant who did not trust the post-Embargo period. "The prospects since the removal of the Embargo have been such," he wrote Martin, Hope & Thornley, "that I have had no inducement to make any Shipments—I have therefore been entirely inactive in hopes that prospects may again brighten and encourage me to do something" (Levi Coit to Martin, Hope & Thornley, July 19, 1809, Levi Coit Letter Book II, N.Y.P.L.). Reinoehl noted the bad fortune of the Crowninshield family when they traded in other than western European ports in the 1809–1812 period. (John Reinoehl, "Post-Embargo Trade and Merchant Prosperity: Experiences of the Crowninshield Family 1809–1812," *Mississippi Valley Historical Review*, September 1955, pp. 236–246).

26. Isaac's contemporary, the Philadelphia Quaker Nathan Trotter, preserved nominal membership in the Society during his seventy-odd years, but heeded the demands of his temporal calling so exclusively that only dry crumbs were left over for the rest of his Quakerism. After a successful career as a metal wholesaler he turned his metal business over to his sons. Then, instead of retiring, he spent the rest of his life—and considerably increased his fortune—as a private banker discounting notes. Trotter's recent biographer comments that "he gave some time, though not very much, to matters which were not connected with his family or profits. He served for one year, 1817-18, as Guardian of the Poor . . . Trotter did his duty as he saw it, but during his lifetime he gave relatively little to charity and at his death he left his entire fortune to his wife and children" (Tooker, *Nathan Trotter*, p. 22). Raistrick noted a tendency of the children of successful English Quaker businessmen to leave the Society: "Young men and women . . . acclimatised to the fashionable drawing rooms of their fathers' customers and associates and were accustomed to a standard of life more consonant with the support of the bankers' position and credit than with the plainness of Friends" (*Quakers in Science and Industry*, p. 341). He further notes the not always harmonious relation of business and religion: "In some degree . . . these positions were reciprocal, that as wealth and secular power increased, spirituality . . . decreased, the accumulating wealth within the Society forced a partial retreat" (*ibid*, p. 348).

INDEX

Haviland, Benjamin, 24
Le Havre, France, 115, 116
Haydock, John W., 29
Hazard, Thomas, 76, 138
Helsingör, Denmark, 118, 120, 128
Henderson, James, 73
Henry & John Hull, 48
Hercules (ship), 86
Hicks & Doughty, 73
Hicks & Loines, 27
Hicks & Post, 85
Hicks, Jenkins & Co., 107
Hicks, Benjamin (son), 148
Hicks, Edward (cousin), 13, 149–151
Hicks, Elias (cousin), 1, 13, 19, 56, 61, 139, 141–147, 152, 159, 166, 164
Hicks, Elizabeth (daughter), 133
Hicks, Elizabeth (sister), 13
Hicks, Isaac: *biographical and personal:* birth, 11; early Long Island experiences, 11–12; education, 12; move to New York, 24; marriage, 24; personality, 12, 80, 81, 86, 87; retirement, 132, 133, 162–168; farm and home, 133, 134; books, 134, 135, 139; heart attack, 144; will, 148; relations with sons, 148, 149; relations with wife, 151, 152, 154, 155; death, 153
—— *business career:* his advantages: of the times, 2–11; family, 12; as a Quaker, 14–25; tailor, 12, 25, 26; school teacher, 12, 13; grocer, 25–27; partnerships, 112, 157, 158; Hicks & Loines, 27–28; Loines, Alsop & Co., 28–31; *see also* Loines, Alsop & Co.; begins Alsop & Hicks, 30; ends Alsop & Hicks, 73; *see also* Alsop & Hicks; capital, 27–29, 108, 109, 111, 115, 122, 125, 126; business journeys, 61, 101, 102; information service, 61, 62; begins firm of Isaac Hicks, 74; oil business, 74–87; cotton business, 91–107; drops commission work, 107; reputation, 66; honesty, 69, 81, 156, 157; stock ownership, 130, 131; bank director, 130, 131; lobbyist, 130; real estate, 130, 131
—— *as a Quaker:* upbringing, 13–20;

membership, 19, 20, 24; collector for Meeting, 135; African Free School, 138; views on slavery, 137, 138, 157–159; Meeting committees, 139, 140; Clerk, 140; religious journeys, 143–146, 152, 153, 166; religious beliefs, 144–149; reputation as a Quaker, 156; sale of alcohol, 159, 160; use of courts, 161
Hicks, Jemima, 152, 154
Hicks, John (son), 149
Hicks, Mary Mott, 149
Hicks, Robert (son), 149
Hicks, Samuel (brother), 13, 85, 90, 113, 133; *see also* Hicks & Post; and Hicks, Jenkins & Co.
Hicks, Samuel (father), 12–14, 134, 150
Hicks, Sarah (wife), 24, 103, 133, 145, 146, 151, 152, 154
Hicks, Valentine (brother), 13
Hicksites, 136
History of Pennsylvania (Proud), 135
History of the Rise . . . of the . . . Quaker (Sewel), 135
Hodgson, William, 17
Holman, Captain, 125
Holmes, James. *See* James Holmes & Co.
Hone, John, 127, 128, 131, 132
Hone, Philip, 127
Howland, Thomas, 37
Hudson, New York, 33, 47, 48, 55–62, 72, 73, 80, 88, 128, 129, 131, 145, 160
Hudson Packet (sloop), 46, 57
Hudson River Valley, 36, 143, 151
Hull, Tiddeman, 46
Hunter (packet vessel), 95
Hunter (ship), 63
Hunting, Benjamin, 60
Hussey, Isaiah, 136
Hussey, Sylvannus, 33
Hutchins, John G. B., 10, 177
Hutchinson, John, 33

Immortalitie (frigate), 118
Imports, U. S., 9, 10, 88, 89, 99
Impressment of seamen, 116, 125
India, 63

214 Index

Whitney, Eli (inventor), 91
Whitney, Eli (merchant), 36
Wilkes, Charles, 49
Willitts, Thomas, 156
Wine, 25, 26, 103, 118, 120; Fayal, 74; Teneriffe, 88; French, 118

Wing, Cornelius, 161
Woodstock, New York, 106
Woolman, John, 134, 159

Yellow Fever, 73, 706